DATE DUE

DEMCO 38-296

WOMEN IN THE WEST

Series Editors

SUSAN ARMITAGE
Washington State University

SARAH J. DEUTSCH
Clark University

VICKI L. RUIZ
Claremont Graduate School

ELLIOT WEST
University of Arkansas

The

COLONEL'S LADY
on the
WESTERN FRONTIER

The Correspondence of
ALICE KIRK GRIERSON

Edited by
SHIRLEY A. LECKIE

UNIVERSITY OF NEBRASKA PRESS
Lincoln and London

The paper in this book meets the minimum requirements of
American National Standard for Information Sciences—Permanence
of Paper for Printed Library Materials, ANSI Z39.48-1984.

Library of Congress Cataloging-in-Publication Data

Grierson, Alice Kirk, 1828–1888.
The colonel's lady on the western frontier : the correspondence of
Alice Kirk Grierson / edited by Shirley A. Leckie.
p. cm. – (Women in the West)
Bibliography: p.
Includes index.
ISBN 0-8032-2886-4 (alk. paper)
ISBN 0-8032-7929-9 (pbk.)
1. Grierson, Alice Kirk, 1828–1888—Correspondence 2. Frontier
and pioneer life—West (U.S.) 3. Officers' wives—West (U.S.)—
Correspondence. 4. United States. Army—Military life—
History—19th century. 5. West (U.S.)—History—1848–1950.
I. Leckie, Shirley A., 1937– . II. Title. III. Series.
F594.G765 1989
978'.02'0924–dc19
[B]
88-27912
CIP

THIRD PAPERBACK PRINTING: 1995

To Bill
and
To Mathew, Kim, Maria, and Becky

Contents

Illustrations

Preface

At the close of the Civil War the reorganized and vastly reduced Army of the United States turned its attention to pacifying the Plains Indians of the trans-Mississippi West. For the next quarter century a succession of Indian wars were fought to protect the miners, farmers, town builders, and proliferating railroad lines invading the hunting grounds of these nomadic tribes and dooming their way of life. By 1891 the Indian wars were for all intents and purposes over and, as Frederick Jackson Turner noted two years later, the frontier era in American history had passed.

A surprising number of army officers' wives recorded their experiences as dependents of the Indian fighters on the western frontier. For the most part these women were of middle-class family background who accepted without question Victorian standards of ladylike behavior. Thus they not only chronicled their trials and tribulations in maintaining the proper standards of domesticity in the masculine world of the army, but also told a story of meeting a series of personal crises which challenged their ability to adapt.

Most of these women were young brides when they entered military life. Their husbands, with the exception of those of Margaret Carrington, Ellen Biddle, Eveline Alexander, and Elizabeth Custer, were junior officers, and this accounts somewhat for the physical hardships they experienced. But other factors mitigated their circumstances considerably: their youth and the relatively small size of their families. For, given the crowded conditions of post life, the lack of adequate health care, the problems inherent in educating children at remote posts, and the poor pay awarded officers by a niggardly Congress, even small families were difficult to raise on the western frontier. Several of the wives who published their memoirs—most notably Elizabeth Custer and Frances Roe—had no children at all.

The letters of Alice Kirk Grierson reveal a different story. At thirty-eight she was no longer young when her husband entered the reorganized United States Army after a distinguished career in the Civil War. Furthermore, she had already borne four children, one of whom had died in infancy. At the time, she was still living with relatives because her husband's business failure had left the Griersons "virtually without a dollar" and, worse yet, deeply in debt. Thus turmoil, uncertainty, and stress were not strangers to her. She was, however, a tough and intrepid woman.

As it turned out, those were the qualities she would need for her new life on the western frontier. There, as the colonel's lady, she would bear three additional children and encounter the difficulties of meeting the needs of family members of varying ages and extraordinary vulnerabilities.

Like other women of her generation Alice Grierson was a product of Victorian standards and mores. Nonetheless, a tremendous strength lay beneath the veneer of conventional virtues. She may have lived her life primarily as wife, mother, daughter, and sister, rather than as self-interested individual pursuing personal ambition, but she always remained her own person. The force of Alice's character shines through her correspondence.

I am indebted to many institutions and people for their assistance. First of all I wish to thank the Illinois State Historical Library, the Tom Green County Historical Society, and the Texas Technological University for giving their permission to reprint these letters. Thanks are also due the University of Oklahoma Press for permission to use letters that appeared in part in *Unlikely Warriors: General Benjamin H. Grierson and His Family.*

The staff of the Illinois State Historical Library, especially Cheryl Schnirring, were most patient and helpful. Jackie Wright of Springfield, Illinois, researched difficult questions in the Jacksonville area and provided gracious hospitality during visits to Springfield. Mary Williams of Fort Davis National Historic Site contributed great effort, assistance, and expertise on the Grierson family, and the debt I owe her is beyond calculation. Wayne Daniel, historian of the Fort Concho Museum, helped locate both materials and pictures. As always, Sara D. Jackson, of the National Archives and Records Service, steered me to the proper sources for personnel files and other military records.

Closer to home the staff of Interlibrary Loan of the University of Central Florida patiently and with unfailing good humor tracked down rare books and documents. I am especially grateful to Cheryl Mahan and Nancy Myler. Karen Lynette, of the Information Support Center of the College of Arts and Sciences, carefully retyped this manuscript more times than she cares to remember and always with great patience and a discerning eye for possible errors.

Bruce Dinges and Sherry Smith both read this manuscript and made valuable criticisms. Finally, two people were essential to the writing of this book. Sandra Myres first suggested that Alice Grierson be allowed to tell her story in her own words. As I began this project, I relied heavily on the insights and ideas in her publications. The other person who contributed far more than he will ever know was my husband, William H. Leckie. He supplied faith in the outcome, expertise on military questions, and assumed many of the burdens of running a household in order to give me the time needed to work on this endeavor. I have received assistance from many people, but the shortcomings and mistakes of this work are entirely my own.

Introduction

Alice Kirk Grierson was born in 1828 into a prosperous, upper-middle-class family of Youngstown, Ohio. Family records contain little information regarding her mother, Susan Bingham Kirk, but a good deal on her father, John Kirk, who made his fortune through merchandising and shrewd real-estate investments. A "conscience" Whig, he had been associated with temperance, the Underground Railroad, and movements to assist fugitive slaves in the 1840s and 1850s. These activities, an outgrowth of his involvement as an elder in the Disciples of Christ Church, had an abiding influence on his entire family.[1]

Alice was the oldest of thirteen children, and since her father believed in improving the status of women, he gave her the finest education within his means, sending her first to Huron Academy in Milan, Ohio, and later transferring her to a female seminary in Hudson, Ohio. After graduation Alice, like many educated young women in that era, taught school, first in her hometown and later in LaFayette, Indiana, and Springfield, Illinois.

Despite her father's misgivings, in 1854 she married Benjamin Henry Grierson, talented musician, bandleader, music teacher, and childhood friend from Youngstown. The wedding marked the culmination of a long courtship notable for its separations and reconciliations, largely because Ben lacked both piety and prospects. In the end, however, the strong physical attraction between them overcame Alice's religious scruples against marrying a man who was not a devout Christian.[2]

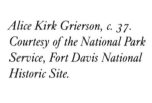

Alice Kirk Grierson, c. 37. Courtesy of the National Park Service, Fort Davis National Historic Site.

Both Ben and Alice brought to their marriage a strong desire to achieve marital happiness. Doubtless, Alice had been taught at her various schools that to succeed as a proper wife she needed to exhibit the qualities of "true womanhood": piety, purity, domesticity, and submissiveness.[3] Her piety was unquestioned, and she tried hard in the early years of her marriage to convert her husband. Seventeen years passed before she gave up entirely; nonetheless, there were no hard feelings on her husband's part. It was commonly believed in that era that women were morally superior to men, even while they were perceived as physically and intellectually inferior. Thus Ben Grierson viewed his wife's exhortations as the attempt of his "better half" to improve her less perfect partner.[4]

When it came to the matter of purity, Alice was outwardly conventional but not repressed. Many of her early letters to her husband contained warm expressions of love, such as: "Wouldn't I like to kiss, hug, love and almost devour you if I could only have you to myself today but I suppose you are safe from any such demonstration at present." Such declarations made it clear that she welcomed and enjoyed marital relations.[5] As for domesticity, she was a conscientious but not enthusiastic homemaker who found household tasks restricting, burdensome, and unending. "It is no wonder women in general have so little energy, they live so shut up in the house, they have no chance to grow hardy."[6]

The quality that gave her the most trouble was submissiveness. By nature she was frank, often brutally so. Moreover, since she and her hus-

Benjamin Henry Grierson at the end of the Civil War. Courtesy of the National Park Service, Fort Davis National Historic Site.

band both valued their relationship highly, and because he was strongly attached to her and viewed her as his moral superior, she exerted significant influence when it came to decision making. Her forthrightness, combined with her family's advocacy of women's rights, hardly made her an ideal candidate for submissive wifehood. However, Alice never dominated or henpecked her husband. To the contrary, she struggled valiantly to uphold his position as head of the household and often assented to his desires. At the same time, she was aware of her need to be able to state her opinions freely and to remain an individual in her own right, an effort that was not always easy.

In an attempt to increase his earnings following the birth of their first child, Ben Grierson entered business in Meredosia, Illinois. Any chance for success was destroyed by the depression that swept through Illinois after the panic of 1857. By the time Civil War broke out, the Griersons, deeply in debt, had lost their homestead and were residing with their two sons in the home of Ben's parents in Jacksonville, Illinois. Nothing in Alice's upbringing had prepared her to deal with these circumstances, but her stoicism enabled her to accept poverty without complaint as the manifestation of Providence. As she had told her father earlier when he had warned of impending financial disaster, "if prosperity is the best thing for us, I believe we shall have it, and if adversity, I hope we shall profit by its severe teachings."[7]

Ben Grierson joined the Union Army in 1861 as an unpaid aide in an

Illinois infantry regiment. His leadership ability catapulted him quickly to major and then colonel of the Sixth Illinois Cavalry. Alice learned for the first time what it meant to be a soldier's wife. Struggling to raise her sons alone, she watched with anxiety as the death toll in America's bloodiest war mounted.

Nonetheless, despite the dangers, there were compensations. In addition to a steady paycheck the army brought fame and recognition. In April 1863, while General Ulysses S. Grant sought to invest Vicksburg, Grierson led a diversionary raid through Mississippi. The six-hundred-mile dash through enemy territory was one of the great cavalry achievements of the war. By drawing as many as thirty-eight thousand Confederates away from Grant's army, it contributed significantly to the fall of the Southern fortress. Alice saw her husband emerge as a national hero whose picture appeared on the cover of *Harper's* and whose rank advanced to brigadier general. Another devastating raid the following year won him promotion to major general.[8]

When the war ended, Alice encouraged her husband to accept a position as colonel in the postwar army. Since he was now forty and she, at thirty-eight, had just given birth to their fourth child, long-term security seemed most important. Ben assumed command of the Tenth Cavalry, a regiment of black soldiers and white officers. Although neither understood clearly at first, the postwar army would call upon both husband and wife to render arduous service at the outposts of civilization.[9]

Fortunately, Alice brought to her new position a number of assets. These included her family upbringing, which would enable her to relate comfortably to other officers' wives of similar background.[10] In addition, her sound education would demonstrate its usefulness as she socialized with a wide variety of military and civilian personages. And finally, since she had met her share of personal tragedy (in addition to the business failure her second son, John Kirk, had died in infancy), she had developed a tough resiliency. This, more than any other attribute, would prove essential for enduring the vicissitudes of army life on the western frontier.

She was destined to experience her share of hardships as she lived at times in tents and bore her fifth child at Fort Riley in Kansas and her last two at Fort Sill in Indian Territory. As the wife of the commanding officer she would enjoy amenities and comforts not available to most other army wives, but she would also shoulder additional responsibilities. Among them were the tasks of setting the standards for other officers' wives, maintaining good relationships among the officers' families, functioning as chief hostess at each of her husband's posts, and serving as an informal second adjutant to her husband, especially during his absences. In addition, Alice Grierson would take on one other burden not usually assumed as enthusiastically by other officers' wives: an unflagging commitment to furthering the welfare of the enlisted men in the regiment.[11]

Finally, Alice would be obliged to care for her own family. This in itself was an arduous task given the number of her children and the primitive conditions at western posts. As the recollections of army wives make clear, women faced inadequate housing, the lack of staples such as fresh eggs, milk, and vegetables, and a scarcity of household help. Female servants transported from the East were notoriously unreliable, for they either returned home quickly, tired of the monotony and isolation of post life, or more commonly, found husbands on post and left domestic service. Of necessity most officers' wives relied heavily on off-duty enlisted men, known as *strikers*. But strikers were primarily soldiers, and given their long working hours even the commanding officer's wife occasionally found herself without assistance.[12]

Thus the life of a colonel's lady on the western frontier was demanding and rigorous in spite of the perquisites of military caste. For the most part Alice Grierson performed her duties without complaint or even comment. At times, however, the conflicting demands placed upon her proved more than she could bear, and her stoicism dissolved to reveal a troubled and sometimes anguished woman. One difficulty persisted. She felt tremendous tension as she sought to balance her roles as wife, mother, and person in her own right. Undoubtedly, other commanding officers' wives faced similar problems, but individual circumstances made Alice's ordeal especially severe.

Her family was larger than those of most officers' wives on the western frontier. And since Alice's childbearing extended over a seventeen-year period, in the first few years at isolated posts not only was she either pregnant or nursing, but she also had to contend with the problem of educating her older children at the same time that she adjusted to her new duties as wife of the commanding officer.[13] In her own words, she found it "hard ... to learn to harmonize public life with nursery duties, and other family cares." Eventually, the strain became so great after the birth and death of her seventh child that she left Fort Sill and went back to her parents' home in Chicago to recuperate. During this separation she wrote her husband a series of candid letters describing her discontent and calling for changes to make her situation more bearable. After gaining some concessions, she returned, and her life entered a new phase. She enjoyed a brief and welcome two-year respite when Colonel Grierson was placed on recruiting duty in Saint Louis. Then the family was assigned to Fort Concho.

In 1875 Fort Concho was a run-down, isolated post on the high plains of west Texas, and neither Colonel Grierson nor his wife viewed this change of station as other than a sentence of exile. In large measure they were correct. Through his support for the so-called Indian Peace Policy, Grierson had antagonized the "powers that be," notably Philip Sheridan, commanding general of the Division of the Missouri.

The seven years at Fort Concho brought grueling military duty to the colonel and a succession of tragedies especially painful to Alice, including the death of one child and the descent into mental illness of two others. A conscientious mother, she undoubtedly wondered if the family had not paid a heavy price for the financial security of her husband's military career.

In 1882 headquarters of the Tenth were transferred from Fort Concho to Fort Davis. At this picturesque post amid magnificent scenery Alice and her husband found an environment so enjoyable that they considered making it a permanent home. With this in mind and to provide some future for their children, Colonel Grierson plunged heavily into ranching. At one time he either owned or leased more than forty-five thousand acres of land in west Texas.[14] A fine soldier but a poor businessman, he succeeded only in increasing the family's indebtedness. To add to their difficulties, numerous relatives constantly required assistance. As the person responsible for maintaining close kinship ties, Alice never doubted that she and her husband would provide as much help as possible, notwithstanding their own growing obligations.

Despite her increasing anxiety over finances, Alice enjoyed their later assignments, Fort Davis and Whipple Barracks in Arizona Territory. Both were located in beautiful settings and more benign climates than Fort Concho. In part, however, her later stations were more pleasant because life on army posts was changing. The advance of the railroad to remote areas brought the comforts of civilization.[15] After a brief stay at Fort Grant, also in Arizona Territory, Colonel Grierson was made commander of the District of New Mexico.

This appointment brought the Griersons to the territorial capital of Sante Fe, where they had access to a wide variety of social circles and events. But Alice found her pleasure in life diminished. By now Colonel Grierson needed additional income to cover his investments and to assure an adequate retirement. He sought promotion persistently and just as persistently was passed over. His position as colonel of a black regiment and his stand on Indian affairs continued to cost him, for Sheridan had become commanding general of the army.[16]

Alice cared little about promotion for its own sake, but it was an ordeal to watch her husband repeatedly build up his hopes, endure suspense and uncertainty, and then experience disappointment. At this point her health began declining. A long-standing ailment became more troublesome and painful, but since she was not a complainer it failed to receive adequate attention. By the time doctors recognized the seriousness of her condition, she was beyond their help. On August 16, 1888, she died. Twenty months later Colonel Grierson obtained his long-sought star.

Although Alice never knew of her husband's promotion, her unwavering support, assistance, and counsel made it her achievement as well as his. Three months after his appointment, Benjamin Grierson celebrated his sixty-fourth birthday by retiring, as mandated by law, thereby ending a career that had spanned almost three decades, the greater part of which had been spent in the West with Alice.

In one sense, however, their life together was not over. Alice had left behind a large correspondence to husband, children, relatives, and friends which described the conditions she and her family faced in the frontier army. After her death her husband preserved most of the family letters, as well as many Alice had received from others. What emerges from them is an ongoing account of the challenges and difficulties faced by one commanding officer's wife in the trans-Mississippi West.

Sources and Methodology

The correspondence of Alice Kirk Grierson is located in four repositories. The largest collection exists in the Benjamin H. Grierson Papers at the Illinois State Historical Library in Springfield, Illinois. A second collection is in the Benjamin H. Grierson Papers, 1827–1941, in the Southwest Collection at Texas Technological University in Lubbock, Texas. A third collection, only recently opened to the public, was formerly in the possession of the late Susan Miles of San Angelo, Texas, and is currently on extended loan to the Fort Concho Museum from the Tom Green County Historical Society at San Angelo. Finally, the Fort Davis National Historic Site is the repository of miscellaneous documents, including genealogical studies and some undated correspondence. I have used abbreviations ISHL, TTU, TGCHS, and FDNHS in brackets at the end of each letter to indicate the collection from which it was derived.

The letters themselves were written for family and friends and not for publication; many were dashed off hurriedly, sometimes without any signature. Some letters were undated, and in these instances I have given them a date in brackets based on their relationship to other letters in the various collections. I have modernized archaic spellings, substituting *stayed* for *staid*, *wagons* for *waggons*, and so forth, and have regularized the capitalization. I have also corrected occasional misspellings such as *Calafornia* or *vaccinnation* and some names, such as *Smither*, which Alice often spelled inconsistently. Since paragraphs were usually nonexistent, they have been introduced to aid the reader. Finally, I have modified the punctuation in those cases when there was an obvious slip of the pen or when an error obscures the meaning of a sentence, and have regularized the position of punctuation in relation to quotation marks and the use of periods after abbreviations such as *Mrs.* and *Dr.*

Although the number of letters that has survived is amazing, some are missing. At times I have had to rely upon responses to Alice's letters to discover what happened and to carry the narrative forward. Moreover, for some periods of her life the correspondence is sparse, usually when she was with her husband for extended times. Since she was a prolific letter writer, she undoubtedly corresponded with others, but those letters were less likely to be salvaged.

The reader will notice that I have used ellipsis points to indicate deleted portions of letters. The missing material sometimes consists of prosaic details, such as household accounts, sewing supplies, tax bills, or orders for fuel or hardware. More commonly it contains passing references to a myriad of distant relatives or friends who could not easily be identified and whose introduction would only confuse the story. Alice's letters also include numerous references to officers, physicians, and clergymen who served in the West. An alphabetized appendix at the back of the book provides a brief biographical background on each of these figures. Any additions to the letters, such as first names, corrected spellings, or proper titles, are indicated by brackets.

My goal in editing these letters has been to prune them sufficiently so that the major conditions and concerns of Alice Grierson's life on frontier posts become visible and her personality and character emerge as clearly as possible. Of special interest is the nature of her relationship with her family, especially her husband and children, and how it changed over time. Finally, and most important, it is my hope that this edition of letters and correspondence will allow Alice Kirk Grierson to speak for herself and to tell the story of her experiences in the West as fully as possible in her own words.

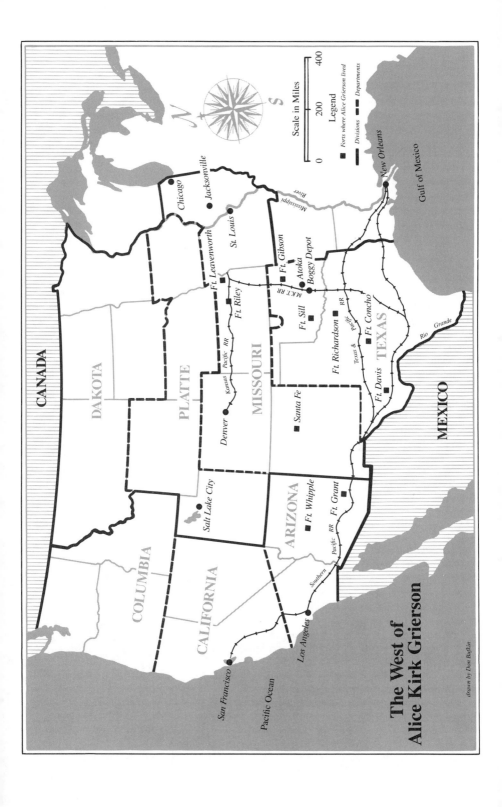

The West of
Alice Kirk Grierson

drawn by Don Bufkin

Legend
■ Forts where Alice Grierson lived
▬ ▬ Divisions
▬ ▬ Departments

Scale in Miles
0   200   400

CANADA

Pacific Ocean

San Francisco

Los Angeles

COLUMBIA

CALIFORNIA

ARIZONA

Ft. Whipple

Ft. Grant

Southern Pacific RR

Salt Lake City

DAKOTA

PLATTE

Denver

Kansas Pacific RR

MISSOURI

Santa Fe

Ft. Riley

Ft. Leavenworth

St. Louis

Chicago

Jacksonville

Ft. Sill

Ft. Gibson

Atoka

Boggy Depot

M.K.T. RR

Ft. Richardson

Ft. Concho

Ft. Davis

Texas & Pacific RR

TEXAS

Rio Grande

MEXICO

Gulf of Mexico

New Orleans

Mississippi River

Chapter 1

EARLY YEARS ON
THE FRONTIER

In March 1866 Benjamin Grierson, recently mustered out of the Union Army, appeared before the Congressional Joint Committee on Reconstruction to present testimony on conditions in the Southern states. Although he spoke with conviction regarding the need for continuing federal protection for freedmen, he was far from certain about his own future.[1] He wrote Alice seeking her view on his reentry into the army.

Since their marriage was based on mutual respect and affection, he would not have chosen a career objectionable to his wife. Nonetheless, Alice carefully phrased her reply so that the final decision remained her husband's. She also urged him to build her a home, an understandable desire given the loss of their homestead earlier. Clearly, Alice failed to comprehend that the army would bring frequent changes of station, thereby rendering her desire for a permanent home unrealistic. Still, the Griersons did expand the family home in Jacksonville, where Ben's father still resided.[2]

The bantering tone of Alice's letter was unusual. Although she advocated temperance, she had been drinking ale as medicine for a sore throat. As the letter progressed, her spirits improved. By the time she reached the point where she had just read the letter to her oldest child, her scrawl was almost illegible.

Chicago March 12th 1866

My dear Ben

Yours of the 6th & 7th were received last Friday evening—that of the 8th—this morning. I am exceedingly pleased with your testimony given before the Reconstruction Committee, & can imagine that your "Yes & No Sir's" were given with a decided vim. I knew your evidence had appeared in the Chicago papers of the 7th but had not seen it.

I strongly incline to the opinion that you will enter the Regular Army, and that it will be best for you to do so—Still we will see.

I am glad you are having a pleasant time in Washington—you will of course say as many good things, for or in my behalf to our mutual acquaintances as you choose, also give them my kind regards &c. . . .

What crotchet do you think has got into *my* head? Nothing more nor less than, as you "*have at present no occupation*" of trying to revive in *your cranium,* a crotchet which to any certain knowledge has twice within the last eleven years had tolerably full possession of it—namely *housebuilding*—and if you can't at first sight—"see it" —I do hereby warn you, to fully arm, equip, & in every possible way prepare yourself for a regular siege from me, on this subject —and to prevent all possibility of misunderstanding, I do clearly express to you in the following words, my wish that you—Ex Brevet &c, do in the shortest *convenient* time, *immediately* proceed to build your "beloved wife" Alice K. G. &c—a house, on a lot—near the Institution for the Blind—in the town of Jacksonville. . . .

Said house to be modelled in all its main features like the house in which said Alice is at this present time, most comfortably ensconced, waiting with extreme serenity the arrival of her Lord and Governor the aforesaid Benj——H——Ex Brevet &c so on—At which time she does propose in the most unimpassioned manner of which she, the said Alice is capable, of laying before this same famous personage (her own dear husband!) the why's wherefores of a proceeding heretofore so unheard of—"from Ancient History down to the present time."

. . . I was miserably weak, last week, & scarcely able to be out of bed the first three days, have bought, & drank five bottles of Ale, and feel much stronger—but my mouth is quite sore—showing me the exceeding importance of taking the best care of my health. The children are very well—All send love—Your *loving,* "beloved wife."

Alice K. G.

I have just read this letter to Charlie & asked his opinion of it. Most *unhesitatingly* he pronounced it "a love letter." Do you agree with him in opinion?

[ISHL]

Grierson received the highest recommendations from both Ulysses S. Grant and William Tecumseh Sherman. When he was offered the colonelcy of the Tenth Cavalry, one of two cavalry regiments to be staffed by white officers and black enlisted men, he readily accepted. His Civil war experiences had taught him to respect the fighting abilities of blacks.

He left Washington and returned to Illinois by way of Youngstown, Ohio. During his travels Alice's letters failed to reach him, and in exasperation he sent her an irate note ordering her to "write immediately." Alice's response from Chicago, where she was visiting her parents, was quick and straightforward and indicates her rather unusual views, given the times, regarding the proper relations between husband and wife.

[Chicago, April 4, 1866]

My dear Ben,

... I want *always* to have my husband the male head of the establishment I live in, and I of course want to be the female head. I have several reasons for this feeling which are too long to write, but which I will tell you.

Before we were married I told you I wanted a certain amount of money of my own, to use just as a husband does, exactly as he pleases, or thinks right or proper. We sat on the porch at the back of the house when I told you, and if you pass the old brown home possibly you may recall it. You know of course there never has been such an arrangement, and I never have been, and don't know that I ever shall be quite satisfied without it, unless you should come *really* to think the money you earn, as much mine as yours, which you certainly do not now. . . .

I don't know how satisfactory this letter may prove. I have at least written *immediately* as you requested. Did you expect *your letter* would inspire me to write one "gay and festive" *kind* and *loving?*

I have great faith however, that as you recall the scenes of other days, and the "Little May" who shared many of them with you that instead of hardening your heart against me you will soften enough to write me *in less than eight days* from the date of your last—indeed I should not be *much surprised* to hear that you had deliberately and wilfully, fallen in love with me over again, so deeply too, that you almost entertained the absurd idea, that an earnest—truthful —woman might perhaps have as *clear*, and *just*, notions of right and wrong in even business matters as a man.

I am very sure at all events that you will gratify me by writing "by return of mail," and keep me "posted" as to your plans and whereabouts. I think you don't know how little heart one has to write when they feel no assurance that the letters will reach the person for whom they are designed, for a long time if at all. . . .

. . . I have dreamed of your being here several times. It is getting late, I must go to bed, so "good night my love good night."

Yours affectionately
Alice K. G.

. . .

Sunday Morning

Dear Ben,

When I first read your letter yesterday afternoon, I was so angry I thought I would not answer it at all, but in a minute I was able to laugh over it and hope you will agree with me that I have acted more sensibly.
[ISHL]

In September 1866, after reporting for duty to General Winfield S. Hancock, commander of the Department of the Missouri, Colonel Grierson proceeded to Fort Leavenworth, Kansas, to begin organizing his regiment. By mid-November Alice had arrived with their children, Charlie, Robert, and Edie, aged eleven, six, and fifteen months, respectively. Their lives in the frontier army had begun.

Alice found Leavenworth an old established fort with comfortable quarters and ample opportunities for social activities. The post itself, located on high ground overlooking the Missouri River and fertile prairies, was situated in the midst of a rich, agricultural area. Thus fresh vegetables were readily available and additional articles could be purchased in Leavenworth City three miles to the south.[3]

They had been together only a few months when Ben was called home by his father's terminal illness. During his absence Alice assumed responsibility for keeping him informed of the progress being made toward recruiting and training black soldiers, progress that was impeded by the prejudice of the post commander, Colonel William Hoffman.

Organizing the twelve companies proceeded slowly, due to Colonel Grierson's insistence on a high quality of recruit. Selecting the officers of the Tenth also posed problems, for many refused to serve with blacks. In her husband's absence Alice kept a watchful eye on the arriving personnel and duly reported her observations in her letters.

As far as the Griersons were concerned, one of the most important men to obtain as an officer for the Tenth Cavalry was Samuel Woodward. He had served as Grierson's adjutant in the Sixth Illinois Cavalry during the war, and it was the colonel's hope that he would eventually fill that position in the new regiment as well. Several months would elapse before Woodward could assume his duties, but thereafter for two decades he would serve his commanding officer as trusted confidant and Alice as close friend and adviser.[4]

Like many officers, Woodward had earned a brevet, or honorary, title as major in the war, though his actual rank was that of lieutenant. When he joined the reorganized army, Woodward was always referred to as *major*, just as Ben Grierson and John W. Davidson, the Tenth's lieutenant colonel, were often addressed as *general* because of their Civil War brevets.

This profusion of actual and honorary titles existed throughout the army in this period and complicated the matter of observing correct protocol. For example, Frances Roe, the young bride of Lieutenant Fayette Roe, became so confused during a social occasion at Fort Lyon in Colorado Territory in 1871 that she addressed the commanding officer as *mister*, much to the consternation and embarrassment of those assembled.[5]

Fort Leavenworth Apr. 11th 1867

Dear Ben

... A paper came to you from Washington, this morning, containing a notice of your confirmation as Brevet Maj. Gen. ...

Gen. Hoffman had, to use a rowdy phrase, "been after Lt. Alvord [acting adjutant of the Tenth]—with a sharp stick"—ordering him two or three days ago to draw arms for his company without fail next day. I suppose he has sent in the requisition for them today —has been issuing clothing to the company—drilling them twice a day, and so forth.

Lieut. Spencer was thrown from his horse—or, *he says* his horse fell with him—night before last, his head cut, and back bruised so that he can do nothing for the present. I believe his hurts are not considered serious. Lieut. Graham went to Kansas City—but was telegraphed back here to inspect horses, fifty of which had arrived. . . . Gen. Davidson, I suppose you know, is confirmed Lt. Col. of the 10th Cav. . . .

Yesterday morning we had near an inch of snow, today is so lovely a Spring day as one need wish. Mrs. Alvord, Charlie, and I, intend going to the city this afternoon. I want to get a hat for Charlie, which I had not time to get on Saturday, when I got his and Robert's clothes. I also want to get some garden seed. . . .

I understand Gen. Hoffman is rather distressed because he expects Gen. Stanley with the white troops to leave here the 18th and does not expect his own here until the 20th—only colored troops being here in the meantime—he gives that as the reason for hurrying Lt. Alvord to get their arms.

I presume I shall be moderately *delighted* to see you on your return and if I make no loud demonstrations of joy—probably Edith will make enough for both as she seems to wonder what keeps papa away so long.

A letter came from Maj. Woodward yesterday in which he regrets not having seen you as you passed through St. Louis and apprehensive that he may not be in town as you return. I send this to his care thinking you will be more likely to get it, than if I send it to Jacksonville.

Hoping you will not have occasion to extend your absence longer than you spoke of in your letter.

I am yours as ever
Alice K. Grierson

[ISHL]

The work of recruiting enlisted men and officers continued slowly, but as the companies were formed they were dispatched to aid in countering the Indian threat to outlying white settlements in Kansas and to the Kansas and Pacific Railroad, then under construction. As the following letter indicates, the completed units had already attracted their share of laundresses.

Until 1878, military regulations allowed each company three to four laundresses, who were paid by officers and men. A hard-working laundress could earn as much as thirty to forty dollars a month; many were married to enlisted men, who were paid only sixteen dollars a month. Nonetheless, their living conditions were usually abominable, for they resided with their husbands and numerous children in tents, sod houses, dugouts, or hovels behind the barracks or close to stables or creeks. Since these women were not considered "ladies" in the caste-ridden society of the army, they did not socialize with the officers' wives, save for occasional appearances at post hops. On the whole, they were poorly treated by army officials, as the following incident makes clear.[6]

Fort Leavenworth May 21st 1867

My dear Ben

Your note of the 16th informing me of Father's death came Sunday morning, that of the 15th telling me of your arrival in J—— was received yesterday (Monday) morning. I am glad you reached home before Father's death and that he knew you.

I hoped you would be at home today, but Lt. Alvord told me last evening that you had applied by telegraph to Gen. Hancock for an extension of your leave until the 1st of July. Lt. Alvord went into Dept. Head Qdrs. just after your dispatch had been received—they were hesitating about granting you an extension, not having heard of Father's death, but upon being informed of it, assented to your request.

They rushed Company C off in great haste—tried to get it off Friday morning but did not succeed until Sunday noon as the weather was quite rainy. The first time they were mounted, they started off on their march to Ft. Riley. Gen. Hoffman made Lt. Spencer Quarter Master of the company, and sent him along. Spencer tried to get off from going, but went in an ambulance at last.

Mary [Alice's maid] informed me Thursday evening that she was going with the company. I paid her off with great satisfaction, glad to get rid of her, she went as one of the laundresses, although Gen. Hancock ordered no laundresses to be taken. Capt. Byrne told the men to put their trunks in one of the wagons and told the women to walk on until they were out of sight of the Fort, and then they might ride.

Gen. Hoffman and Dr. Irwin were highly incensed that you put the man whom Dr. Irwin had as Hospital attendant, into the company. Gen. Hoffman ordered Lt. Alvord to take his name off from the list, so that he could remain. Lt. Alvord told him he would not venture to do such a thing when your signature was affixed to the paper.

Gen. Davidson has finally received his commission as Lt. Col. He says he is going South soon, and is going to take every recruit with him—hopes there will be a good many here. Ten or eleven recruits came from Philadelphia the day after you left. Lt. Alvord detailed as many of them for various purposes as possible, as Gen. Hoffman ordered him to detail eight men for teamsters. The Philadelphians are disappointed—as they expected to be made noncommissioned officers.

No officers have reported since you left, but the names of four more lieutenants were published in the N.Y. Tribune last week. . . .

yours as ever

Alice K. Grierson

[ISHL]

Alice welcomed her husband back to Fort Leavenworth in early June. Late in July, orders arrived transferring headquarters to Fort Riley in Kansas. For the Tenth Cavalry it signaled the beginning of two decades of service on the Great Plains.

The move occurred none too soon, for Alice was expecting her fifth child the first of October. After a brief trip she found that her new home was more attractive than Leavenworth. One observer, Jennie Barnitz, the wife of Captain Albert Barnitz of the Seventh Cavalry, was at Riley about the same time and described the fort as "beautiful." Officers were housed in fairly spacious, "well finished" stone dwellings with piazzas in front, separate kitchens in back, and cellars underneath. The post even offered such amenities as a library and reading rooms.[7]

In mid-September Grierson received orders summoning him back to Fort Leavenworth for the court-martial of George Armstrong Custer, lieutenant colonel of the Seventh Cavalry. Custer was charged with dereliction of duty for having left his command at Fort Wallace, Kansas, "without permission" to join his wife Elizabeth at Fort Riley. Additional charges included "marching his men excessively . . . all on a journey of private business" and, even more serious, "excessive cruelty and illegal conduct in putting down mutiny in the 7th Cavalry by shooting deserters."[8]

Ben had been gone a few days when Alice received a package from her father in Chicago, along with a letter admonishing her to practice celibacy following the birth of her child during the period set forth in the Old Testament. Advice from John Kirk on health, nutrition, and child care was not uncommon. Nor was it uncharacteristic for him, as a devout member of the Disciples of Christ, to draw his tenets and guidelines from the Bible.[9] It was, however, unusual for him to write this bluntly on intimate sexual matters. He did so because he feared for his daughter's safety, a fear that was fully justified given the medical facilities on most posts.

This was Alice's first experience in childbirth on the frontier, and she had to endure not only labor but its possible complications afterward. Many officers' wives believed that, with few exceptions, doctors in the frontier army were more adept at treating gunshot wounds and amputating limbs than delivering babies or caring for mothers.[10]

[Chicago, September 19, 1867]

Dear Alice

I knew nothing of your wants until I wrote the first sheet that I read to your mother, when she called my attention to your letter. I inclose your An. Ex. Co. receipt for the Abdominal Supporter & the Hair Net. If the supporter should not be of the right size it can be exchanged. I got one of medium size. . . .

. . . In connection with the Abdominal Supporter, I think you will do well to read, mark, and inwardly digest the Levitical Law, contained in the 12th chapter of Leviticus. Why a woman should be unclean 66 days when she bears a maid child, and only 33 days when she bears a manchild, has always been a mystery to me, but such is the stubborn fact. I have taken the trouble to consult sundry able physicians on the subject, but none could give any light. My theory is this, that when a female child is born, it partakes more of the mother, and consequently reduces the system more, and thus requires a longer time for the system to recuperate.

Again, I have no idea that a pious Jew ever had sexual intercourse with his wife during the blood of her purifying, within the 33 or 66 days. In my opinion, the violation of this good old law, has been the cause of thousands of premature deaths, and untold miseries to women, after childbearing.

J. K.

A hint to the wise is sufficient.

N.B.No2 If this Jewish law had never been violated, healthy women would not require Abdominal Supporters. Nor any thing of the kind, in my opinion.

[ISHL]

Alice delivered Benjamin Henry Grierson, Jr., safely on October 3. Six days later she wrote her husband, still at Leavenworth, describing her recovery and the assistance given her by a woman she barely knew.

Fort Riley Oct. 9th 1867

My dear Ben

It is just a week since I last wrote you. Yours of the 4th, 6th and the note of the 4th were all duly received. . . .

I am getting along very nicely, grow stronger every day. . . . B. H. Jun. is just as good as can be. I think looks so far, more like Mother Grierson than any one else—has long upper lip, sort of a double chin, large nose, high forehead, and beautiful black hair, as luxuriant for his size as yours, it grows at the side of his temples like yours. I hope he will have eyes the color of yours but can't now tell what they will be.

I do not think it will be "old and young Ben," I will allow neither in my hearing. I would like to have him named for you, and the initials the same in writing, but think Henry a prettier name than Benjamin or Ben, and Harry I think rather pretty for a baby.

Mrs. Mahar went to Leavenworth to her husband yesterday, she said she would try and see you and tell you just how we all were. She was very attentive to me after the baby was born, stayed right in the room ready to do all the little waiting on I or the children needed. I was very glad she was here.

I stayed in bed three days, then got on the lounge to have my bed made, and found it so comfortable, and such a pleasant change from the bed, that I have lain on it most of the time since during the day. . . . I am very careful of myself I assure you. The children are much pleased with "little buvver" as Edith calls him, she is very jealous of "Mama's baby," that is, don't like to see any one take him from me.

I suppose you had better bring, a knife to Charlie, cars or a steamboat to Robert, and if you could find a box of thick, square, alphabet blocks for Edith, I think she would be pleased with them. Do you have to go again to Leavenworth for the trial of others? I wish you might not have to.

If Capt. Alvord is assigned to Co. M. and they go away soon I shall miss them very much indeed, particularly if you are away. I felt somewhat lonely last evening, it was chilly and very dark part of the afternoon. The children were great company for me but I thought it would be much nicer if you were here. I believe Alvord and Woodward have kept you pretty well posted.

Yours affectionately Alice K. G.

. . .

The baby has a long hand and beautiful long slender fingernails.

Yours Alice

[ISHL]

Following Custer's court-martial, which concluded a few days later with a verdict of guilty and a sentence of dismissal from rank and command for one year without pay, Colonel Grierson returned to Fort Riley.[11] By the end of October, news arrived that the Southern Cheyennes and Arapahoes, the Comanches, the Kiowas, and the Kiowa-Apaches had signed the Medicine Lodge Treaties. With these tribes amply supplied with government annuities and confined to two large reservations, away from white settlement and the transcontinental railroad currently under construction, the long-term prospects for peace appeared excellent.[12] The easing of tensions allowed Alice and her family to enjoy the amenities of a well-ordered post.

The peace was short-lived. Disputes arose, for Congress, preoccupied with impeachment proceedings against President Andrew Johnson, was slow to appropriate the necessary funds. Thus annuities were late in coming, and by the spring of 1868, disillusioned Kiowas and Comanches were again raiding the Texas frontier. In the face of growing hostilities, Colonel Grierson was appointed commander of the District of Indian Territory and ordered to move his headquarters to Fort Gibson. From there he was instructed to search for a site for a new fort farther west, suitable for policing the tribes of the southern plains.[13]

The move to Fort Gibson took ten days. Upon arrival Alice and the children discovered that their new home was a small post in which the officers' quarters had fallen into disrepair. The only housing available was a pair of tents, although work had begun on more permanent quarters.[14]

Alice did not even enjoy her husband's company. He left immediately on his exploring expedition, but as always during their separations she kept him well informed on both family and military matters.

Fort Gibson June 19th 1868

Dear Ben

Yours of the 11th duly received. Lt. Munson has just informed me that there is to be a mail starting for Ft. Arbuckle at 1 o'clock, so I will send a line to inform you of our flourishing conditions. We have been very well since you left, except one or two days this week the baby has not been quite well, he has a new tooth, and a fourth one almost through which with the hot weather is sufficient reason for his slight illness.

The ice in the cellar gave out last Saturday. I have been sharing mine this week with Dr. Crarey, as I felt in duty bound to do. Lt. Josslyn has promised to send him some from the icehouse hereafter. It will however be gone from there in a short time. I think if you are not here by the 10th of July you will probably see no more ice in Fort Gibson this summer.

I have not yet moved and scarcely expect to before the 22nd or 23rd, may possibly move tomorrow. I suppose the plastering of the basement is finished, but probably the doors and windows are not yet in. I see very few persons except Mrs. Alvord, and the Chaplain, instead of being lonely however, the quiet is very refreshing to my nerves—the new house on account of the hammering will be less agreeable than this. . . .

. . . Robert wants me to tell you he has had a nice skiff ride. There was a sail in the boat, and he went up the river two or three miles. He sends you 25 kisses, ten to Capt. Alvord and ten to Maj. Woodward. . . . Robert is going to take this note up to Lt. Munson.

Yours as ever

Alice K. G.

[ISHL]

Many of the army wives, such as Elizabeth Custer or Frances Roe, who came in contact with black soldiers exhibited fear and prejudice. Alice was not without bigotry, but she never felt afraid of the "buffalo soldiers," as they were called, a name given them by Cheyenne Indians.[15] Instead she was extremely protective, rising to their defense whenever any officer or officer's wife treated them unfairly in her view. Meanwhile, she had a battle of her own to fight. Having moved out of the tent into the basement of their unfinished home, she found herself protecting the children from falling plaster.

Fort Gibson July 5th 1868

Dear Ben

I have sufficient material for a long letter to you, but have not the opportunity of writing it—am not very well. Maria [Alice's maid] has been sick for several days, so I have the baby to take care of &c.

Yesterday was a 4th of July long to be remembered. Sergeant Brown, Innes, and Woodson were put in the Guard House through Mrs. Alvords influence. Sergeant Brown was soon released but remains under arrest, in his quarters with leave to go to the kitchen. I sent for Lt. Munson last evening, who said he would see Maj. Bryant this morning, and learn how long Innes and Woodson are to be kept prisoners. Lt. Munson also allowed Innes to be brought over here as I wished to hear his side of the story from himself.

From all I hear, I think Mrs. Alvord (and I went to see her) has acted very unwisely. I expressed my opinion very decidedly to her, and told her that I felt very sure you would disapprove of her proceedings, and I thought her husband would also. She thinks Innes treated her with great disrespect, and impertinence in not hitching up Frank in the buggy so soon as she wished a few days ago.

I believe Mrs. Alvord intends going to meet Capt. Alvord on his return, and should you hear from herself, or the Capt. her version of this story I hope you will be very guarded in expressing approval of her conduct until you hear the other side of the story.

Our basement rooms have proved less desirable so far, than they seemed to promise before we occupied them. The baby has had two narrow escapes and Edith one, of being crushed by falling plastering. About noon yesterday there was a furious storm of wind and rain, which came driving in at the windows and doors above, causing a quantity of wet plastering to fall ruining the looks of one of our parlor chairs—that green carpet chair, injuring numerous books, and other articles, among them that red carpet.

I have not allowed it to disturb my serenity, however. I have a perfectly clear conscience about having tried to take care of our worldly goods since we broke up at Riley, and shall not fret over them. Shall consider we are fortunate if the house is completed without any broken bones, or other serious accident to any of the family. . . .

Unless you hear of this guard house matter from Capt. or Mrs. Alvord, probably you had better not mention it until your return. We heard last week that you were encamped in safety in the Wichita Mountains, and hope you may return safely by the 15th or sooner.

Yours as ever

Alice K. Grierson

[ISHL]

Shortly thereafter the colonel returned to Fort Gibson, and Sergeants Innes and Woodson were released. Several months later Alice decided to return to Illinois to place Charlie with her parents so that he could attend school in Chicago. She did so reluctantly, but he was now thirteen, and no educational facilities existed at Fort Gibson. Separation seemed to be the only solution to the problem that sooner or later plagued every military family with children at frontier posts.[16]

Ben accompanied his family east to cast his vote for Grant in the fall election and then returned to Indian Territory, where more trouble had erupted. Other southern plains Indians had left their reservations. Cheyennes and Arapahoes, enraged by the government's failure to distribute annuities at the promised time, were raiding settlements along the Saline and Solomon rivers in northwestern Kansas.[17]

Alice had planned to rejoin Ben at Fort Gibson in early January, but inclement weather and an illness of Edie's forced her to remain in Jacksonville. For the first time Alice expressed fear in a letter that continuing separation could injure her relationship with her husband. She was not receiving mail regularly from him.

Jacksonville Dec. 16th 1868

Dear Ben

I have been thinking so much this week of going to Gibson. I want so very much to be there, and yet the going is by far the most formidable work I ever attempted. . . .

. . . One serious objection to our staying here through the winter is that we will not be any better acclimated to the Indian Territory than we were last spring, and be just as likely to have Fevers and Ague, as last summer. The main thing is that it is unnatural and wrong for families to be so separated. I never see John and Elizabeth [Ben's brother and sister-in-law] together, but what I see the bad effects of their having lived apart all these years. Louisa [Semple, Ben's widowed sister] notices it too. . . .

I wish you were satisfied to stay in Fort Gibson until the Military Authorities send you some place else. Just think how much worse off you would be if they would send you to Alaska or California. I hope you will get your pay, and send me another $100, so that I will not have to borrow of John if I go. I am quite sure he has used up his ready money, so that he has very little himself. . . .

I rather think if I hear from you that our quarters have a little more room for us, and are somewhat nearer finished, and if you send me money, that I will get up courage enough to go from the 5th to the 15th of Jan.—say as soon after the 5th as the weather and health permits. I would not of course leave here in severely cold weather, if I could start just after a cold snap when it has moderated, I might perhaps get along without serious inconvenience, I must try and get some overshoes lined with wool, as our feet would be most likely to suffer.

I shall not expect you to come farther than Baxter's Springs to meet us, nor will I expect you to start until you hear from me more definitely than this. I have $60.00 still.

It is after 10 o'clock and I must go to bed. Pa says Charlie is a very good boy.

Yours affectionately
Alice K. G.

[ISHL]

The next day Alice received a backlog of letters from Ben indicating that, because of the outbreak of Indian troubles, he would spend little time at Fort Gibson. The need to establish a new fort farther west was now not simply desirable but urgent and would prolong their separation.

Alice had news of her own.

Jacksonville Dec. 17th 1868

My dear Ben

Yours of the 4th, 5th, 6th, and 7th were received this morning. I had quite a feast reading so much. After I read them all over to myself, I read them aloud to Louisa. Your storm at Fort Gibson commenced sooner than ours; we had snow on the 6th but the high wind not until the 7th and 8th. I hope your journey, whatever its length, may be made in safety. I wish you might overtake Major Kidd's command, but it is not very probable you can.

I am very decidedly of the opinion that you had better not come to Olathe or Kansas City, as it is by no means certain that the children would all be well enough to start on such a journey, on the arrival of a telegram—just now Edie has a cold, and for two nights past has had an ugly, croupy, cough, such as I would not like at the beginning of such a trip. Neither do I feel quite sure of my own health. I can scarcely believe I am in a "family way," yet if I am not soon unwell, I shall fear an attack of flooding, such as I had that spring you were in Paducah, or else be settled in the belief that the other "is what's the matter."

I am now resting in the hope that the elements and every thing else may combine to allow us to go to you sometime in Jan. I shall wait to hear of your arrival, or of the probability of your return to Gibson. If I am obliged to stay here all winter, the time will not seem so long if I have the hope that I may go to you before Spring. A bird was singing today as if Spring had already come—it is quite warm and the snow melting very fast, now is the time for mud and high water.

Louisa wants me to tell you what a very good girl Edie is. Louisa bought some toys for Robert, Edie and Harry for Christmas, and yesterday made a nice little muff and comfortable for Edie's doll. . . .

I intend writing to you twice a week, hoping the letters may reach you sometime. Edie wants to send you a dozen little kisses.

Yours affectionately
Alice K. Grierson

[ISHL]

At last both the weather and the children's health permitted the journey. After a train ride to Saint Louis, Alice and the children, accompanied
by Louisa Semple, boarded a river steamer bound for Memphis, a stop
along the way.

St. Louis Feb. 11th 1869

My dear Ben

Here we are on board the Memphis Packet Luminary—all
"Hunky Dory" as Edy says—so far. They say the boat will leave
at 5 o'clock and that it connects with the White River boats. We
don't feel as brilliant as we probably will after a good night's sleep
as Louisa did not even lie down last night much less sleep and I
was only undressed a little more than an hour. . . .

. . . I received on Tuesday your letters written from 8th to 12th
Jan., on the way to Fort Arbuckle, also a note from John asking
me if he should return to Jacksonville to assist me in getting off.
Harvey [Fuller, Ben's brother-in-law] did all that was necessary,
and was very kind. Edie had a second chill Monday but has had
none since. If our journey continues as pleasant as it has been so
far, we shall be very fortunate.

Yours as ever
Alice K. Grierson

[ISHL]

The small party remained at Memphis a few days visiting friends and
then boarded a steamboat that brought them down the Arkansas River
to Fort Gibson. In Ben's absence they were met by their friend Samuel
Woodward, Alvord's replacement as adjutant.

Alice's arrival coincided with the appearance of Colonel DeLancey
Floyd-Jones, Ben's successor as post commander at Gibson whom Alice
addressed mistakenly as Colonel Jones. The demand for housing now
exceeded the supply, setting in motion a constant shuffling as the highest-
ranking officers with the longest periods of service claimed the more
desirable quarters, "ranking out" the families of junior officers. Only the
commanding officer's family was entitled to a separate dwelling with four
rooms and a kitchen, but even these quarters were small.[18] As Alice's letter demonstrates, she was willing to share her home with Colonel Floyd-
Jones (she had already turned one room over to the chaplain). She was
even more eager to give it up entirely to rejoin her husband.

As always, Alice continued to intercede for the buffalo soldiers, this time for Mat Moss, who would one day join the family as a striker. As was customary in the army, he would then be referred to by his last name, whereas nonmilitary servants were always called by their first names.

Fort Gibson Feb. 26th 1869
½ past 10 P.M.

Dear Ben

Louisa and the children are all in bed, and I have since read your long letter of the 24th for the 2nd time. I read it so disconnectedly this afternoon, as there were a number of persons in, and so much talking done, that I could only get the main substance of the letter, without remembering all the details. It is too late to answer it tonight, but as there are so many things to be said, I thought it well enough to tell you tonight that we arrived about 2 o'clock this afternoon, "right side up with care." As soon as the boat "Ft. Smith" landed, I saw the buggy and horses on the hill and knew some one was waiting for us, but as I could not see you among the crowd, I knew you could not be here. . . .

. . . I assure you I am glad to be here, although you are gone, for two weeks steamboating, at one time, is quite sufficient for moderate people. Maj. Woodward assisted us from the boat to the buggy, and drove up for us, as the horses were feeling so well that Bill [a servant] did not care to have the responsibility of so precious a load. The Chaplain had the house warm, and things in order, and comfortable for us, also went to the commissary and got all we need until tomorrow after breakfast.

It has been two months now since I have had a servant and it is quite a luxury to have Bill, and tomorrow Maria is coming to help part of the day. I shall have either Maria, or Bill's wife, I suppose. . . .

. . . If this letter should reach you before you see Gen. Sheridan, I want you to think twice before you urge him to allow your HeadQuarters to remain here nominally. Of course we can't tell what changes will occur within perhaps a few months after Grant is President, but I am strongly inclined to think you will never *live* at Gibson again.

I have not the least intention of going back to Illinois, for years, if you remain in the Indian Territory, and I would, over and over, rather live in two rooms at Arbuckle, if you are most of the time at Medicine Bluff, than to have this whole house, nearly two hundred miles farther from you. I like Ft. Gibson well enough, and these quarters very well, but it is far more desirable to me, if it is unwise or impracticable, to be with you, to be just as near as possible.

I am very sure that since my arrival here, I have *felt* positive indications that we may make our calculations for the arrival of a young stranger by midsummer, and if we are to emigrate either to Medicine Bluff, or nearer it the sooner the better. Louisa, and all our acquaintances here can testify that I have not "taken on," either that you are not here, or at the uncertainty of future prospects.

There are several questions, however, which in my mind have been settled for years, and others, which though decided more recently, are still on the list of settled questions. I shall certainly intentionally leave nothing undone which will add either to the comfort of Louisa, myself, or the children. I intend to unpack and use most of our things, shall spread down all the carpets, hang the pictures, and make the house as homelike as possible, but shall put just as few tacks in the carpets as will answer the purpose, and shall hold myself and our possessions in readiness for marching orders at short notice. . . .

The Chaplain would have moved yesterday, but I asked him to stay until the rooms were wanted. I asked Maj. Woodward to say to Col. Jones that if he wished to occupy half of these quarters he was at liberty to do so. Whether he does occupy them or not, I shall feel better satisfied that I have made the proposal. If you were to be here, I would much prefer having the house to ourselves the main part of it at least.

Since writing the above, Col. Jones has called—he tells me that Mrs. Alvord intends moving in with Dr. Delaney's family, and that when she does, he will for the present move into her quarters; he is now staying at Major Bryant's. All of the officers and ladies of the garrison have called to see us, except Major Bryant, and his mother who never makes calls.

Monday Morn
March 1st

Dear Ben,

I have been so much interrupted in writing this letter that is not a very satisfactory one to me. When I once get the housekeeping in regular running order it will probably be somewhat easier for me to write.

Mat Moss sent me a letter yesterday, asking me to use my influence for his release, as he killed Maybee [a buffalo soldier] in self defence. I know of course that I can really do nothing about it, but if he is to be tried by Court Martial can't you have the court appointed soon, so that if there is a chance of his being cleared, he can be out of that wretched Guard House as soon as possible. The Chaplain is still here, as I prefer he should stay until I want the room. . . .

. . . The children are pleased to be here, and see familiar things, and faces. Harry has quite a bad cold, but I shall try and cure him as soon as possible.

I scarcely slept at all on Friday night, thinking of the many changes that have taken place, and are still to come. I shed some quiet tears all to myself, over our mutual disappointment, in not meeting here. You must remember that I think the comfort of a family depends much more upon the family *being together* in love, than on the house they are quartered in, and that I am unwilling to be separated from you any longer than is absolutely necessary. It may be that we would all be healthier at Medicine Bluff or Arbuckle than here. I have no wish to dictate, but suggest.

I have sent for some men to help move heavy furniture, boxes &c and must be ready to direct them, so goodbye for the present.

Yours affectionately
Alice K. Grierson

I hoped I would get a letter from Charlie, before I sent this, but the mail due yesterday has not arrived that I have heard of. So I know nothing of him since we left Jacksonville.

[ISHL]

The site Colonel Grierson had chosen and General Philip Sheridan had approved earlier for the new post was located at the confluence of

Cache and Medicine Bluff creeks on the eastern edge of the Wichita Mountains. Described by one observer as a "beautiful locality ... wild, romantic, and full of nature," the region inspired Ben's enthusiasm. In his letters he wrote of the gently rolling hills, the groves of hickory, oak, and cottonwood, and above all the "sparkling mountain streams."[19] But eager as he was to have Alice and the children join him, much work remained to be done before even the simplest accommodations could be constructed. He had no additional appropriations from Congress, no labor force save his soldiers, and the nearest railroad was three hundred miles away.[20]

In the meantime, Alice tried to make herself as comfortable as possible at Fort Gibson, although Colonel Floyd-Jones waited impatiently for her quarters. Three months had passed since she had last seen her husband, and there was still no word from Charlie.

Fort Gibson March 5th 1869

My dear Ben

We have now been here a week and are settled quite comfortably. We are dreadfully annoyed by smoke; it is sometimes almost intolerable. A carpenter has been at work here more than two days, putting catches on the windows and doors—when he gets some buttons on the hall doors it will be still better. The locks are not yet here.

Your letters of 20th and 23rd Jan. have been received from Jacksonville—also your note by Capt. Alvord and the one from the Seminole Agency. Capt. and Mrs. Alvord are occupying the attic at Dr. Delaney's. I believe Col. Jones has not yet moved into the quarters from which Mrs. Alvord moved. Edie thinks this is not the right Fort Gibson, she wants to go to the Fort Gibson where Papa is. Louisa has the back parlor for her room. I and the children sleep in the other back room and we use the front room as a reception room, or parlor. . . .

I hope if quarters are built for us at Medicine Bluff that there will be no basement. I detest basement kitchens, and four rooms, and a kitchen on the ground floor, with attic rooms makes abundance of room for us; a cellar for a family is quite desirable. The motion, which I spoke of feeling in my last letter, continues. I have had a hard cold which is aggravated by the smoke, Edie and Harry are getting better of theirs. Louisa is reading [Randolph] Marcy's "Army Life on the Border," today, seems quite interested. . . .

I feel very much like lying on the lounge, which I have scarcely had the opportunity of doing since we came.

Sunday afternoon
March 7th

Col. Rockwell decided not to send a courier until tomorrow, so this sheet has not been finished. . . .

Dear Ben, how well I would like to have you here this evening —it is raining out of doors, which makes it seem all the brighter and more cheerful here. Edie and Harry are asleep, Robert is in the basement and Louisa in her room—the lounge is near the fire with a pillow on it—if you were lying there, it would be a homelike Sunday evening. Edie thinks it would be very nice for Papa to come and take us to Medicine Bluff to live with him in a tent. . . .

Bill's wife is living here now. I like to have Bill sleep in the house, so as to make the fires early in the morning, the two can do all that is to be done and, now that things are going on regularly, I quite enjoy having all the hardest and roughest work done for me, I get tired very easily. Maria is ready to come as soon as I need her, and says she will go with us if we go to you.

Monday Morning
March 8th

Not one word from Charlie since we left Jacksonville. I don't know what can make his letters so behindhand, for I think he has certainly written, it will be four weeks tomorrow since his last letter was received. Lewis, Capt. Alvord's orderly, has been on a spree and has gotten into the Guard house. Edie had a chill on Saturday and I fear has another coming on. Harry too is hanging on me, so I have not a very good opportunity of writing. I hope we shall hear from you before very long, though I suppose it will be some time before you can tell when you will be able to come back here.

Yours affectionately
Alice K. Grierson

[ISHL]

Letters to and from Ben were delivered irregularly, but the arrival of Charlie's first letter dispelled some of Alice's concern. Greatly relieved, she directed her energies toward assisting Sergeant Lewis.

Fort Gibson March 12th 1869

My dear Ben

Maj. Woodward has just told me that a mail is to go out in a couple of hours, and, as I did not know in time to write by the last mail, I must say at least a few words now. I have just had the first news from Charlie, though I feel sure he has written before, and the letters have miscarried. . . .

If you have not already said something in regard to our prospects for next July, please make some allusions to it next time you write. The train, which Col. Rockwell is to send to you, only came in yesterday morning and will not get off I suppose before Sunday or Monday.

If Lewis, Capt. Alvords orderly goes out there, and wants to talk to you, I hope you will hear what he has to say—he has a very sore looking leg, which has been so for months. He says he would like to go into the hospital and have a chance to get it cured. Also that he would rather be with his Company than with the Alvord's. He has certainly been detailed a long time, and it seems to me that if he prefers company duties, it is only fair that he should be allowed to go to the Company. Mrs. Alvord told me that Dr. Delaney said if Lewis would ask him for a discharge on account of his leg, that he would have to give it to him. He has been in the Guard house two or three days this week for drunkenness, fast riding &c.

A steamboat is expected this afternoon with a Paymaster on board. It is now a few miles up the Verdigris. The wind today is fast drying up the mud, which looks more favorable for a wagon train than for a few days past.

I hope we shall soon hear from you as we have had no news since Capt. Alvords arrival now nine days since. Our stove in the front room makes us much more comfortable, as the smoke was almost intolerable. We are on the whole as comfortable as we can expect to be without you.

Yours affectionately
Alice K. Grierson

[ISHL]

Two days later Alice still had received no word from her husband. By now she was protecting not only Sergeant Lewis but Maria, a laundress who occasionally worked for her as a maid.

Fort Gibson March 14th 1869

My dear Ben

No news from you since Capt. Alvord's arrival, except that some traveller from California met you between Arbuckle and Medicine Bluff; that of course was better than nothing. We are all reasonably well, and weather quite mild since our stove was put up.

The more I think of it, the more strongly am I of the opinion that you had better take us with you the first time you come to Gibson, at least as far as Arbuckle. Personally I would prefer a few weeks, or even months, living in tents, to remaining here, or even at Arbuckle—yet I am neither impatient, nor headstrong in regard to the matter. It is simply my deliberate opinion that it will be the best thing for you, and me, and the children. I am pretty sure Louisa inclines to the same opinion. I only hope you are sufficiently tired of "roughing it" alone, to be willing to accept the best company (for you) when it is offered. . . .

I hope you have received the letters I have already sent promptly. Maria has not been living here, since my return, as I had spoken to Bill last Fall about his wife, and told him I would try her when I came back, and felt under obligations to keep my word, and I thought for a month we certainly did not need more than two servants.

Yesterday Maj. Woodward applied to Maj. Bryant (Col. Jones has gone to Fort Smith) for a guard to arrest Maria, and take her and her baggage across the Arkansas River with orders to the ferry-man not to ferry her to this side again. Maj. Woodward believes that Maria on Friday night set fire to a small unfinished cabin near the stable, now occupied by the Detachment horses, and burned it down. The evidence against Maria is to Louisa, the Chaplain and me very far from being conclusive.

After dark last evening, quite to my surprise, Maria came here, said she was arrested and had not the slightest idea for what until she got back to town, and heard she was accused of burning the cabin. She had been here but a short time, when Maj. Woodward came in and spent most of the evening. Of course he was not pleased when I told him she was here, but I think I shall give her a fair chance for we all feel sorry for her, and she is the most efficient servant either in the nursery, or kitchen, that I have had in the Army.

The Alvords are somewhat troubled today, the Captain being ordered by Maj. Bryant to return the Commissary stores which he purchased yesterday, as it was done in the absence of Lieut. Rees, and was considered to be in unauthorized quantities. Alvord says he shall not return the stores, and if Maj. Bryant arrests him shall not notice the arrest. Perhaps all this will be a bore to you, but it has been "the talk" with us for the last twenty four hours.

A violent storm of wind has come up and it is getting quite cold. I miss you more on Sundays than on any day of the week and think how much we would all enjoy it if you could have a cosy place on the old green lounge. I hope we may see you in the course of a month.

Yours truly
Alice K. Grierson

[ISHL]

On March 18 six companies of the Sixth Infantry arrived at Gibson, accompanied by officers and their wives and children. Colonel Floyd-Jones decided that, as the commanding officer replacing Colonel Grierson, he was entitled to "rank out" Mrs. Grierson. Accordingly, he ordered Alice to vacate her quarters.

Alice, remembering that she had offered to share her quarters with him earlier, invoked higher authority and refused to move.

[Fort Gibson, March 18, 1869]

Col. Jones

Since sending the enclosed note to your Quarters this morning, I have received another in reply to which, allow me to say that the quarters occupied by myself and family, are not only held by the courtesy of yourself, but by direct permission from Lieut. Gen. Sheridan, who said he would if necessary issue a "Special Order" permitting my husband to retain these Quarters, or any others in the District which he might choose for his Private Quarters.

I have no wish to be either selfish or troublesome. I heartily

35

regret that it is necessary for one to occupy Quarters any where by either courtesy or permission and will most joyfully vacate my present ones at the earliest possible day.

Very respectfully

Mrs. Grierson

[ISHL]

Colonel Floyd-Jones gave up any further attempts to remove her, and Alice and the children remained in the commanding officer's home until they left Fort Gibson.

As March progressed, Alice's anxiety increased. With each passing day her pregnancy became more advanced, making the projected move more difficult and potentially more dangerous. Moreover, she found it increasingly irksome to be the sole parent to three young children.

The family was discovering how different, and at times breathtaking, the climate was in Indian Territory. In addition, there were new illnesses to cope with—among them malaria.

Fort Gibson March 29th 1869

Dear Ben

Nothing new or strange since I last wrote—not a word from you since your letter of the 10th, finished the 11th, this makes time seem rather dull. There have been prairie fires on all sides lately. Yesterday evening we had a hard rain, with wind, lightning, and distant thunder, between the moonlight, lightning and prairie fires. There was a brilliant, and many colored sky, quite splendid, Louisa enjoyed it of course.

Yesterday afternoon, Louisa, Edie, and I went in the buggy to church and heard the Chaplain preach. Edie could not sit very still on the hard seat, but on the whole behaved very well for the first time at church. We all dream often of seeing you, and Edie woke up the other morning saying she saw Charlie, that he was under the front steps, and could scarcely be persuaded she had been dreaming. Harry likes Maria very much, and stays nearly the whole day with her, which is quite a relief to me. . . .

Robert thinks he would like very much to go out with Maj. Woodward. I said once maybe I would let him go, but as I think you will surely be in soon, I think I had better keep him until we all go. He needs you very much, he is very positive that his own opinions are better than any other persons, and makes himself very disagreeable in some respects. He has four boys to play with now, which is I think a good thing for him.

Evening—Edie was sick again this afternoon, had a slight chill I suppose & I have sent for Quinine for her. She is feeling very well; just now she and Harry are playing "hide and seek" with Aunt Louisa. Robert has gone fishing with Maria. I took a ride this afternoon. Mrs. Moore, wife of the senior Capt. of the 6th Infantry, went with me, she is a very pleasant little lady. I hear Capt. Moore wishes to be sent to Medicine Bluff.

Tuesday Morning—I heard that there was a courier in from Wichita last evening about flour, and felt disappointed that there was not a letter for me. . . . Edie is standing beside me, and says "tell him I am well"—she seems very bright this morning, I hope she may escape a chill tomorrow.

Afternoon—Woodward has been in, says he will call in the morning and take this—nothing new, the day has gone as most of them go—we had a ride—have had several calls, have done a little sewing, and so forth. We are longing for letters for a variety as well as for news.

Col. Jones is drilling his Regiment this afternoon—suppose for the first time, as he was a stranger to most of his officers. Col. Moore (whose family has been staying at Col. Rockwells) is having tents put up today, as two wagons arrived last night bringing tents, and will move into them tomorrow probably. I wonder when our moving will be, and when we shall see you.

Yours as ever
Alice K. Grierson

[ISHL]

At last Alice began receiving the backlog of letters from Ben. At the same time, additional officers and their wives and children were arriving, and two families now lived in her basement.

Fort Gibson Apr. 4th 1869

Dear Ben

Yesterday morning before I was up, our orderly brought me Charlie's letter of Feb. 21st, almost six weeks on the day, also one from Aunt Betsy Jacobs in Iowa, which came by Jacksonville in very respectable time. After dark last evening, your letters of the 14th, 18th, 20th, and 27th were brought me, the one of the 24th having come the day before. I was of course pleased to get them, but would have preferred not having so long to wait for some of them.

I am glad to hear of the prospect of the permanent Post being built this summer. Mrs. Rockwell's sister Mrs. Card long ago wrote to her from Leavenworth, that Capt. Forsyth was to be sent as Quarter Master to Camp Wichita. . . .

. . . The two families are still living in the basement. They do not disturb us, or interfere in any way with our comfort, as we are willing to have them there, but I have not felt like giving up any more of the house, and don't intend to before your arrival—then of course you can manage affairs of that sort. . . .

We had a nice ride today. Edie getting a bouquet, mostly of yellow flowers, her favorite color. You may remember Robert did not go riding, but gathered a very pretty bouquet, somewhere.

I think we will not send you any more newspapers, but I will probably write once or twice more, lest you may be detained longer than you expect.

Yours as ever
Alice K. Grierson

[ISHL]

As the wife of one of the "humanitarian" commanding officers, Alice faced the problem that her husband's attitudes toward Indian policy differed from those of his commander. General Sheridan believed in strong force and swift retaliation whenever tribesmen left their reservations to raid. Grierson, on the other hand, felt that the Indians were often driven by desperation because the government failed to honor its treaty terms. In his view, strict adherence to treaty terms, especially the timely distribution of promised annuities, was the best way to ensure peace.[21]

In 1869 Grierson was ordered to cooperate with Colonel William B. Hazen, commander of the Southern Indian Military District, in issuing rations and curbing the activities of raiders. Sheridan had ordered that immediate action—including arrest and, in the case of murder, hanging—was to be taken against any Indian involved in depredations. If the raiders were not caught, hostages were to be seized from their respective tribes.

Hazen agreed with Sheridan on the necessity for swift retribution, and before long relations became strained between Hazen and Grierson. Given Sheridan's views, Ben began to fear that Hazen might be granted command over Indian Territory, in which case Ben would have to report to him. If that happened, Ben threatened to leave the army even if it meant the "poor house in the end."[22]

Such a possibility distressed Alice, pregnant with their sixth child. She could not insist that Ben remain in the army without challenging his role as male head of the family, but with care and tact perhaps she could persuade him to reevaluate his situation.

Fort Gibson Apr. 12th 1869

Dear Ben

Not one word from you all last week, but yesterday afternoon your letter of the 7th, by courier arrived. I think you must have been rather blue when you wrote it, and not much wonder. I most cordially hope the Indians will be civil and quiet, until you are well on your way to Gibson at least. I am very desirous of getting to Camp Wichita, or at least as near there as Arbuckle, where we would be within comparatively easy communicating distance. Since the Headquarters of the District, and Regt., are really moved, and the Chaplain gone, (he went last Thursday morning) it seems less like home than before.

I have not been as well as usual for a day or two, (feel better now,) and after your letter came, was more depressed in spirits than I have been in a long time, but it has pretty much worn off. I shall not advise you to resign, unless you are fully convinced it is the wisest thing for you to do. I have known all the time that you would not be particularly gratified to be under command of Gen. Hazen —but you will be as well suited as many other officers with the new order of things I presume. . . .

Last week was the mildest weather we have had, and the leaves and blossoms have come out quite rapidly, and makes the scenery much prettier. Edie was dreaming again last night that you were here. Louisa sometimes tells her maybe some little Comanche girl is hugging and kissing you, and being your little girl, she resents such an idea very strongly. . . .

I opened your trunk one day last week for the first time, and found four pair of moccasins, the smallest pair I supposed were for Louisa, at any rate they just fit her and were a little short for me, so I gave them to her yesterday, and she wore them part of the day, in honor of its being just two months since our leaving Jacksonville. Our hearts would have been heavier, had we known it would be so long a time before seeing you.

If you can't come for us I think we will have to get up courage enough to go alone, which I have no doubt we could do as Mrs. Alvord came from Arbuckle with only Lewis and a servant. If you are still at Camp Wichita when this letter arrives, had you not better "order" us out there, and request Col. Rockwell to furnish us such transportation as is necessary. Poor Edie had a chill Saturday, and has another now. Robert has had fewer lately than through the fall and winter. Earnestly hoping that you may soon be here.

I remain as ever yours
Alice K. Grierson

[ISHL]

Finally, at the end of April, Colonel Grierson returned to Gibson and escorted his family to Camp Wichita at Medicine Bluff. The site was as beautiful as he had described it, but little existed by way of permanent structures. Once more Alice took up housekeeping in tents. Late in July a picket house was ready, permitting the family to move shortly before fourteen-year-old Charlie arrived from Illinois. On August 1 Camp Wichita officially became Fort Sill,[23] and eight days later Alice gave birth to Theodore MacGregor (George) Grierson.

When Alice had counseled her husband to postpone making any decision about resigning until President Grant's Indian policies became clear, she had offered good advice. The new president, responding to widespread demands for reform, implemented a series of changes that collectively became known as his Peace Policy, a departure the Griersons warmly applauded.

Under the new policy, Indian affairs remained under civilian control as long as the Indians stayed on the reservations. Off the reservations they came under army jurisdiction. In an effort to improve the quality of reservation agents, Grant sought recommendations from church groups. When the Society of Friends responded enthusiastically, the southern plains reservations were soon staffed by Quakers. Grant also appointed a Board of Indian Commissioners to oversee the operation of the notoriously corrupt Indian Bureau and the dispensing of annuities. A group of

*Fort Sill, Indian Territory, c. 1890–95. Courtesy of the Western History
Collections, University of Oklahoma Library.*

ten prominent citizens were selected to serve without pay. In concert with
the secretary of the interior it began implementing this policy, which was
designed to transform the Indians into Christian farmers on reservations.[24]

Twelve days after George's birth one of the members of the Board of
Indian Commissioners, William E. Dodge, along with his wife, Melissa,
arrived at Fort Sill to inspect the agency. Since Alice was the commanding
officer's wife, it fell to her to entertain them in unfinished quarters. Several
weeks later she received the following letter from Mrs. Dodge.

Cedar City Tarrytown Oct. 29th 1869

My dear Mrs. Grierson

We were very happy to learn by your good husband's letter that
you are well, for we feared that the result of our visit at your house
would cause you a longer confinement. Please thank him for sending us his photograph, we shall love to give it a good place in our
Album, and should like to see you alongside of him.

We shall long remember with pleasure our stay at your house,
it was so refreshing after our tedious journey and long dwelling in
[Yento], to be received so cordially, and sleep again under a roof.

How is the dear little General! it was quite an astonishment to me to see a babe 12 days old, apparently like one a month old. You recollect his little sister bringing him out in her arms to see us. If he has advanced as rapidly as he did the first week, you must by this time have put him in short clothes. I have taken the liberty of sending you a little clip for him, which I trust will be acceptable, that he may wear it in remembrance of our early visit to him. . . .

Through the mercy of our Heavenly Father, we arrived home in safety and found an unbroken circle, and the different branches of our family all in good health. During our journey we had many discomforts, yet I think we would both willingly bear it all, rather than to have lost the privilege of our varied experience. The memories of the councils, and seeing the Indians at their homes, and learning their characters so much better than we could have done at a distance, has made a lasting impression upon our minds. We trust that the visit of the commissioners may prove a blessing to these poor benighted ones, both temporally and spiritually. We have recently received most interesting accounts in regard to the State of Religion among the Decotas. Missionary effort has been signally blessed, and a large number of them give good evidence that they know and love the saviour. We think plans will be executed in connection with our Missionary Board to send labourers among some of the Tribes that we have visited.

Mr. Dodge read me the General's Report which he kindly prepared for the gentlemen, we were greatly interested in it, and hope it may be of service when they go to Washington. Please remember us most kindly to your sister, and the dear children, also to all the friends whom we had the pleasure of seeing there. We were very glad to hear that Cap. Morrison has arrived safely, for he was very ill when with us. Our united kindest remembrances to the General and believe me,

affectionately yours
Melissa P. Dodge

[TTU]

Alice did not recover rapidly after George's birth. She experienced great difficulty in nursing him, and he was sickly during his first year. Her social responsibilities continued unabated, nonetheless. The Griersons not only shared their quarters with visiting dignitaries, both civilian and military, but felt obliged to give frequent dinner parties and hops.[25]

Late in September Charlie returned to Chicago to resume his schooling. As always, Alice found it difficult to be separated from her child, and her letters reflected her interest in every detail of his life. In return, she sought to keep him informed, writing him not only of family matters but of post events. In the following letters Alice demonstrated her continuing concern for the well-being of the buffalo soldiers, her pleasure over improvements in their still-unfinished quarters, the ongoing battle to keep liquor away from the post, and the arrival of newcomers—most notably the Quaker Indian agents, as well as a young wife encountering the rigors of post life for the first time.

Fort Sill Nov. 16th 1869

Dear Charlie

[I was relieved] to get your letter of Oct. 27th last Saturday. You do not speak of having received any from me, though I think you must, as I thought one or two of mine would be at Chicago on your arrival. . . .

I want to know something of the school, where it is—how many scholars, also your teacher's name. I am glad you got your new clothes—who selected them for you, and why did you not get socks? Do you wear your new pantaloons every day? I am very glad you got through your buffalo hunts safely—it is rather dangerous to be chased by a buffalo. Mrs. Beck has a young son, born the 10th I believe.

Last Friday evening Gen. H. N. Davis, Assistant Inspector General, arrived here, and has been very busily engaged ever since, inspecting all sorts of Government property, the company books, and so forth—it will take him one or two days longer. He occupies the parlor. I made a bed for him on the little iron bedstead Aunt Louisa had going to Harker. He has an order from the secretary of war, requiring him to hear the grievances soldiers may wish to complain of. I am so glad of it. Several soldiers have been to him and I think it will tend to prevent company commanders from abusing their men.

We got our flues built last week, and have the stoves in the kitchen and dining rooms. We have a flue in the parlor, and as yet no stove for it. We are having another Norther, but not so cold as some we have had. Lewis found the buggy blown out into the parade ground this morning. . . .

Your Mother
Alice K. Grierson

[ISHL]

Fort Sill Nov. 23rd 1869

Dear Charlie

We have had but one letter from you since you left, that of Oct. 27th. I hope you will not fail to write regularly, at least once a week. . . .

Last week Sergeant Gibbs of Co. E found that some kegs of whiskey were buried a little way outside of the garrison and told papa of it. He sent out and got it, also arrested the man who brought it, and some other men with him, and seized the train of four wagons. Papa had the whiskey spilt out on the side of the hill, 29 gallons in all—it was villainous looking stuff. Maj. Van De Wiele [Vande Wiele] will take the men prisoners, and the wagons to Vanburen, Arkansas and turn them over to the U.S. Authorities there. . . .

Papa took me down to the Agency on Saturday to see Mrs. Tatum, and some of the other Quakers and Quakeresses. They all live in the one Agency house. . . .

. . . Papa has got hold of more whiskey today, and found a carbine, pistols, cartridges and so forth which he supposes have been exchanged for whiskey.

Love to all

Your Mother
Alice K. Grierson

[ISHL]

Fort Sill Dec. 5th 1869

[Dear Charlie,]

No word from you yet, that of Oct. 27th being the only one I have received from you since you left. I can't account for it and feel very much disappointed. Papa had a letter from Aunt Louisa of Nov. 20th, which is the only news we have had from Illinois since Uncle John's letter of Nov. 1st.

We have had company for a week, and I was so busy that I

neglected writing to you last week. Col. Lee and his wife were here almost a week. Col. Lee is Commissary for the Indians, and has rooms in one of the new warehouses for Indian stores. He has but one arm, having lost his right one, at the battle of Gettysburg— he has been in the Freedmen's Bureau at Alexandria D.C., having relieved Capt. Alvord there four years ago. We like both Col. Lee and his wife very much, and think them quite an acquisition to our society.

Major Yard and his bride arrived a week ago. The Major brought nearly three hundred recruits, mostly for the infantry. Lieutenants Murdock and Thompson also came in charge of the recruits, they were a month coming from Fort Scott. It has been a pretty rough experience for Mrs. Yard, she has always lived in New York City, and had no idea at all of what soldiering was, had never seen a tent. They have been here to dinner and to breakfast. I like Mrs. Yard and think she has borne the discomforts of her trip bravely. Major Yard is ordered to Arbuckle, with companies C - L - and M. I am very glad Mrs. Yard has the prospect of a house to live in before long. . . .

Papa is just having a review, I have heard it said that there are more troops here now, than at any Post in the United States. . . .

Last night an opossum got after one of our chickens, and Lewis set his dog on it. It ran under the house, but Lewis managed to get it. Papa says it is the largest one he ever saw. Lewis has it tied up by the barn. We see by the papers there has been a very heavy fall of snow in Chicago, I wonder if the Rail Roads are blocked up in Northern Illinois. I do hope the next mail will bring letters from you. Harry is beginning to put words together now, so that we hope he will talk sometime. Love to all.

Yours affectionately
Alice K. Grierson

[ISHL]

Lawrie and Mary Ann Tatum, the Quaker agents, were now at work supervising other Quakers in a host of activities designed to change the Indian way of life. Joseph and Lizzie Butler conducted classes for children in a recently constructed, one-room schoolhouse, and a large patch of land had been cleared to teach agriculture to adults. This last endeavor was futile, for the Kiowas and the Comanches, longing to continue their way of life based on the buffalo hunt, had no interest in farming. The Quakers were also trying to encourage the Indians to adopt new styles of clothing, but this too proved difficult. Lawrie Tatum later reported that when the Indian men were first given trousers they tore out the tops and used the lower parts as leggings.[26]

Fort Sill Dec. 19th 1869

Dear Charlie

Your letter of Nov. 12 came last night, making two which I have received from you since you left. I also received a letter from Mrs. Dodge enclosing a beautiful little white dress for the baby, which has been six weeks getting from New York. Papa received a letter from Uncle John of Dec. 2nd, which was very quick time.

I am glad you got into the Brown School so soon, and hope you have not fallen far behind your class by being out of school. I shall like to know your standing in all of your reports. . . .

Mr. and Mrs. Tatum and their little Willie were here to dinner on Friday. The Quaker women have made some red woolen sacks for the Indian women to wear, and they seem quite pleased with them. The Quakers want them to wear something a little more convenient, and comfortable than blankets.

Papa and I were at Col. Moores to dinner today, had a nice turkey—they are so cosy and comfortable in their tents.

Do you carry your papers in the morning or in the evening, and how much do you get for carrying them? Love to all.

Your Mother
Alice K. Grierson

[ISHL]

While the Kiowas and Comanches were on the reservation, ostensibly under Lawrie Tatum's supervision, war parties from their camps continued raiding into Texas. Tatum at last asked for military assistance from Colonel Grierson, and the Kiowa chiefs Satank, Satanta, and Big Tree were arrested. Satank was killed on the way to prison while trying to escape, but the other two were tried and convicted for their crimes, and some semblance of peace was restored. The Kwahadis, a band of Comanches who had never come onto the reservation, continued raiding, however, and their example soon kindled renewed rebellion among some of the Kiowas. Clearly, Grant's Peace Policy was in grave danger of collapsing.[27]

46

George had scarcely been weaned when once more Alice was pregnant. On June 23, 1871, she gave birth to her seventh child, Mary Louisa. The infant suffered from intermittent fevers and chills, and the constant attention she required left Alice exhausted.

Mary Louisa had not improved when Colonel Grierson, leading nine companies of buffalo soldiers, mounted a joint expedition with units of the Fourth Cavalry under Colonel Ranald Mackenzie. Their goal was to drive the Kwahadis back onto their reservation and in the process extinguish the rebelliousness among the Kiowas. Accompanying this expedition was eleven-year-old Robert Grierson, experiencing his first taste of military campaigning.

The campaign proved difficult and frustrating. Instead of Indians, the soldiers encountered searing heat and prairie fires. Aggravation mounted until word arrived that Kicking Bird, a Kiowa chief and peace advocate, had returned some stolen mules to Tatum.[28]

At Fort Sill the heat continued almost unabated, as Alice's letter to her husband and son indicated. During August that year the temperature soared to a record high of 109 degrees.[29]

Fort Sill Aug. 14th 1871

Dear Ben

Your letter by the forage officer (begging his pardon for the name) came before Mr. Jones left, but I thought I would not answer it until today. I am not at all surprised that your health was no better at the time of your writing, but hope it may have improved before this. I don't feel well this morning, did not sleep much last night. I must contrive to get more open air, even sitting on the porch as I am now doing is a great improvement on being shut up in the house. . . .

I don't see how Robert could possibly ride all the way to Otter Creek without being blistered and lame. Certainly it is the first time he ever has astonished one by his horsemanship. I hope if he experiences no serious ill effects from this performance, that he will continue to ride until he becomes a good rider.

I am very glad his desire to see buffalo was so soon gratified, but think if his wish to shoot one is not accomplished for years, it is of no great consequence. When he learns to shoot I think it ought to be under a very careful "inspector." Edie thinks she would like to be at Otter Creek too and enjoy life as Robert is doing and see buffalo. She says your letter is such a good one.

The baby seems brighter this morning and less feverish. I would be so glad if she could get along without medicine. I suspect if you could see her just now you would think her as pretty a picture as most you see at Otter Creek.

Afternoon. I have been sleeping, but sleep with the thermometer at 94 and swarms of flies, bent on making a living, does not make one feel very brilliant on waking—still after being up half an hour I feel much better than I did before.

I have missed you more today than I have anytime since you have been away. I would like to see your camp, and the "big country" around, and would not object to seeing a few buffalo. I hope Robert will send the letters he promised by the next opportunity. The men are working at the fence today. I hope will get it finished sometime. George has just given me a good smack for you.

Yours affectionately
A. K. G.

I am glad you have the use of a chair, hope Capt. B[aldwin] has one too.

[TTU]

Fort Sill Aug. 15th 1871

My dear Charlie

I enclose papa's letter written on your stationery, as it will give you the latest news of Papa & Robert....

Kickingbird came in with the mules on the 11th, and Major Schofield says, "we are at peace with the Kiowas." It is said that Gen. MacKenzie has ten companies of cavalry, and two of infantry out at camp. I cordially hope the Indians will commit no more depredations and that there will be no war made against them.

Five prisoners escaped from the Guard House the first night papa was away, but three of them, soldiers have returned and given themselves up. I think both the others were citizens, and are said to have gone to Texas. Major Schofield and Captain Norvell have gone hunting young turkeys this morning.

Did I tell you Papa got a nice large water cooler, (or whatever the name is) at Mr. Evans, and we have had ice every day but one since you left. We don't get very much, but it is put in the cooler and none of it is wasted. We have it on the table in the hall behind

48

the front door. It is a great convenience, and the ice a great luxury. We have had no rain yet but there have been thunderstorms around us, which has cooled the air, so that yesterday the thermometer did not get above 94. I sent your picture down to *Mr. Soule* yesterday to be framed, will send for it today.[30] The men are working at our fence this week, so I hope it will be finished in the course of events. They have dug the trench for the posts so that wagons can't now come inside of what is to be the backyard, and Kate got her clothes dried yesterday without dust. . . .

Wednesday

I had a letter from papa last evening. He with his troops is going up the North Fork of Red River and Gen. MacKenzie with his, up the Salt Fork, expected to be away about three weeks. Robert caught two fish, without hook, line, or net, just with his hands. The first was over two feet long, and very large. He had a great struggle with it in the water, and after he got on shore it flopped back into the water, but Robert jumped in, caught it by the tail and carried it in triumph to camp. Next morning he caught another in the same way. Papa thought his fishing equal to his catching the buzzard in Gibson. Robert is going on the expedition with them.

Love to all,
Affectionately your mother
Alice K. Grierson

[ISHL]

Several weeks later Mary Louisa had not improved. To add to the strain, rumors of military disaster circulated in the garrison, but Alice refused to give way to panic.

Fort Sill Aug. 31st 1871

Dear Ben

As Major Schofield intends sending out a mail to "Officers in the field," I will write you a short letter, to let you know we are in tolerable health, though neither Louisa, nor the baby are as well as we would like. . . .

There is a rumor in the garrison that the Indians have stampeded most of your horses, but I shall not believe it, until I hear it from good authority.

Tucker, the soldier who has taken care of Capt. Walsh's and our cows so long, shot one of ours three days ago because she would not come home just as he wanted her to. She had to be killed, the butcher made beef of her. The soldier says he will pay for her. Mrs. Norvell, Edie, Harry and I took a long walk yesterday, and a shorter one this morning, I know I would feel better to walk some every day. . . .

I hope you have had no collision with the Indians, and will feel much refreshed by your trip. I hope Robert has enjoyed his soldiering, also that he will be glad to get home, and [be] kind to his brothers and sisters after he gets here. The mail is waiting. Good bye.

Yours as ever
A. K. G.

[ISHL]

Ben returned from campaigning, having failed to encounter a single Indian on the Staked Plain but understanding too that Grant's Peace Policy was in shambles. Shortly thereafter, on September 16, Mary Louisa died. Alice was inconsolable.

Over the next several weeks events from the East absorbed Alice's attention. Recent letters from her father disclosed that her mother, Susan Bingham Kirk, was losing her mental faculties. Moreover, her sister Ellen, having married Ben's nephew, Harvey B. Fuller, Jr., was expecting her first child. And finally news reached her of the great Chicago fire of October 8–10, which destroyed two-thirds of the city's businesses.[31] Among those who sustained losses was Alice's brother, Tom Kirk, whose hardware store's entire inventory was reduced to ashes and rubble.

Given these circumstances, Alice decided to visit Chicago. The trip offered a welcome change of scene and the diversion of seeing numerous relatives again. It also provided an opportunity to spend time with Charlie, who was often moody and rebellious, according to recent letters from Ellen. Alice took Edie and Harry with her, leaving Robert and George in Louisa Semple's care. Alice also left behind a husband who believed that she would return shortly after New Year.[32]

Such a trip was an arduous undertaking, requiring at least six days of travel, three of them by stagecoach. But there were some compensations in the scenery and wildlife along the way. And it helped that advance notice had gone out that the colonel's lady was en route. Thus though Alice traveled unchaperoned, accompanied only by two children, she was relatively safe even on the frontier.

Arbuckle Oct. 27th 1871

My dear Ben

So far so good—we are getting on nicely, though 22½ hours to Arbuckle, does not seem very fast travelling, when Major Forsyth made the journey in fourteen hours, without changing team. . . .

Last night was quite cold, we needed every one of our wrappings, and I have opened our trunk and taken out some extra ones for fear we may have still colder nights. I put on woolen stockings over my cotton ones and canton flannel drawers over my muslin ones and then should have suffered with cold, had it not been for the buffalo robe.

On the whole we had a very comfortable night, considering riding in the stage all night is a new experience for us. Harry being just the length of the seat, is most comfortable. I held Edith's head on my lap part of the time, and part of the time I sat on the floor and let her have the whole seat. Tell Mr. Robb I was very glad to have the stage to myself the first night at least. The roads are excellent, neither mud, nor dust, except a little mud in a few low places 25 or thirty miles from here.

Soon after daylight we stopped at Dr. Stearnus (I believe) and had quite a comfortable breakfast, got thoroughly warmed, and when we started again the sun was shining brightly, and we have all been as merry as crickets.

When we stopped at other places to change horses, the drivers attended strictly to their own business, allowing me to climb in and out of the stage and lift the children in and out at my leisure, which of course I was both able and willing to do. Dr. Stearns (I suppose) was, however, more polite, and assisted me. I paid a dollar for our breakfast and "thank you" [a gratuity] for the politeness. I am writing this by invitation at the Sutler's desk, with ink, instead of on a cracker box with pencil, as I was prepared to do.

I hope Louisa is as well as usual, and that George is not very troublesome. Tell Robert we saw two deer before sundown, running along a little ravine. It made me think of the song "I'll chase the antelope over the plain &c." Harry and Edie were much pleased at seeing the deer and wanted me to write to him about it, but I am afraid I won't have time to write to him today. Also tell him that just before the sun went down, we were on rather low ground and could see the sun just over the hill behind the stage and the full moon in front of us just over a hill. We also saw a flock of ten wild geese this morning. They were on the ground when we first saw them but as the stage came near they flew away.

Tell George, Mama and Edie throw each a handful of kisses to him and all of you. Edie wants me to tell you she had a slight "cold in her head" last evening. Love to Louisa & Robert.

Yours truly
Alice K. Grierson

[ISHL]

Tishomingo Oct. 28 1871

Dear Robert

I wrote to papa yesterday from Arbuckle, and as I have a little time here before the stage goes out, I will write a little note to you. The stage driver told me last night that he tried to get the mail agent to Arbuckle to let him stay there until evening, and then ride all night because he did not think I could get a bed here, but the agent made him leave Arbuckle at the usual time. I told him I was glad of it. I would rather ride in the daytime and stop even part of the night. I asked him if there was a room here with a floor in it. He said "Oh! yes, you can have the floor and a fireplace." I said "very well, I can spread down my buffalo robe and shawl and that will be better than riding all night."

We arrived here at 2 o'clock and I was happily disappointed at finding a room ready for me, with a good comfortable bed, bureau, washstand, chair, rag carpet, &c. It seems papa had told Mr. Carlton the road agent, that I would probably come through this week, and he had told a Mr. Renney, and Mr. Renney said I should have a room at his house if I came, though he does not keep a house for the accommodation of travelers. We had a very nice breakfast this morning, Harry enjoyed it very much, and ate a long time after the rest of us were done.

You see the stage started before I finished my note, and we are now at the "new Boggy Depot Hotel" waiting for the stage to take us to Gibson, we may have to stay half the night here, or possibly all night, they can't tell when the stage will be here until it comes.

It is called one hundred and forty miles from here to Gibson, and one hundred and sixty from here to Fort Sill, so more than half our stage ride is over, they say the rivers are falling, and if we get along as well the rest of the way as we have so far, I shall be very glad.

Edith and Harry have been better so far than they are at home. I have nothing to do but attend to them, and they have not had as many bumps, falls, and *squalls*, as they do at home. Edie felt quite forlorn after you and papa left us that evening, she thought living in the stage three or four days and nights was not going to be very fine, and had a big cry, but I finally told her that she would have a long cry if she was going to keep it up all the way to Chicago, and that if she did not hush, I would spank her—so there has been no more of it since.

As the driver was watering his horses in Sandy Creek two or three miles from here, Edie said "Oh! see those pretty stones across the creek, it looks as if a stone house was buried." The stones in the bank were in regular layers, and looked as if there was mortar between them.

Yesterday near the Washita this side of Arbuckle, we were passing a piece of tangled underbrush, bushes, vines, weeds, grass, and some trees. Harry said, "O! what a wrinkled up garden." I got some of the handsomest scarlet berries, for the children today that I ever saw, they are about as large as some of the wild grapes you get, grow on a vine in thick clusters, also some black berries which Edie thought were grapes. As we were passing along the road, an old colored woman told me they are called bamboo berries. Edie also thought some dogwood berries were haws, but found when she tasted them they were almost as bitter as quinine. She thought it would be a good joke, to take the red skins off some, and put them in a pill box and give them to someone for pills.

We have just had a very good supper, we arrived just before sundown. Tell Kate I have seen neither bread nor butter since we left home, except what she put in the box for us. We have some of it yet, they have hot biscuit every where. I have seen no white sugar since we left home except at Mr. Renney's this morning.

I wish you would tell Annie Verbisky that I meant to have sent Edie over to see if she would shake hands, and make friends with

Edie before we started, but there were so many people at our house, and the stage early, so soon forgot it. I have been writing on one of my tin cracker boxes, so you must excuse the writing. Love to Auntie and Georgie and Papa of course.

Your Mother

Alice K. Grierson

[ISHL]

Among the risks of traveling in frontier areas was the possibility that heavy rains would cause the rivers and streams to flood and make the roads impassable.

Ft. Gibson Oct. 30th 1871

Monday Afternoon

My dear Ben

Here we are, and if the balance of our journey is as prosperous as it has been so far, we will be at 53 Warren Av. to sleep, Wednesday night, Nov. 1st, as you thought we might. But I tell you we hit the right time for starting exactly. It commenced raining last evening (Sunday), rained steadily all night, and has all day and seems likely to rain indefinitely. The streams are rising rapidly.

[ISHL]

Three days later Alice reported that they had arrived safely in Chicago the night before. She was distressed to see how much her mother's memory had deteriorated, but it was good to be reunited with her parents and with Charlie.

Thursday Morning

Nov. 2nd 1871

53 Warren Avenue—I am writing by gaslight, after having a fine night's sleep, hoping the letter may go in this morning's mail.

Just as I had commenced writing, the stage came to take us to Gibson station seven miles from the old fort—it was dark when we reached there—pouring rain, and I got my feet wet, and by the time they were dried I was glad to lie down on a mattress on the floor and sleep. We were eight hours at Tishimingo, four at Boggy Depot and eleven at Gibson station, no other stops of more than

54

an hour and a half or two hours. We all kept well, and the children behaved firstrate all the way.

I wrote to you at Boggy and told you that we had the stage to ourselves, to that point—from Boggy to Perryville there was but one passenger beside ourselves, a Mr. George Reynolds of Lawrence Kansas, formerly Indian Agent for the Creeks and Seminoles for five years—He says he knows you very well as it is only two years last August since Capt. Baldwin became his successor at the Seminole Agency. Mr. Reynolds was very kind to us indeed, you could scarcely have done more for our comfort than he did. From Perryville to the station we had six gentlemen passengers beside Mr. R—he, the children and I occupied the back seat from 2 o'clock Sunday until the end of our stage journey, Monday evening. From the time it commenced raining at dark Sunday evening, the children and I were not out of the stage *for any purpose* until we reached Gibson, 22½ hours.

Mr. Reynolds is a contractor for the Missouri, Kansas and Pacific R.R. that is for the building of it. He got a pass for me from the end of the road to Sedalia, the place where the M, K, and T [Missouri, Kansas, and Texas rail] road crosses the Missouri Pacific, this was very unexpected to me, and saved seventeen dollars so that my fare was $20.00 to Chicago from the end of the R.R. instead of $37.00. We changed cars at St. Louis, the only change, had a fine sleeping car, and breakfast in the "Palace dining car" on the St. Louis, Alton and Chicago road, and supper between 8 and 9 OClock at 53.

Pa's head has whitened very much since I saw him. I asked Ma if she knew me, she said no, and I said "don't you know Alice?" "Oh! yes" she said. She is very quiet but smiles and seems pleased to see us, has not changed much in looks. Charlie came out to the carriage and helped us into the house, of course they were not expecting us so soon, thought I would scarcely be here before the middle of the month. Rufus [Alice's youngest brother] had just gone out visiting before I came and I did not see him until this morning. Charlie has gone to notify Ellen (who lives a mile and a half farther out) of our arrival. Rufus will notify them at Tom's, as he goes to the store, Tom lives a quarter of a mile nearer the city than this, on the nearer side of Union Park, Washington Street.

Tom don't know yet what his loss is, Charlie said Tom thought not over $20,000. Charlie said he was singed, scorched and looked blue enough the day after the fire. Pa lost nothing, Rufus and Harvey nothing, they are employed at the same wages as before the fire. Uncle Thomas Lord sent $500, to Pa to distribute personally, it has made a good deal of work for him but he has given it where it was much needed. This is only to notify you of our arrival, I will write very soon again.

Yours as ever

Alice

[ISHL]

While Alice was away, Robert wrote once a week describing the various events on post and the stream of visitors that led to constant shuffling of quarters. Although only eleven, Robert was extremely perceptive. Neither the overindulgence in alcohol among officers nor occasional flirtations among their wives escaped his attention.

Fort Sill I.T. Nov. 5th 1871.

Dear Mamma

Papa is teaching me how to play chess. Yesterday Kate, Taylor and I went down to the lower Stone. Kate rode my pony. I rode the black horse. Taylor rode another pony.

The Ladies Raid.—Five Ladies and Six children all went to a camp down on Cache Creek on a gloomy morning. So of course one of them was Mrs. Norval [Captain Norvell's wife]. It was ten miles. Before they got down there it began to rain and blow a regular Norther very cold. When they got down there all the Officers had to give their tents to the ladies. The next day Major Schofield rigged a government wagon up with blankets and buffalo robes for them. Lieutenant Orlaman [Orleman] was drunk and he went to put Mrs. Myers into the wagon and he turned her heels up and her head down. Mrs. Myers said I'm afraid you can't put me in. He said *oh yes I put you in.* The Officers had to lift the young ones out of the wagon on the way here right before the Ladies.

You may guess what fore. They got in here in the evening and it was so muddy that Dr. Kilburn had to carry Mrs. Norval in his arms from the wagon to our porch. Mrs. Norval said she enjoyed the trip very much. I am getting along well with my lessons. Auntie will tell you about Georgey.

[ISHL]

Fort Sill I.T. Nov. 12th 1871.

Dear Mamma.

I'm very glad to hear from you. Georgie went nearly wild with his letter. There has been a great fuss about quarters. Major Schofield and his Servant went to their quarters on Monday the 6th in the evening. Dr. Kilburn didn't come in here after all. It rained for two or three days here and made mudpuddles every where. After the rain we had a very hard frost and the ice on the mudpuddles was a quarter of an inch thick. On last monday Captain Nolan and his family and Lieutenant Cooper and his family came to our house. Each of them had two children and there were two Servants women. Ten people in all. They didn't stay here all night. It was wash day. We are all well. Papa says he will not be turned out of his bed for every body that comes. He has ordered a bed fixed up stairs for the Pay-Master and others.

[ISHL]

Fort Sill IT. Nov. 25th 1871.

Dear Mamma.

I can play chess pretty well now. Tell Edith, Harry and Charlie that I killed a mouse that lived in a frying pan and called it, its house. They found some coal and gypsum down at the stone quarry. Taylor has got to be a Priest he puts a long tailed overcoat on every morning and evening. Auntie has been sick for three days and two nights. There was a race a few days ago between Captain Little's horse and Lieutenant Spencer's horse. Lieutenant Ward was the one to ride Captain Little's horse and another man was to ride Lieutenant Spencer's horse. Captain Little's horse ran away with Lieutenant Ward and Lieutenant Spencer's horse threw the man off. So that settled the race. I was down there of course on my pony.

Every body is well but Auntie and she is better now.

Georgey is very good.

Yours Truly
Robert K. Grierson

[ISHL]

By early December Colonel Grierson eagerly awaited his wife's return. But Alice was in no hurry to reappear at Fort Sill before spring at the earliest. Explaining her prolonged absence in her letters, she contrasted the relaxed pace of her life in Chicago with her many tiring duties at Fort Sill. She also revealed a great deal of dissatisfaction, some of it directed at her husband.

Chicago Dec. 13th 1871

My dear Ben

Your good and welcome letters, of Nov. 29th and Dec. 2nd, were received Monday afternoon, and I am very glad to find you realize the fact, that I am, (and will be for a long time) in great need of rest and quiet. Nerves that have been for eleven years at least, getting in the state mine are, at present, and that have arrived at such a pitch of sensitiveness, as mine have been in for the last eighteen months, will need large, and long continued doses of rest, and quiet, to soothe them into a desirable state of composure.

I have not been confined to bed, since my arrival here, from over exertion, neither do I expect to be. You must remember that I am relieved of many cares here, which I have at home, restless little George, first and of "foraging" for the family, also of the never ending kitchen brawls, of which you are having a fair specimen. ... Then I am not obliged to make a single article of clothing, nor for the house, unless I choose, and I *have not chosen yet*, to make anything, but a pair of sheets, and the strain of having to cut, and make almost every article for the children, and the house at Ft. Sill, was greater on me, than you can estimate. ...

... I mean no unkindness to you, nor do I say it reproachfully, but simply say what I honestly believe true, that your disagreeable habit of jingling your cup, when you wish it refilled at the table, has hurt me more than all I have done, since I left Ft. Sill, put together.

Our breakfast here on weekdays, is usually from six, to half past

58

six o'clock, so that Rufus may walk the mile and a half, to the store, by seven. I dress the children, make my own, and Charlie's bed, attend to my room, comb Ma's hair, put on her collar, and see that she is decently, and comfortably dressed, scrape lint for Pa's hand, bandage, and do it up, and have the rest of my time to shop, write letters, and "rest & be quiet." I have not notified any of my acquaintances of my presence here, not even my friends the McClures. There have been lectures, by Dr. Cordova, Dr. Lord, and Mark Twain, in the church just by us, but I have not heard them, though I would have liked to, had I felt able. I think, I perhaps average an hour more of sleep at night than I did, so there is hope of my wakefulness coming to a close in the course of events. . . . Love to all.

Yours affectionately
Alice K. Grierson

[ISHL]

This was unwelcome news to her husband, who now wrote her almost daily describing his growing unhappiness. Nonetheless, Alice remained adamant; she would stay in Chicago through the winter and longer if possible.

Her letters revealed that new influences were working on her. She subscribed to the *Revolution*, a journal formerly produced by the National Woman Suffrage Association's leaders Elizabeth Cady Stanton and Susan B. Anthony. Under a masthead that until recently had read "Men, Their Rights and Nothing More! Women, Their Rights and Nothing Less," the *Revolution*, now more conciliatory, still campaigned vigorously for equality for American women.[33]

Alice had also sent for *Golden Age Tracts*, pamphlets written by Theodore Tilton and devoted to advancing the status of women and winning them the suffrage. Among them was a biography of Victoria Woodhull, who had recently declared herself a candidate for president. Almost a year earlier Woodhull had appeared before the House Judiciary Committee to argue that women were citizens and thus under the Fourteenth and Fifteenth amendments entitled to vote.[34]

Undoubtedly, this idea attracted Alice, but Woodhull raised other issues even more pertinent. Matrimony, she argued, was a matter "of the heart and not of the law."[35] Thus marital relations should always arise from mutual desire rather than a wife's subjugation to her husband's demands. In the pages of the *Woodhull & Claflin's Weekly*, published by Woodhull

59

and her sister, Tennessee Claflin, writers contended that wives had a moral right to limit the frequency of sexual relations. This was especially true when unplanned and unwanted pregnancies could destroy a woman's health and prove injurious to her present and future children.[36]

These ideas held strong appeal for Alice, but it was difficult to state them bluntly. By sending her husband an article on suffrage and following it up with Tilton's biography of Woodhull, she could raise the question of women's rights in a theoretical and nonthreatening way. She was not trying to win her husband's support for the suffrage, for she already knew that he believed women were entitled to the vote. Rather, in a very real sense she was seeking "domestic feminism," that is, greater control over her personal life, especially in the area of childbearing.[37]

Alice's letters touched on other health matters. While smallpox was raging in Chicago, even young George at Fort Sill needed protection, and she was taking steps to ensure that he received it. She also made many references to her recent bouts with insomnia, a common symptom of prolonged depression.

Chicago Dec. 18th 1871

My dear Ben

I slept firstrate last Thursday night, very little Friday night, finely Saturday night, and firstrate last night. This is the best sleeping I have done, since before I left home and, I not only feel much refreshed, but greatly encouraged, to hope that my sleepless fit is coming to a close. Your letter of the 8th finished the 9th and Louisa's and Robert's of the 8th came this P.M.

I am sorry to hear Louisa continues to have chills. I hope she will not work quite so hard to entertain George hereafter. I suppose it is scarcely a thing to be hoped for, that Taylor and Kate [servants] will quit worrying her with their frequent quarrels.

You have doubtless learned before this that it will be unnecessary for you to make further preparations for sending to Gibson for me and, if you are disappointed that I have decided to remain all winter you are at least relieved from any necessity of leaving Maj. McKibben in command of the post on my account. I still remain of the opinion that it is best for all concerned that I stay here until you can come on your six months leave, that is if you succeed in getting it next year. I am glad you are convalescing, and that Robert is enjoying his new suit. I hope he will like his Sunday ones when he gets them. . . .

. . . Our arms are so nearly well now, they are no longer trouble-some. The Doctor's going to put up part of one of the scabs for me to send to you, so that George can be vaccinated with another that is good. There is so much Small Pox in the city that Charlie is going to be vaccinated again, as he has but a small scar, and it is eight or nine years since he was vaccinated.

I subscribed for the Golden Age, and two copies of it have come. I like it so far as I have read it. I also sent to Mr. Tilton for five copies of his "Life of Mrs. Woodhull." I will send a copy to you when I mail this letter, and I want you to read it, to please me, it will not take you more than an hour. I think Louisa will like to read it too. I will enclose in this an article on suffrage, by Wm Lloyd Garrison, which is one of the best I ever read on the subject. . . .

. . . I requested "Woodhull & Claflin Weekly," and the Revolution, to change my address from Ft. Sill to Chicago, but as yet I have received neither of them.

Dec. 19th Tuesday Morning

The ground is white with snow again this morning, so the bells will be jingling noisily today I suppose. I hope every mail hereafter will bring you a letter from me, or some one of you.

Yours affectionately
Alice K. G.

[ISHL]

Ben's letters grew more loving as he entreated his wife to return as soon as possible. "I never was as lonely and miserable in all my life before, when separated from you, and I never want to be separated from you again."[38] He saw no reason why she should remain in Chicago all winter and proposed instead that she return by mid-January and make another trip later in the year. Alice now found the courage to write her husband a delicate but candid letter revealing the real reason she wished to remain in Chicago longer. She feared another pregnancy.

The Griersons had attempted to limit the number of their children, but Alice's reference to "an incomplete act of worship" provides evidence that they relied upon coitus interruptus, the most common form of birth control in the nineteenth century.[39] Not only had it proven ineffective, as seven children demonstrated, but it offended Alice's religious scruples. Like many nineteenth-century women she was caught in a painful dilemma. Contraceptive methods appeared to divest sexuality of its procreative aspects and therefore seemed counter to natural and religious law.[40] At the

61

same time, the mutual attraction between Ben and Alice continued to be strong, and Alice accepted it as "inevitable" that once reunited they would enjoy marital relations. It was the "consequences" she feared.

In the following letter Alice also disclosed how she had felt about her pregnancies. None had been planned, and the last two births had left her deeply depressed.

Chicago Dec. [20] 1871

My dear Ben

There is no use in planning for another trip for me, in all probability after I have been with you a few months I shall be in no condition for travelling, if it can possibly be avoided. There is no use in "going it blind," when we both have eyes to see, and commonsense to comprehend the facts of the case. Both of us will know one thing, which will inevitably occur, if the good Lord permits us to meet again, and are both well aware of the *possible* consequences which may follow.

We are the temples of "the living god," and these temples must never again be desecrated by an incomplete act of worship, (union). I think it is desirable that the parents of every unborn human being, should, from the first hour of their knowledge, that by their own voluntary act such being exists, accept the fact with at least quiet joy, and thankfulness.

Charlie's existence I accepted as a matter of course, without either joy or sorrow. Kirkie's with regret, for so soon succeeding him. Robert came nearer being welcomed with joy, than any other. Edie was gladly welcomed so soon as I knew her sex, but I was exceedingly thankful she did not come until the close of the war. Harry succeeded her too soon to give me as much rest, as I would have liked, and it was so hard for me, to learn to harmonize public life, with nursery duties, and other family cares, that I used to feel as if I had scarcely natural affection for Harry, and told you before he was a year old, that I would rather die, than have another child, yet no sooner was he weaned, than Georgie came into life, but I was neither tempted to commit suicide, nor the fearfully frequent National crime of abortion.[41]

I was so greatly debilitated in the spring, before he was a year old, that Dr. Kilburn [Kilbourne] did not think I could nurse him through the summer nor did I think I could have done so except for the constant stimulant of Sherry wine, which I used by his consent, and your approval. I believe if I had not been nursing him, he would have died, when he was so ill in August, and came so near doing, although the wine may have saved his life. I firmly believe it injured me, as so soon as I weaned him, and was again immediately pregnant, my nerves became irritable to such a degree, that life has ever since, been nearer a burden to me, than is at all desirable.

When our precious baby died, you said to me, "bear up, darling, she was with us for some purpose." How often I think of your words, and what is the purpose, for which she was with us? I can think of many purposes which her brief life may have been intended to accomplish but one thing I shall always believe, and that is, if it had been possible for us only to have had our own family last summer, that she might have lived. Or had I been possessed of a great deal more philosophy, and religion, than I was, so that I could have taken life as it came, *without any fretting*, she might have lived, but you well know, I was neither saint, nor angel, and I did the very best I knew how, both for her and myself, and the results you are well aware of.

Now if I remain here until the 1st of March and return to Ft. Sill by, or before the 10th, I will endeavor to be in such a state of body, and mind, as to accept whatever the Lord has in store for us, joyfully, thankfully. But whether I am again a Mother or not, I hope you will agree with me, both in theory, and practice, that quiet home joys entirely within our reach, are just the best, and most to be sought after, of all earth's good gifts. Mr. Helmer said in his excellent sermon last Sunday, that in good and loving homes, paradise was trying to retain a foothold on earth.

I hope you can believe me when I say, I do not wish to take advantage of being "mistress of the situation" but really desire to do what is for the very best good, of all parties concerned. When I first wrote you that I might stay all winter, I could see from the tone of your reply how annoyed you were, but after thinking of the matter over night you wrote a manly generous letter, like your better self. So now, you must think over all sides of the question, and see if we can't come to a decision.

good bye, dearest.

[TTU]

Alice's letters and her extended stay were having their intended effect on Ben. Anxious to bring her back home immediately, he pondered ways to improve her situation at the post, mainly by obtaining additional household help. In an incautious moment he also revealed that he believed it was her father's influence that kept her in Chicago.[42] As she sought to dispute her husband's view, Alice revealed her deepest fear. If the strains at Fort Sill were not alleviated, it seemed possible that she might suffer her mother's fate.

Chicago, Dec. 27th 1871

My dearest Ben

Yours of the 18th is just received. I intended writing a description of our tree, and Christmas doings generally, to Robert, this afternoon but will defer it to tell you that I am open to "compromise," and suggest two, which have been shaping themselves in my brain since I wrote to you yesterday. Fortunately I did not lie awake last night to concoct them, and I have been as busy as a bee all day, with my light pleasant, household duties, but not so busy with my hands, but what my brain has been actively at work, and the burden of my thought has been you, "My honey," and all the rest at Ft. Sill, whose house is in the quarters of the Commanding Officer.

First let me say that Pa has *no* claim on me whatever and never has the slightest thought of making any—but he is a grey headed man of sixty five years, who has seen all of his thirteen children, except five, wither away into the grave, and who sees the wife of his youth, and Mother of his children, sitting before him daily, and sleeping beside him nightly, who although physically well, is so utterly wrecked mentally that frequently she can't dress herself without his assistance, or that of some one else. . . . Of course as I am of his blood, flesh, and bones, as well as Ma's, he can't see me in what *he knows* to be a critical state of health, without being very desirous that I should have the best opportunity of regaining my wanted health and strength.

My darling husband, I should have gone into my grave, if I had not gone home to my Father's house, when Kirkie was a baby, and stayed there for months. I am in no immediate danger of death as far as I can judge, now, but there are things which *to me* are *incomparably worse than death,* of which *I may* be in danger if I have not sufficient rest. To be a helpless invalid for years, or to lose my memory as Ma has, or my reason, are calamities from which I earnestly pray the good Lord may deliver me, and if it is his will, I would much prefer death, to life with any of the above ills. When I die, God grant it may be so that my friends can bury me in the earth. . . .

[ISHL]

Alice's ongoing complaint that the demands placed on the post commander and his family were unreasonable received confirmation from Louisa Semple. The colonel's sister found the role of post hostess not only arduous but thankless as well.

[Fort Sill] Dec. 22nd 71

Dear Alice

I received yours of the 12th but can not answer except in a rambling way as it may fall. I am glad you are so well and enjoy yourself and employ yourself so much to your liking. . . .

I have avoided expressing my opinions in relation to your return in Jan., or prolonging your visit until some indefinite time when Ben shall apply for a leave. I left it to yourselves though I did not anticipate that anything except some involuntary obstacle would detain you so long. But on occasions when I have something to say that no one else will say or think, I am apt to say something for consideration, acceptance, or prompt rejection, with possibly long afterthought—whichever it may be does not concern me as the saying does. I think then you had better stay till Spring or as much longer, as will be necessary in your own opinion to effect restoration in your case, for if you return before that you will not be well.

Next, stage drivers, teamsters, soldiers and others had frozen and amputated limbs from travelling in the Territory last winter, and women have been nearly chilled to death even in the month of March. The children might suffer, if not yourself.

The third reason is that when you return you come back to the repulsive life of the garrison, where you are liable any and every day to be invaded by from one to ten persons, men, women, children and servants—who take it as a matter of course—make you their convenience as long as they please, and abolish even the ceremony of thanks by the remark that it is the custom of the army, and where you and Ben cannot call your rooms or beds your own but may be driven from them worse than poor tradesmen or laborers.

Army officers who come for special duties are only occasional visitors, stay but a short time, and seldom have children or women, black and white with them. They may be entertained at least patiently, but the idea of the family of a Post Commander being made the servants of a whole regiment of shiftless things, is simply disgusting and intolerable and it is time some one should try to make them perceive it. . . .

[ISHL]

The unremitting social duties at Fort Sill had weighed heavily on Alice, and she now sought to ease her burdens. Her patience with guests who wore out their welcome had long since expired, and in the case of Captain Caleb Carlton and his wife she had taken drastic action.

Chicago Dec. 28th 1871

My dear Ben

It is between 3 and 4 o'clock in the morning but I can't sleep for thinking of you, so you may as well have the benefit of some of my thoughts. I am glad Louisa does not intend "to present herself as the entertainer of a lot of revellers, able to dance two or three nights in a week, until 3 o'clock in the morning, and gorge themselves with indigestibles." When I do come home, I mean with your approval, to send round a circular, similar to the following. Those officers and ladies of the garrison who wish to see me, after my — months are respectfully requested to call at the house of the Commanding Officer, ___ evening, between the hours of six and nine o'clock.

Very respectfully
Mrs. Grierson

There are persons in the garrison, disagreeable to me, who have intruded upon me, and bored me, at times when they ought to have known better, and I am determined they shall not do so hereafter, if I have wits enough to contrive suitable methods of preventing them. I shall want at best two or three days, perhaps a week, after my return to recover from the fatigue of the journey, and visit with my family before receiving calls from any "outsiders" whatever. "Don't you think so neither." I also want you to use your best endeavors to prevent *our home,* from being either a hotel, or a boarding house. I am social by nature, and believe hospitality to be a sacred duty, and enjoy company, and entertaining guests, to the best of my ability, but I am unwilling to make a martyr of myself for any individual, or any garrison.

In a delicate, and ladylike, way, I invited the Carltons, out of our quarters, into their own, (which I never told you before, though I told Louisa at the time what I said). Both Louisa and I believed they would not have gone that week if I had not said what I did to them. I knew they were incomparably better able to take care of themselves, than I was to have the care of providing "victuals and drink" for them. I have never been sorry for a single minute, for saying what I did, but when I found they were a little hurt about it, I told them you knew nothing of it, and must be exonerated from all blame. I would not like to be talked to, as I talked to them, but I would never give any one the occasion. I like the Carltons, better than any family, that ever came to the regiment, for the same length of acquaintance.

I am glad you can write to me, when Robert and George are behaving in an uproarious manner. Has George learned to be a civilized boy at the table or is he still such a wild Comanche, that he has frequently to be sent away? . . .

. . . Charlie is excused from singing in school because his voice is changing. It is a critical time of his life, and I am glad of this visit here, on his account. Edie is such a baby that I think a short time in a large school will be of real benefit to her. . . .

Yours truly and affectionately
Alice K. Grierson

[ISHL]

The Carlton episode disappointed Colonel Grierson, but he began to understand that hospitality, however admirable a virtue, had its limitations.

While Alice remained in Chicago, Robert continued his stream of letters, describing in detail the problems of the post school. It was difficult if not impossible to obtain competent teachers at frontier forts. And as always, Kate and Taylor continued their battles, which degenerated into brawls.

> Fort Sill, IT.
> Jan. 5th 1872.

Dear Mamma.

I was to go to school the 2nd of this month. I got my books and went over to the school room and behold when I got there the teacher was gone and no body knew any thing about him. A few days ago I saw him riding in an apple wagon. There is a horse gone out of one of the Cos. Papa thinks he has taken it and sloped as he calls it. . . .

Tell Charlie that I ran three races on my pony and I got beat once, and I beat twice. Papa got a letter from you to day. . . . I have written a letter every week since you went away and I would like to know if you get a letter every week.

> Your Son
> R. K. Grierson

[TTU]

> Fort Sill IT.
> Feb. 2nd 1872

Dear Mamma

There is another school teacher here now. He was going to teach school the 1st of this month but the school room wasn't quite done and he will not commence till Monday. Papa says for me to go. They have been putting up ice at Medicine Bluff. They began last monday and got done yesterday and they are building a house over it today. The reason they dont bring it in here and put it up is because it would melt when they bring it. The pile of ice is 90 feet long 20 feet wide and 10 feet high. Tell Charlie that one man fell head over heels into the creek. Taylor and Kate had a fuss three days ago.

Taylor was going away but he could not leave little George he says. We are all well.

Your Son

Robert K. Grierson.

[TTU]

Early in March Alice returned to Fort Sill. She was distressed to learn soon afterward that her mother had died only a few days after her departure. Despite her sadness she felt relieved; her mother's suffering was over.

Her return brought to an end one phase of her life as a commanding officer's wife. Not only was her husband more aware of the frustrations she faced, but events had been set in motion which would bring about other changes. In the spring the Griersons, along with four companies of the Tenth, were reassigned to Fort Gibson, where additional troops were needed to drive intruders out of Indian Territory. By the onset of winter the situation had been brought under control.

Thus when General Sherman offered Grierson a temporary assignment as superintendent of the Mounted Recruiting Service, the colonel readily accepted. In January 1873 the Griersons said farewell to the garrison and took up residence in the Saint Louis Armory.[43] For the next two years the entire family was reunited. During this period the four older children attended public school and corrected many of the deficiencies of their previous education. Finally, a long-sought goal was achieved when Charlie graduated from high school and won admittance to the Military Academy at West Point. When he finished he would enter the army with an advantage his father had lacked. As Charlie left for West Point in the fall of 1874, Alice felt that her oldest son's future was bright, and thus encouraged she held strong hopes that her middle-class dream of upward mobility for all her children would one day be realized.

Chapter 2

❧

FORT CONCHO

Life in "the Most God-Forsaken Part of Uncle Sam's Dominions"

Alice expected to return to Fort Sill when her husband's recruiting duties ended. Instead Colonel Grierson received orders transferring his head-quarters to Fort Concho in West Texas, a change in assignment brought on largely by his continuing support for the Peace Policy.[1]

Other factors were involved as well. The Tenth Cavalry had its share of cliques and feuds, and in Grierson's absence Lieutenant Colonel John Davidson had proved inept at managing personnel. General Sheridan was particularly incensed at the way Davidson had handled the "scandalous intimacy" between Elizabeth Myers, the wife of Lieutenant J. Will Myers, and Lieutenant Quincy O'Mahar Gillmore. The latter, a recent graduate of West Point, had been brought before a "public court" to discuss his affair with Mrs. Myers and was forced to resign. In the wake of this and other incidents Sheridan decided that the time had come to scatter "the nest at Fort Sill."[2] Thus Ben found himself exiled, as his brother John saw it, to "the most God-forsaken part of Uncle Sam's Dominions."[3]

Alice remained in Jacksonville while her husband reported for duty at Concho late in April 1875. Upon arriving, Ben concluded that his brother's assessment had been correct. The general vicinity of the fort was "a flat, treeless, dreary prairie," broken only by a few "straggling growths of mesquite." As for the post, "if such it may be called," it was in deplor-able condition, for in the past few years there had been a constant turnover of commanding officers. Dilapidated buildings, sagging porches, broken

Fort Concho, 1876. Courtesy of the Fort Concho National Historical Landmark, San Angelo, Texas.

windows stuffed with rags and old blankets, and trash-strewn ditches were everywhere. Weeds, some three feet high, covered the entire post, including the parade ground, but this was actually a blessing since they hid the numerous deposits left by dozens of dogs.[4]

The nearby town was even more depressing. San Angela (San Angelo after 1880), "a horridly wicked portion of the universe," was a collection of hovels, grog shops, gambling dens, and bawdy houses and offered neither amenities nor wholesome recreation. The countryside abounded with Anglo and Mexican bandits and cattle and horse thieves. And although the southern plains tribes had been decisively defeated in the Red River War of 1874–75, Kickapoos, Lipans, Mescalero Apaches, and a few renegade Comanches still threatened wagons, trains, and stagecoaches passing through the area.[5] Facing an enormous peace-keeping task and suffering indignities under Sheridan, Ben once more gave serious thought to leaving the army.

Fort Concho Texas
June 25, 1875.

My dear Alice.

The Goths & Vandals, I have read somewhere, had a custom which they followed or carefully observed—which was, that when they had any question of importance to settle or decide, they invariably debated the matter *twice* (if of importance to the State), once drunk that their councils would not lack *vigor* or *vim* & *spirit*, and once sober that, due regard should be given to *discretion*. It turned out that in this way a just or correct medium was got at, in coming to their decision or conclusion.

Now I have been discussing in my own mind for sometime, being at times rather disgusted with the Army & Army life, as to whether or not it would not be well for me to get drunk & argue the case with myself, pro & con, & then examine into the matter again when I am duly sober . . . as to whether or not I had best remain for the balance of my life in the Army.

Now as I am tolerably well advanced in years and hardly think or deem it prudent for myself to get drunk, as I have been a very temperate man so far, & if once *gloriously* drunk I might conclude that was a happy condition, & then become a drunkard, I have thus far concluded therefore not to discuss this matter when I am drunk, and as I can not fully decide in my own mind what is best to do in the matter, and as you & I are *one*, the thought *struck* me that you might perhaps get *drunk* & *discuss* the matter with that *other* and *better half* of *my self*, & then write me the result, of your council with yourself when *drunk*, that is if you can remember your argument when you get *sober*.

Now if I knew that I should be compelled to stay a very long time at Fort Concho or in the Dept. of Texas, I think that either *drunk or sober*, my decision would be to resign & get out. . . . Whether you get *drunk* or not in order to discuss and think over this matter, I wish you would let me hear from you on the subject.

I wish you had a fortune of about 5 or 10 million, so that I could help you take care of it. In fact I would be willing to hire out to you for life, on one condition and that would be, that I should never be separated from you during life, & *good behavior,* that is *of course* your good behavior. Now if I had a fortune & I was not married to you, as I am already, I would marry you instantly & then *hire you for life* with the distinct understanding that you never should *separate yourself* or be separated from me, that is so long as *you behave* yourself, of course.

Perhaps you may conclude that this "*Turkey talk*" is all one way & that in any account, *You only get the Turkey Buzzard.*

B. H. G.

[ISHL]

*Cadet Charles Grierson.
Courtesy of the National Park
Service, Fort Davis National
Historic Site.*

Years earlier Alice had always tried to state her opinion in such a way that she appeared to leave major decisions regarding her husband's career entirely in his hands. Now her answer was direct and unequivocal: the family needed the steady income from a military career.

Jacksonville July 6th 1875

Dear Ben

Yours of the 25th, 26th, and 27th came yesterday morning. I shall certainly not get drunk, in order to give you my opinion of your remaining in the Army. I think it will be a long time before you get an equally good position, and salary in civil life, consequently think you had better let "well enough" alone.

I know it would be a very easy thing to spend a few thousands more than we have, or are likely to have, but it would be a good deal harder to have less than $350 a month in clear money, "to go and come on." We had better make up our minds that *we are not rich,* and should not indulge in luxuries. . . .

. . . I had a postal card from Charlie yesterday—he says their standing was published the last day of June—he was 29 in Math, 28 in French, 30 in general—had gained a little. There were 5 men of the 1st class—4 of the 2nd, and 7 of his class "found" deficient —so he is better off than some. . . .

[ISHL]

*Robert Grierson, c. 17.
Courtesy of the National Park
Service, Fort Davis National
Historic Site.*

By September, after a separation of almost six months, Alice arrived at Fort Concho with Edie, Harry, and George. Ben proudly showed them through their recently renovated quarters, still smelling of fresh plaster and paint. Only one factor marred Alice's relief at rejoining her husband: Robert remained in Jacksonville boarding with the Longs, a family that now occupied the Grierson home. Hardly an ideal arrangement, it was the only way Robert could attend high school, since there was no school on post. Alice consoled herself that her father and his second wife, Ann Bayne Kirk, would soon leave Chicago and settle permanently in Jacksonville. In the meantime, Louisa Semple occupied a room adjacent to Robert's in the Grierson homestead.[6]

A young cousin, Olive McFarland, accompanied Alice to Fort Concho to serve as governess, maid, and companion. More important, she hoped to find a husband among the officers of the regiment, and her first letter to Robert included an assessment of her current prospects. "Nice young officers are not very plenty here at present. They are all out on the scout. They are expected back the 1st of Nov. The only two unmarried officers I have met are Major Woodward and Capt. Lee."[7]

Back East the shortage of young men since the recent war consigned

Edith Clare Grierson.
Courtesy of the National Park
Service, Fort Davis National
Historic Site.

many females to spinsterhood.[8] Matrimonial prospects, however, improved significantly on frontier posts, given the relative scarcity of eligible young women. Indeed, even a young woman not "prepossessing in appearance" could win a proposal in a matter of days.

Fort Concho Sept. 24th 1875

Dear Charlie

Just as I wrote the date of this letter, I happened to remember that it is the 21st anniversary of our wedding day—I had not thought of it before.... I believe all the officers and ladies who are here, have called except Mrs. Keyes, and I was told she is not making calls on account of the recent death of her father.[9]

Suppose you have heard of Major Schofields engagement to Miss Bullock, it was made on an acquaintance of seventeen days. Miss Bullock called here last evening with her sister and her sister's husband. I do not think her prepossessing in appearance, though she seems bright. I am rather surprised that Major Schofield should have been so deeply smitten in so short a time.

We are almost in order, and are really very comfortable, although we have less furniture, than we have had at any time in the army. Olive commenced teaching the children Tuesday, as there is no

Harry (Benjamin Henry, Jr.) Grierson. M. C. Ragsdale photograph/Fort Concho Museum.

school here, and they had not looked at their books for three weeks. . . .

Affectionately your Mother
Alice K. G.

[TGCHS]

Because Fort Concho was one of the more remote posts, boredom posed an ongoing challenge; unrelieved, it heightened tension and frustration. The Griersons thus encouraged the garrison to take every opportunity for enjoying healthy recreation. Colonel Grierson took special pains with the regimental band by arranging much of its music and, when time permitted, directing it himself. Alice contributed her efforts toward planning post dinners and hops. And since the area around Fort Concho abounded in wild game and the two Concho rivers provided excellent fishing, the Griersons often joined other families in overnight hunting, fishing, and camping excursions. Alice described to Charlie one expedition in which post families were able to combine all their favorite outdoor activities with a concert and dancing.

At the same time, Alice constantly exhorted her oldest son to apply himself rigorously at West Point. Given the economic instability of the

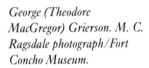

George (Theodore MacGregor) Grierson. M. C. Ragsdale photograph/Fort Concho Museum.

time, she valued the comparative security of a military career more highly than ever.

Fort Concho Oct. 11th 1875

Dear Charlie

Your letter of Sept. 26th was rec'd Saturday evening—it came Friday afternoon but we had gone on a fishing excursion and did not return until the next evening. Our family of seven, including Anderson who drove, Capt. Keyes, wife, two children, and servant, Capt. Nolan, wife, two children, driver, & soldier, Capt. Lacy [Lacey], two children, and a Corporal, Lt. Morrison, wife, two children, servant, and soldier, and Dr. Smart, with Sergeant Brenner and fifteen of the band as escort, two six mule wagons, and drivers making between 45 and 50 men, women, and children. Each family had a tent and their own provisions, and mess arrangements.

Our family were the most successful in catching fish Friday afternoon. I threw in a line, and had a bite first thing, but drew up the hook too soon and lost the fish, but either the same fish or another caught at the bait again, and I was more careful and got as fine a bass as was caught. The children too caught a number of fish. George got a turtle, but as it was hardly large enough for soup, he put it back in the creek, after playing with it awhile.

In the evening we had music and dancing. The music was by the string band, though there were a few brass instruments. Mat Moss had papa's guitar—he played, sung, and danced for us, also several other soldiers, Mathew, Leonard, Wright, also Dr. Smart. They took the board, which we used as a table, and put it on the ground, and the soldiers did their fancy dancing on it. The officers and ladies danced on the ground.

Saturday was very windy, so it was not so agreeable, neither was the fishing so good. Papa wounded an antelope, and Dr. Smart another but they did not get either one. We however spent the whole day out, and did not get home until near tattoo, had quite a pleasant excursion, take it all through.

Of course it will seem tedious and monotonous to you often, I presume, before it comes time for your furlough. But remember, it would be tiresome to be at college four years, or learning any trade or business. Think how faithfully Rufus, Harvey and Gurdon, have worked all these years, and their salary is not, nor is likely to be what yours will as soon as you are a 2nd Lieut. Then there is much more variety in the education you are getting, than if you were just working at one trade, or sort of business, and if you were at college, you would not be sure of a situation as soon as you graduated.[10]

Papa has but very few dollars of his Sept. pay left, but as soon as he gets the Oct. pay, I will ask him to send you some money to help put you out of debt. I hope you will be as economical as you can well be. Papa has used up all the bonds he used to have, and our taxes are heavy, and only papa's salary for all expenses except Robert's board. . . .

Affectionately your Mother
Alice K. Grierson

[TGCHS]

The wedding of Allie Bullock and Major Schofield took place as planned and was a festive occasion, as Alice's letter to Robert indicates.

Following the ceremony the couple left for Fort Stockton, where the major became the commanding officer. Their happiness was short-lived, for seven years later Major Schofield killed himself, using the Smith and Wesson revolver he had modified for army use.[11]

Fort Concho Nov. 9th 1875

Dear Robert

Your letter to Olive of the 28th Oct., and postal card to me of the 29th, came yesterday afternoon. . . .

We have today attended the wedding of Maj. Schofield, and Miss Allie Bullock. It was quite a stylish affair. The wedding cards were very pretty, and we received them Saturday morning, they did not come until Friday afternoon, so they sent out the invitations as soon as possible after their arrival. The hour appointed for the wedding was 9 o'clock this morning, but of course it was nearly ten, before the ceremony was performed. Capt. Lee was groomsman, and Miss Sallie Badger, daughter of the Chaplain, bridesmaid. The bride was dressed in light blue silk, with a long white veil, orange blossoms in her hair, and at her neck. The bridesmaid was dressed in white swiss, trimmed with white cherry blossoms. The rooms were darkened, and lighted by lamps. The house was prettily trimmed with evergreens. The ceremony was the Episcopalian, and was quite long, but passed off very well.

After the congratulations, a very nice breakfast was served. There was bread, butter, coffee, two kinds of salads, turkey, ham, hot oysters, pickles, bride's cake, fruit cake, jelly cake, and champagne. Major Schofield had chartered a stage to take himself and wife to Ft. Stockton, and soon after the breakfast, the bride went and changed her wedding dress, for her traveling one, and we stayed until they got into the stage and drove off. It is only a little over six months since Lt. Hunt married one of the Chaplain's daughters at this post, and Capt. and Mrs. Dawson of the 9th Cav., who were present at the wedding this morning, were married at this post a few years ago, so it is quite a post for weddings. Maj. Woodward escorted Olive. . . .

It is so cold that we have fire in the diningroom today, for the first time. Olive made a nice lot of molasses candy for the children this afternoon. It was real good, and I would like it if you could have a plate of it. We expect to have a reading here tomorrow evening, similar to those we used to have in Jacksonville. I enclose a list of names of persons present at the wedding. Love to all.

Affectionately your Mother
Alice K. Grierson

[ISHL]

The holiday season called for elaborate celebrations. Although Alice maintained that she and Ben were less inclined to give parties at Concho than they had been at Forts Sill and Gibson, her letters indicated that the reverse was probably true. Diversions were needed on post, given the dearth of polite society and the lack of opportunities for respectable socializing in San Angela.

Fort Concho Dec. 28th 1875

Dear Charlie

I presume I will be too busy to write you by Saturday's mail, as we intend our party to come off Friday evening, so I will write a few lines today....

Papa went hunting yesterday, and expects to get enough game for our party. It is rather windy but otherwise very mild and pleasant. Olive is busy making a white Swiss dress for Friday evening.

One of the doctors here told me yesterday that five men had been killed just across the river in St. Angela within a week. Human life is not valued very highly on the frontier. I suppose whiskey is the cause of many of the quarrels; the officers drink a great deal more here, I think, than at Ft. Sill or Fort Gibson.

Our woman, who set fire to her tent, drank, smoked, and chewed, and was accused of continually treating the soldiers. Fanny, the woman we have now, seems a good deal more like a human being.

Do you have any vacation during the holidays? Our children had the day before Christmas and will have the day before New Years without lessons but that is all. Their lessons however are never more than an hour or two.

A soldier gave George a pretty little brown puppy Christmas. George says it is a pointer and thinks a great deal of it.

Affectionately your mother
Alice K. Grierson

[TGCHS]

Fort Concho Jan. 3rd 1876

Dear Robert

I have been so tired since our party Friday evening, that I forgot the mail goes out this morning, but will write a few lines now, and possibly can yet send it by the stage. Thursday evening, just after papa had given the invitations for the next evening, there came up a severe storm—it rained all night, all day Friday and most of Friday night. They sent an ambulance for the people, and a step-ladder for them to use in getting in and out.

The dancing was as lively, as if the weather had been pleasant. Including ourselves, and the musicians, about fifty were here to supper. We kept "open house" New Years day, and "received" fourteen calls, all of the callers went into the diningroom, and drank coffee, and ate a lunch.

Fanny, our woman, cooked eight turkeys Thursday, and boiled a ham. On Friday she roasted a venison ham, one of Antelope, and also a goose. We had three fruit cakes, three marble cakes, two jelly cakes, and two whitecakes with citron in them, besides biscuit, pickles, canned pears, preserved quinces, apples, raisins, and expensive fruit candy, coffee, tea &c.

I am very glad it is over, and think it will be a long time before we will get up such another supper. Papa is not so much for giving parties, as he used to be at Forts Sill and Gibson, and as we have readings here once in two weeks, and they can dance always then, it is not necessary for us to give parties often. Edith is very fond of dancing, and gets frequent opportunities, as there are so many more gentlemen to dance than ladies. . . .

Saturday and Sunday, were bright and sunny, and the mud is pretty well dried up. Love to all.

Your Mother
Alice K. G.

[ISHL]

Even a military career was not absolutely secure. In virtually every session Congress discussed further army reductions, creating fear and uncertainty among the officers. Morale, already low because of poor pay and limited chances for promotion, continued to erode.[12] Since Ben was a colonel, however, Alice knew it was unlikely that he faced dismissal. Thus she was making plans for the new year, which she hoped would include a visit to the Centennial Exposition in Philadelphia.

Fort Concho Jan. 18, 1876

Dear Charlie

I think I have not written to you since receiving your letter of the 2nd. . . .

Papa thinks you had better not read many novels while you are at West Point. I have just finished "The Caxtons," by Bulwer. Papa has made a great talk about me reading novels, so I intend reading travels, and history for awhile. I have not heard much said by officers about the reduction of the army, and have no idea what sort of business papa would go into if he should be "dropped." There is always more or less talk about reduction of the army at almost every session of Congress.

Papa is not sure that he can go to the Centennial at all. I expect to go to Jacksonville at any rate, so that you can come home. I shall be sorry if papa cannot go, as it will be so long since he has seen you, but shall hope that he can go, until it is positively settled one way or the other.

We attended a pleasant party last Friday night, given by Doctors Bedal and Smart. The circular said "Gen. Grierson, and family" so Edith insisted that she was invited, and papa let her go. There were only five ladies there who danced, two of those did not dance much, so Edith had plenty of opportunities for dancing and for playing cards when not dancing.

We have had rain and mud for over a week, but the sun is shining today, and the wind blowing so hard that the mud will soon be dried up. It rained the evening of the party, so that we went and came home in an ambulance but it did not pour as at our party. . . .

A woman was here today from San Antonio, who wants to teach music, and "*literary*"—she explained that the last was school. I think she has come to a very poor place to teach either music or *literary*. . . .

Affectionately your Mother
Alice K. Grierson

[TGCHS]

Cliques represented a constant threat to post harmony. In order to minimize friction, Alice scrutinized all invitations to make certain that neither she nor any member of her family appeared at gatherings that excluded other officers or their families.

Fort Concho Feb. 4th 1876

Dear Charlie

Yours of Jan. 23rd just received, papa and I send our congratulations that you did well enough in Mathematics to get into the second section. Papa says, tell you that *he expects* you, *to keep on* doing better, than you expect, *that he knows it is in you,* and that *you can* do so. We also had a letter from Robert of the 27th Jan.—he stood first in every thing but Analysis, and was second in it. . . .

Lieut. and Mrs. Colladay gave a party to all the garrison on Tuesday evening, except Capt. & Mrs. Nolan, and Lieut. and Mrs. Morrison. They were kind enough to invite Edith, and Katey Lacey but *not* Katey Nolan. So papa is Col. of a *Regiment*, he does not propose to place himself at the head of a *clique*, even to please Mrs. Colladay. So an hour or so before the time for the party, papa and I sent our compliments to Lieut. and Mrs. Colladay, with regrets that we could not be present at the party, (in writing of course).

Mrs. Colladay "does not *admire* Mrs. Morrison," and has quarreled with Mrs. Nolan, so Lt. Colladay publicly slights the officer longest in the regiment, except papa, whose record during the war, and since, has been firstrate, also a staff officer, selected by papa after many years faithful service, as best entitled to the position of Quarter Master, Lt. M. This is a game in which one can "follow suit, *or trump,*" and papa and I holding the highest cards, "trumped, and won."

It was a beautiful evening for the party, but our absence was a much greater damper to the enjoyment than the wet weather of previous parties. Olive found a fox squirrel up stairs the other day, which is still living with us—we suppose it is a stray pet squirrel, but how or when it got here we don't know.

Affectionately your Mother
Alice K. Grierson

[TGCHS]

*Officers and ladies of the Tenth in masquerade dress as described in
Alice Grierson's letter of February 29, 1876. M. C. Ragsdale photograph/
Fort Concho Museum.*

Alice and the other officers' wives missed no occasion to plan a hop.
Valentine's Day was celebrated with a masquerade ball, and the next day
everyone who had participated gathered in the Griersons' backyard for a
photograph.

Fort Concho Feb. 29th 1876

Dear Robert

Papa received a letter from Uncle John this morning, dated the
19th.

I enclose a stereoscopic view of the group taken in our back
yard, in fancy dress. The lady on the right, is Mrs. Morrison,
dressed as a Shepherdess—her dress skirt, and sash were of bright
plaid, the waist of black velveteen, a tall crook in her hand, fur
pouch and a horn at her waist. Next is Maj. Woodward as "Jack
of Clubs," his coat and pants were calico, sewed over with cards.
By him stands Olive as "Queen of Hearts." Lieut. Col. Douglass
is sitting down, dressed in calico, with a hat and veil, representing

Barnum's "Bearded Lady." Just back of him stands Mrs. Little, as "Red riding hood," a scarlet cloak about her shoulders. The next are Captain and Mrs. Nolan, and Ned Nolan. Capt. Nolan was an Irish Gentleman with green coat, white pants and trimmings, and a sort of cocked hat. Mrs. Nolan was dressed as a French peasant, with bright stripes around her dress, and a high Normandy cap made of Swiss muslin.

Then come papa, Mama, and Edith, all sitting, Lt. Morrison as "Old Nick," with his elbow on his knee, back of us. Mrs. Kislingbury as a Gypsy stands behind me, and little Ben Keyes is leaning against my arm. Mr. Loeb the sutler, sits next to Edith, in a costume of blue velvet, blue cap, and feathers. Mrs. Keyes stands next, her skirt was nice blue silk, and the overdress of handsome brocade silk. Lt. Lebo as a "Jockey," is the last on the left, his cap was sky blue silk, and blue silk "frogs" on his jacket. You see the artist has not mounted the picture properly, as only Lt. Lebo's arm shows in one half of the picture. Papa's pants were red velveteen and the cape of brown velveteen. You see there is no grass in our backyard, and a high stone wall around it. Edith is shading her eyes with her hand from the sun, which was so bright that it seemed as if it would blind all of us.

Papa killed an Antelope on his hunt the other day, and came home at about ½ past ten o'clock, instead of staying out all night. Several officers and ladies have just started out for a buffalo hunt, to be gone several days. They wanted us to go along, but as we saw so many buffalo in coming here last fall, and saw several hunts, we did not care to go. The hunting party is gotten up for young Mr. Gassman who has been visiting here for three or four weeks. Love to all.

Affectionately your Mother
Alice K. Grierson

[TGCHS]

Shortly thereafter St. Patrick's day offered new opportunities for a variety of games and festivities. And as always, Alice was hostess to a succession of military families en route to other stations.

Fort Concho March 19th 1876

Dear Robert

No letter from you the last two mails. I have been too busy the last week to write to you; Gen. Buell's family were here four days, and have been here a good deal since they went down to camp, and Miss Lane has been here all the time. . . .

Friday was St. Patrick's day, and the officers got up a horse race, pony race, foot race, sack race, and a wheelbarrow race. The races were a little way outside the garrison and we all went in the large carriage and looked at them as did most of the other families of the garrison. A colored soldier won the footrace, and when he got well ahead, he looked over his shoulder at the others, in a very comical manner. The men of the wheelbarrow race were blindfolded, and two of them ran together, tumbled down, and upset their wheelbarrows. When they got up, one of them instead of going forward in the right direction struck out in a right angle across the prairie, and ran a long distance, Wright following him, and shouting that he was ahead.

After the races were over, several Irish soldiers, and two or three colored soldiers, made desperate efforts to climb a greased pole, finding they could not possibly succeed singly. The Irishmen climbed on each other's shoulders and almost reached the top, then the colored men followed suit, and succeeded in getting a piece of paper fastened on the top of the pole. Then they tried climbing singly again, and each would mark with a pencil, as high as they could reach. A white sergeant climbed the highest.

I had a letter from Charlie Thursday evening—he stood higher than ever I believe in his classes last month. . . .

Affectionately your Mother
Alice K. Grierson

[TGCHS]

By contrast, the news from Robert in Jacksonville was distressing. His letters, describing the treatment he received from the Longs, contained a litany of complaints. Earlier he had noted the lack of fuel, and now he reported on the poor food. If neither of these items excited Alice's sympathy, he was quite sure that references to drinking and cursing would arouse her fears regarding the moral environment of the household.

Jacksonville, Illinois Feb. 7th, 1876

Dear Mamma,

Your letter of the 22nd and 30th of Jan. came today. . . .

Yesterday I stayed to dinner at Uncle Harvey's. For about a month or so after Longs came they had pretty good fare, it got worse and worse, and is miserable now. They take and put the coffee in the pot, boil it, and it is half passable on the first morning, then they take and boil the grounds over again for the second morning, when it is awful. I know enough about coffee to know that that isn't the way to make it. The coffee isn't fit for anything in the first place anyhow. They have liver half the time, and I have to eat it whether I like it or not. They have biscuits more than they do bread—and it isn't good to eat biscuits so much I know. I want at least good coffee, if nothing else.

Mrs. Long is going to board Dr. & Mrs. Crayter next week; today they had some of Mrs. Crayter's clothes on the line. Mrs. Crayter has a baby only 3 weeks old. I suppose it will be boarding all the time. I shouldn't think you would want our house turned into a boarding house. Maybe Longs will have something better to eat when Crayters come.

I used to take lunch to school but I haven't for some time now. Sarah (darn her I wish she was in the bottom the Red Sea) and the young ones make remarks about how many biscuits I eat etc.

Mr. Long gets drunk every now and then—that's where what money he gets goes to. He gets tight—not clear drunk. The other day Sam told me to shut my damn mouth—the young ones swear worse than any man I ever heard. I don't intend to be talked to that way by any young one. . . .

[TTU]

Soon afterward the Longs vacated the Old Homestead, leaving Robert with little supervision and only his Aunt Louisa for company.

Within a few months Alice, the children, and Olive McFarland arrived in Jacksonville. Unfortunately for Olive, she had set her sights on Major Woodward, a confirmed bachelor, and returned home without a husband. After an excursion to the Centennial Celebration in Philadelphia, Alice enrolled the three youngest children in Jacksonville schools. The lack of educational facilities at Concho had set them back considerably.

Jacksonville Sept. 10th 1876

Dear Ben

Yours of the 28th Aug. came Friday, also one of Sept. 3rd from Charlie. . . .

. . . Harry went to school two whole days from choice, and George went all day Friday. Edith is in the second grade, and is anxious to be promoted to the third grade so she is doing her best to be perfect in her lessons each day. Louisa has been working quite hard since she came home. I suppose will be sick before she is done with it.

Yours affectionately
Alice K. Grierson

[TTU]

As the winter approached, Alice recognized the necessity for returning to Concho before bad weather set in. Moreover, the longer she stayed in Jacksonville, the more impatient her husband became. By late October Ben had obtained passes for her return. Army families commonly received tickets from railroad and stagecoach companies at reduced or no cost because it was the military that protected transportation routes against Indian attacks and destruction of property.[13]

Fort Concho, Tx
Oct. 27, 1876

My Dear Alice

I wrote a letter today & mailed it this evening to go out in the morning at 8 o'clock, via Fort Worth, & enclosed therein a pass for yourself & party from Austin to Fort Concho, in Stage kindly & voluntarily furnished one by Mr. Taylor, the Gen. Manager of that line. I also enclosed a card giving names of places & distances on that route.

Please write me in the receipt of same & let me know whether or not you deem it best to come to Concho by Austin, and I can then write or telegraph you so that we can fix upon the time for you to start. When you receive the pass, if you decide to come that way you can select your own time and come either in November or Dec.

When is Robert's birthday? Is it in Dec.? I do not remember—of course it will be lonely for Bob after you leave Jacksonville. I have no doubt, but he would be glad to have you stay at Jacksonville, long as possible. But you & he must not forget that I am out here *alone* & you must try & so arrange matters as to satisfy as near as possible the claims of all parties concerned. . . .

Yours affectionately

B. H. G.

[TTU]

"To satisfy as near as possible the claims of all parties concerned" was difficult. Alice was reluctant to leave Robert behind after providing him with some semblance of normal family life. Nonetheless, she prepared for her departure by drawing up a list of last-minute purchases. Ben had suggested that she bring back ornate draperies and lace curtains, but Alice was determined to simplify army housekeeping. In her case, Victorian standards of domesticity had long since given way to practicality.

Robert, sensing that her departure was imminent, found ways to signal his unhappiness.

Jacksonville Nov. 3rd 1876

Dear Ben

. . . I will try and get the coat binding, gloves, &c, but lambrequins, lace curtains, &c I don't think I will. For my own part, I don't want them at all, and would much rather invest the same amount in a larger supply of table linen, towels, sheets, pillowcases, and other beddings. For of all these things we always have rather a scant allowance.

Housekeeping in the Army, or rather house furnishing, should be just as simple as possible in my opinion. We had less furniture at Concho than ever before, and it was a comfort to me all the time, to think there would be less to pack, and otherwise dispose of, when the inevitable moving came.

Robert got into trouble at school with Mrs. Ramsey, and she told him to go to Mr. Block's room, (and report I suppose) but instead of doing so, he came home. It is the second time she had told him to go to Mr. Block's room, and neither time did he obey, but the first time he did not come home. I don't know what they will do to punish him—he went to school this morning. I told him it would not do of course for pupils to take matters in their own hands—that he must do what he was told of course—that his father and mother expected him to behave like a gentleman and not like a rowdy.

Afternoon

The sun came out this forenoon and has been shining brightly ever since. It is past time for Robert to be home from school. I thought perhaps he would bring another letter from you—probably they are settling up with him for his yesterday misdemeanor.

I suppose you have Charlie's report for last month—he said he stood five in Philosophy, 12 in Chemistry, but was down to thirty in drawing—he says the class stand nearly the same in drawing.

Edith sends you another note—she says she forgot to say that she thought it would be a good thing to have part of the wall painted, for a blackboard. One of board would be much better though. . . .

Affectionately yours
Alice K. Grierson

[TTU]

Alice decided to leave on November 15 even though she had found no family to rent the Old Homestead and her arrangements for Robert were makeshift at best. To replace Olive McFarland she was bringing Ben's niece, Helen Fuller, as the new governess.

The Griersons were staunch Republicans, and even the children took an avid interest in the disputed election between Rutherford B. Hayes and Samuel J. Tilden.

Jacksonville Nov. 9th 1876

Dear Ben

Your letters of Oct. 31st, and Nov. 1st came yesterday, the first one in the forenoon, and the other in the afternoon. We will consider it settled that we are to go by Austin, and in the stage from there, and if I can conveniently telegraph to you from Austin which stage we will take, I will probably do so.

I have had quite a long talk with Pa and mother, and John and Elizabeth, as to what arrangements I had better make for Robert, and we do not see anything better for the present, than for me to employ Kate [a servant] to cook, wash, iron, mend, take care of his rooms, lamps, &c for which I am to pay her, two dollars per week, and she can have fire in the kitchen, and a lamp evenings, and continue to take the key of the kitchen door, when she leaves

Helen Fuller Davis. Courtesy of the National Park Service, Fort Davis National Historic Site.

the house, as she does at present. If anything better suggests itself before I leave, I will act accordingly. John sent up two men this morning, at my request, who put up the stove in the parlor.

I think I will let Robert have a birthday tea party, Saturday afternoon, two weeks "in advance of the almanac," as I am still making all plans to leave for St. Louis on the afternoon of the 15th, of course if any sickness occurs, or any other unforeseen thing happens, the plans may be upset. "The best laid plans of mice and men, gang oft agley."

How do you feel over the election news? Robert had his flag at half mast yesterday, supposing Tilden was elected, but hearing in the evening that Hayes was possibly elected by one vote, he jumped up from his supper with a screech (Edith, Harry and George following suit), rushed out to his flag and hoisted it to the top of the pole, where it remained all night, and still floats, as there is no further news up to this time.

I have given John entire control of the house, furniture (and of Robert), except the rooms now occupied by Louisa. I have made a rough draft of "instruction," when it is completed, I will furnish a copy to John, one to Louisa, and one to Robert, and send one to you. I do this in order to prevent as far as possible any misunderstanding. . . .

Yours affectionately

Alice K. G.

[TTU]

Alice and her party returned to Fort Concho before Thanksgiving in time for the usual round of holiday celebrations. Shortly after the beginning of the new year the garrison at Fort Concho had its first intimation that 1877 would prove difficult.

Fort Concho Feb. 4th 1877

Dear Charlie

Things in general are progressing in the garrison in about the usual manner—papa has gone out with that Englishman Mr. Webb, on a two days hunt.

There is sorrow in one family in the garrison. Mrs. Gasman's baby, six days old, died about noon. Lt. Gasman has been at Ft. Clark and in the field about three months, his company and that of Capt. Keyes, left Ft. Clark for Concho yesterday morning, but the baby has been born, has died, and will be buried without its father seeing it. Old Col. Winston, Mrs. Gasman's father was here playing chess with Helen until after 10 o'clock last evening—he said he felt uneasy about Mrs. Gasman and the baby—that the baby had a cold, but I had no thought of its being seriously ill.

The Ft. Worth mail, which was due last evening, has not yet arrived, I suppose in consequence of the heavy rain which we had on Thursday. Helen was at the Regimental library today, and brought home Thackeray's Vanity Fair, and a volume of Emerson's lectures, and essays. I have read some of the essays this afternoon— a good deal of it is beyond my comprehension, but there are some beautiful ideas, and sentiments which I can understand.

Lt. Maxon and Lt. Smither called here this evening. Lt. Smither seems very cheerful, but some one told me that he feels very sorry to be separated from his little boy who is about three years and a half old.

As ever your Mother

Alice K. Grierson

[TTU]

93

Several days later there was news of other tragedies. Will Myers, whose alcoholism had become more severe since his separation from his wife, Elizabeth, following evidence of her infidelity, had been cashiered two years earlier for drunkenness on duty. He had settled down in the Fort Griffin area, where he was actively seeking reinstatement in the military. On the night of January 17, 1877, he was an innocent victim of a shoot-out in a Fort Griffin saloon between members of the John Larn/John Selman gang and law officials.[14]

Closer to home, Captain Nolan's wife was dying of tuberculosis. And as always, quarters were shuffled as new officers arrived and claimed the lodgings of those with lower rank and seniority.

Fort Concho Feb. 12th 1877

Dear Charlie

The two companies D & F, that have been away nearly four months, returned yesterday. The quarter question is of course the one on hand today. Lt. Davis, and Lt. Turner, have ranked out, (on paper) Lieuts. Maxon, and [unintelligible]. I don't know whom they are going to move, but today is so very wet and disagreeable, that there will be no movings.

Lieut. Myers and some other man attempted a few weeks ago to separate some drunken "cowboys," who were fighting in a saloon in Griffin, and both were shot, Lt. Myers lived but two hours and the other man but a short time. Capt. Nolan read a notice of the affair in a San Antonio paper, and Mrs. Colladay wrote it in a letter to Mrs. Gasman. Mrs. Nolan is very low, Dr. King thinks she cannot live a week. She has quick Consumption I suppose. . . .

I hope you will improve in your marks in drawing, now that you have a different sort of drawing. I would have liked watercolors, I don't know whether I would like perspective. . . .

Aunt Louisa says Robert has improved very much in his Geometry since she has been helping him.

Your affectionate Mother
Alice K. Grierson

[TGCHS]

Mrs. Nolan died the next day. Nonetheless, despite the problems on post the officers and their ladies seized every opportunity they could for recreation. Game was plentiful in the Fort Concho area, and Alice noted that her husband hunted frequently. The large herds of buffalo, however, were fast disappearing and within another year would be gone from the southern plains.[15]

Fort Concho Feb. 15th 1877

Dear Charlie

Yours of the 4th came Tuesday evening. I thought it would be rather late in the season when you received your skates but the weather has been quite cold here, and, judging from it, I should think the river might be frozen at West Point. . . .

Of course I never want you to take the time *from your* studies to write long letters to me, but you had much better be writing to me, than visiting and getting into scrapes at unreasonable times. I am very glad to hear you are doing better in drawing, and hope you will at least regain all you have lost in it. . . .

Mrs. Nolan died a little before 12 o'clock the night of the 13th, papa spoke of it being St. Valentine's day, and it was so near it, that it will be easy to remember the date. She suffered no acute pain for some time, and did not seem conscious that she was dying. Dr. King embalmed her body, and a fine coffin was made for it. Capt. Nolan left with her remains this morning for San Antonio, where she will be buried.

Katie [Mrs. Nolan's daughter] is at school at the Ursuline Convent in San Antonio, and I believe does not know of her mother's illness. The captain said it would almost break her heart. Capt. Nolan gave up his quarters, as he will be away three or four weeks, and he does not want to live in either of the houses he has occupied with Mrs. Nolan. I suppose he thinks it would be too sad.

It is papa's greatest recreation here to go hunting—he is going again with that Englishman Mr. Webb, as soon as the weather clears up. Mr. Webb killed two buffalo when he went out fifty or sixty miles, to a buffalo hunters camp, but he saw no large herds. So many thousands have been killed in this vicinity, for their hides, that they are getting rather scarce. Papa is waiting to take this to the office so good bye.

Yours

Alice K. G.

[TGCHS]

For the nation as a whole 1877 was a hard year. The depression of 1873 continued unabated and produced a large increase in the number of homeless people. Characterized simply as "tramps," they were often blamed, as Alice's letter indicates, for burglaries in the Northeast and Midwest.[16]

Although 1877 was a year that left no officer's family at Fort Concho untouched by sorrow, it was not entirely bleak. In addition to sports activities such as baseball and football for the men, there were parties, post hops, and parlor games for both sexes and occasionally a wedding, always a festive event. By March the post was preparing for the marriage of a servant. She had only recently arrived but, predictably enough, was already engaged to an enlisted man.[17]

Fort Concho March 11th 1877

Dear Robert

Your long letter of the 3rd & 4th telling of the miserable robbery at Uncle John's came last evening. Tramps are certainly very great nuisances and I think Jacksonville will have to contrive some better means of protection against them, than it has at present. I don't wonder Uncle John feels mad.

Dr. Buell is not a relative of Gen. Buell. Mrs. Buell has just been in here—in trouble about her servants, a white German girl, whom she brought out with her from New York. Sergeant Joyce, the Ordnance Sergeant, has seen her a few times, and has offered to marry her, and she has consented on less than a month's acquaintance. I don't know him at all, and papa is not here, so she has gone to inquire of Lt. Cooper as to his character. There is not much safety in bringing servants a long distance, they are pretty sure to be dissatisfied, or to marry. . . .

Katie Nolan knew nothing of her Mother's sickness, but the night she died, she was taken with an uncontrollable fit of crying—said she wanted to see her Mama—that she did not believe she was ever going to see her again—so that it was a long time before the sisters could soothe her. That was quite a remarkable presentiment.

Capt. Lebo called here last evening—he is on his way to Fort Davis. George looked at him with a good deal of interest, and then said "You are the one that used to have the football aren't you?" Capt. Lebo says "yes—Have you no football now?" George said "No, but Robert is going to bring one." . . .

We had quite a merry time Friday evening, playing Verbarium-Memory Strengthener, saying "Theophilus Thistle &c," besides dancing and the usual games. Love to all.

Affectionately your mother
Alice K. Grierson

[TTU]

The wedding took place as planned, according to Alice. She also noted that a recent visitor to the post, Colonel Peck, would soon be in Chicago. It was common practice for officers to pay their respects to other officers' families when they arrived in their hometowns or places where relatives resided. In many ways all were part of a larger family—the military itself.[18]

Fort Concho March 14th 1877

Dear Robert

Sarah Knapp (the servant of Mrs. Buell's of whom I told you) and Sergeant Joyce were married last evening—she had been here three weeks—they were married in haste and whether they will repent at leisure, remains to be seen. Every officer I have heard speak of Sergeant Joyce, speaks well of him—say he is a very steady reliable man. Papa says the only thing he has against him is that he is a Democrat.

The band serenaded the newly married couple, and Harry and George had to stay up to hear it, and felt slighted that we were not serenaded too. . . .

Col. Peck left this morning for Ft. Worth—he expects to be in Chicago several days in a week or so. I gave him Uncle Tom's address, thinking maybe Uncle Tom might like to play checkers with him, if he had the leisure and Col. Peck can tell him about having seen all of us.

It has been warm and bright the last three days, and the roads are splendid, we have a little peach tree which is in bloom.

15th. I had a letter from Charlie this afternoon, but none from you. He is getting along as well as usual. Love to all.

Affectionately your Mother
Alice K. Grierson

[TTU]

Josie Buell may have regretted losing her maid to a soldier, but her spirits remained high, as the following letter indicates.

Fort Concho Apr. 3rd 1877

Dear Robert

We had a good deal of fun here last evening. Mrs. Paulus came in with an old woman who wanted to see the "Ginral, as had care of the soldiers—she had a son, John Jacob Hopkins, who had enlisted, and she thought he had come to Texas, so she came from Iowy, to see if she could find him, and thought mebby the Ginral could help her." She was dressed in a peculiarly country style, and spoke in a very squeaking voice. I asked Mrs. Paulus if she was not somebody dressed up, but Mrs. P. was so sober, that I was not sure but it was really an old woman. Papa and Helen laughed and talked with her, and Helen got her to take off her bonnet, but she had her head tied up in a veil, and had on blue spectacles, and her mouth drawn down in such a funny way, that it was quite a little while before Helen and I discovered that it was Mrs. Buell.

Then we wanted her to go and see Mrs. Markley, and the children wanted to go and see the fun. So papa, Helen, Lieut. Kelton, and all the children went, but Mrs. M. was not at home, and they went on to Dr. King's, and papa introduced her to Mrs. King as an old woman who wanted to see the Dr. Mrs. King was completely fooled, and papa was so full of laugh, that, he excused himself, and said he would go across the hall, and see Lt. Smither and come back soon. They then went to Mrs. Gasmans, and Mrs. Gasman had a cup of tea made for the old lady. Lt. Gasman asked her to excuse his smoking, and she told him she would not mind taking a smoke herself—but when she found that he smoked "LoveJack," she said she didnt know nothing about that kind of tobacky, that wasn't the kind her Hezekiah used to smoke. They then went to Mrs. Markleys, she carried on the joke, but recognized her sooner than any other of the ladies did.

When they came back here, Mrs. Buell played on the piano, and sang a verse of Old Lang Syne, and of Watts cradle hymn, in a style corresponding to her costume. Altogether it was quite a successful April Fool. Mrs. Buell acted the character well, and made very quick and bright replies to all that was said to her. . . .

Love to all

Your Mother

Alice K. G.

[ISHL]

The Griersons welcomed laughter from any source, given the hardships and tragedies at the post. To make matters worse, Congress had recently adjourned without passing an appropriation bill for the army. That meant there would be no pay for months.[19]

Alice's worries extended beyond the world of the post when Robert began sending a barrage of letters complaining of a variety of illnesses. None were serious, but taken altogether they suggested emotional disturbance. They reminded Alice of the adolescent difficulties that had plagued her brother Henry and her deceased sister, Maria. Both had suffered breakdowns in their midteens, and the onset of Maria's illness had been marked by a severe headache and a feeling "that some great crime had been committed."[20]

Jacksonville Illinois

Wednesday April 11th 1877

Dear Mama

I've rec'ed I don't know how many letters since I wrote last. I've been all out of sorts—head and body too. My back's been hurting and I've got such an awful cold and I don't get along at school or any-where else, that I just feel perfectly miserable. I do wish the time'd come when I would be out of Jacksonville.

. . . For the last week I've felt all the time as though I'd killed some body or done some thing else awful. I'm just disgusted with human affairs generally. I never felt so bad in my life before. . . .

I've got the yard to looking nicely nearly all raked up—trees all trimmed etc. A Mr. & Mrs. Green were here looking at the house today and think they'll take it. They'll know Saturday. They are very nice people. Mr. Loar says (he's known them a good while).

Robt. K. Grierson.

[TTU]

A week later comforting news arrived. The Green family had rented the Old Homestead and agreed to care for Robert as if he were their own. Robert's moods, however, continued to fluctuate.

Jacksonville Illinois
April 18th 1877 (Wednesday)

Dear Mama

I feel in a better state of mind than I did a week ago. I'm progressing tolerably well at school. Well I'll tell you how it was in as
few words as possible:——I cut up too much and I wrote a composition that wasn't liked *too* much. Mr. Block gave me a real good
talking to: just what I needed. I can conscientiously say that I did
wrong and that I'm trying to do right now. (I mean since Mr. Block
etc.) I don't feel a bit well and I'll have to quit till tomorrow.

Apl. 19th——

I was real sick this evening and am going right to bed—had
to come home from school today. Greens got considerably moved
today. I saw the Dr. (Jones) who told me not to go to school till I
was well or I'd be sick like I was last year. I'll be all right in a few
days. Don't worry a bit. I'm all right—I think I will be. . . .

Yours affectionately
Robt K. Grierson

The Dr. gave me some medicine.
[TTU]

Alice's father also found reason for concern but thought that the arrival
of a family in the house would bring more structure and discipline to
Robert's life.

Jacksonville, April 27, 1877

My dear daughter Alice,
Fort Concho, Texas,

I know but little of the operations at "Bachelor Hall" during the
past winter. If they had any Irish Revels amongst them, they were
careful to keep it from me.

I suppose that Robt has advised you of the changes. I think the
changes in one respect at least will be beneficial to Robt, as they
have breakfast at six o'clock in the morning. This will, I trust, get
him into better habits of early rising.

I know not what progress Robt has made during the winter in
his studies, as he never lets me see his reports. But he had been
out so much at night that I can hardly see how he could make very

much progress at school. What Robert needs most, as I think, is to
be placed under restraint, to be taught to submit to authority. . . .

Affectionately your father

John Kirk

[TTU]

Alice's apprehensions mounted. Robert, expected at Fort Concho
shortly after school closed, delayed his departure because of one vague
complaint after another. Her most pressing problem, however, lay elsewhere. Nothing had prepared Alice for the following letter from Charlie.
After months of feeling "blue," he had passed his third-year examinations
and was experiencing manic exhilaration.

West Point, N.Y.

July 1st 1877.

My dear Father & Mother

I have been in the hospital since Sunday evening. Now don't be
alarmed or distressed at what I say for I *am* all right—I never was
so well in my life and in consequence have a little surprised myself
in chat, cutting didos, etc. I thank *God* I am a *christian*. I was not
so until a few days ago after I heard Bishop Quintaro's sermon in
which he so forcibly spoke of there being "a *time* we knew not *when*,
a *place* we *knew* not *where*, that *marks* the *destiny* of *man* for glory or
despair." I tell you, my dear father & mother, that my destiny is *not*
despair!! I will write longer and more fully when a more favorable
time offers itself.

I can talk French & Spanish with *fluency*, a thing I could not do
at all four *days* ago. I can write poetry and none of your soft, sadder
juggling rhymes but poetry that's *unsurpassing* in my opinion. I am
not egotistical, selfish or conceited. There is not reason enough to
be that. I *am* going to be the *happiest*, the *best*, morally, mentally and
physically of *God's* creatures here below. . . .

. . . In three weeks I will be the best known man in the United
States, & am already one of the best loved fellows on the Point. I am
going to be also the richest. I thought at first I would have you all
come on this summer but I will not do so. Next Christmas or New
Year's you *shall* make me a call if I am still here, as in all probability
I will, for *I will* not leave West Point without the diploma. I *will*
have that too and all the devils incarnate could not prevent me from

gaining it. I am also going to graduate 1 in my class and they can't help it you see. Am I talking wildly when I say that I am writing class songs. Other songs too that will beat anything *you* ever heard. *I* have read the Illiad, Homer's best, and I truly believe that I can beat him. . . .

All American, I write Grierson

!!America!!

Its past   Its present   Its future!

I don't feel like writing more. I am tired but you'll hear it some-time as sure as fate. My love to all. I'll write—soon. You do, soon.

Yours affectionately

Charlie.

[TTU]

Soon Alice received word that Charlie had been placed in a straitjacket and hospitalized. Immediately, Colonel Grierson left for West Point to begin overseeing his son's care. While away he provided Alice with an almost daily account of Charlie's condition and the progress of his illness.

West Point

July 12th 1877.

My Dear Alice

I arrived here at 4 PM-to-day after a very fatiguing journey. Called at once at Gen. Schofield's office, but found that the General was absent from the Point & will not return until to-morrow afternoon. Capt. Hall was at the office when I called & he came with me to the Hospital where I met Dr. Irwin, whom I learned was informed more of the particulars of Charlie's case. I have also seen Maj. Gardner—& others of them & friends.

The cause of Charlie's sickness is undoubtedly on account of hard study towards the last of the year—or, rather few months previous to the Examinations—then the excitement of the latter & the fatigue undergone in various ways during this *time*. The elation & excitement over his success, all together was too much for him & he gave way under it all.[21]

About the time he wrote the long letters to you & his Uncle John—he also began to talk a great deal—a very unusual thing for him to do—& did many things—not of a very serious nature—but things contrary to the regulations & rules of the Military Academy & was rapidly receiving many demerits.

On the 26th of June he was Officer of the Day—& towards Evening he had to be relieved & taken to the Hospital. After being in the hospital four or five days—he seemed to get much better —so much so that the Doctor permitted him to walk about the grounds near the hospital—by the promenade etc. About the 1st of the month or 2nd he got worse again & had to be placed in a room in the hospital and a detail of soldiers made to take care of & nurse him. He then got better again for a few days & about the 8th or 9, still worse than ever, so that just sufficient force had to be used as was deemed advisable for his own and others' safety.

Yesterday he was better again, & last night he slept very well during most of the night. In about half an hour after my arrival, I went in to see him. He recognized me at once—inquired immediately about you & all the children & talked well—but excitedly & at times wildly. He was however, on the whole, benefitted by the interview & by my presence & has been quiet most of the time since my arrival. He was glad to see me & to hear from home & told me not to be alarmed, for he was all right & would be. I told him I had a letter from you for him—and he wished to see it & read it. . . .

I cannot say definitely what I shall do in regard to Charlie's case—nor have I determined as yet what is best to be done—will consult more fully with the Doctor & also discuss the subject with Genl. Schofield, when he returns. The Dr. informs me that this General is a very kind man & will give Charlie a leave of absence —full year if it should become necessary.

Maj. Gardner speaks in the highest terms of Charlie—says that he was gotten along so well—& has proved himself one of the brightest & most promising Cadets in his Class. The Maj. feels towards Charlie as he does or would towards a Younger Brother. He thinks that it would be best for Charlie to take or have a leave for one year & then join the next First Class. . . .

If he, Charlie, is able to be moved soon & he should receive a leave of absence, as contemplated, we will then have to determine which is best as to where I will take him, whether to Fort Concho,

or to Jacksonville, or elsewhere. Think this matter over and write me what you think in regards to the better course. . . .
With much love for you & all at home, I remain

As Ever

Affectionately yours

B. H. Grierson.

[TTU]

During her husband's absence Alice, as before, did her best to keep him fully informed about both family and post matters. Robert's appearance at Concho after many delays alleviated one worry, and there was other good news as well. After seven months at Fort Concho Helen Fuller had received a proposal from a rough and hard-drinking lieutenant with a booming voice, "Whispering Bill" Davis.[22]

Fort Concho July 12th 1877

Dear Ben and Charlie

Every thing progresses about as usual here. We have taken Robert riding in the carriage the last two evenings, and he rode on the pony, over to Veck's [the sutler] on an errand this morning, but he gets tired very easily, and I think will need care for some time probably.

Gen. McLaughlen, Capt. Keyes, and Maj. Atwood and Mr. Hill, all expect to leave for San Antonio in the morning.

Helen had quite a talk with me on Sunday about Lt. Davis —he does want to marry her, but is willing to give her time to learn to love him if she does not love him already. I told her I was glad he had gone away. I thought it well for both to be separated for awhile, as it will give them a chance to test the strength, and durability of their feelings. Davis needs in my opinion a strong feminine influence as a moral strength or restraint, and Helen has very little physical strength of her own to rely on—so perhaps one is the complement of the other. . . .

Capt. Keyes moved into Kennedy's house and Lt. Morrison intends moving into the quarters Capt. Keyes vacated.

We suppose you are now at West Point, and will be glad to hear how you stood the journey, and we hope to hear Charlie is getting better.

Yours affectionately

Alice K. Grierson

P.S.

Robert is occupying the room up stairs. George and I have the new cots together in the room below, they make a nice bed. Harry sleeps on one of the old cots down stairs also.

If you could know what a comfort it has been to have Robert here this week, and how much it has relieved my anxiety, I think you would be glad you did not telegraph to detain him away a week longer.

[TGCHS]

After much thought Ben decided to take Charlie to Jacksonville for care. Fortunately, they started on July 15. Had Ben waited another day they would have been delayed indefinitely.[23]

Jacksonville Ills.
July 20th 1877.

My dear Alice

... You have no doubt heard of the great Strike of the Railroad Employees & laborers throughout the country. The riot has assumed gigantic proportions. Millions of property has been destroyed—& many persons killed in Penn. & elsewhere.

Many of the Railroads have been blocked up & all freight & passenger trains stopped. It seems that it will take the entire strength of the States' Militia & U S Government troops to back down the rioters and restore things to order. A telegram was just received from Grandpa Kirk from Chicago, stating that there would be no trains out from Chicago to-day—& that the road was burnt up—so it is uncertain when Grandpa can get back to Jacksonville.

It is very fortunate that I made the trip from West Point with Charley. Had I not started just when I did I could not have gotten through. . . .

. . . I have not smoked either cigars or pipe since leaving Fort Worth—& you may be sure that I will exercise the greatest economy in everything.

Love to all, As Ever, B. H. G.

So far as I hear the Strike on the Railroads has not as yet interfered with the persons who travel on the Rails going west, but it may be stopped at any time. I will write often & still trust to look to have the letters go through all right.

I am still greatly in need of sleep and rest.

Yours etc.

B. H. G.

[ISHL]

The next letter from Alice to Ben brought distressing news. Company A, under Captain Nicholas Nolan, had set out on July 10 in search of Indian hostiles. Instead of locating the raiders, the men became lost on the vast Staked Plain of West Texas and were now in grave danger.

Fort Concho Aug. 4th 1877

Saturday

Dear Ben

The garrison was thrown into great commotion last evening by the arrival of Capt. Nolan's 1st Sergeant, and two of Co. A soldiers and the dismal news they bring. You know the last news from Co. A—was, they were going with 28 buffalo hunters, whose stock has been driven off by Indians, to regain the stock, and punish the Indians. The Sergeant says the command suffered dreadfully, were without water over 48 hours, became entirely demoralized, some of the horses died, and when he last saw Capt. Nolan, that he, Lt. Cooper and two men were together, that Lt. Cooper looked at his compass said "we are lost," and fell off his horse from weakness, that Capt. Nolan lay in the sand, and cried, with various other fearful stories. The sergeant says he picked up fourteen men on his way to the supply camp, the officers being from 130 to 150 miles from camp, that the Indians took his horse and gun from him— that he and the two men left the supply camp Thursday morning, and got in yesterday evening, the distance being 130 miles.

Morrison came here soon after dark for Anderson to go and hitch up his ambulance teams. Smither, Tear, and Dr. King went, with twelve or fourteen of the detachment just after taps. The men took four days rations, they took two ambulances, one a yellow one which Capt. Constable brought. Anderson did not go, he has been for sometime in charge of the corral so our garrison is smaller than ever at present.

Mrs. McLaughlen almost fainted when she heard the news, and felt so upset, that she was not willing to stay alone, and Edith stayed with her. She is not at all well, but has not felt unequal to staying alone until last night. Dr. Buell went over to the hospital this morning. No one there is very sick, and the steward can keep every thing in good running order. The officers commissioned the Chaplain to break the news to Mrs. Cooper. I sent for the Nolan children to stay here, but they had gone to Capt. Constable's to stay all night with their children, and Edith said Mrs. Constable was going to tell them the news today.

It is said that Fremont, the librarian, died for lack of water, and that one other soldier had died. They telegraphed to Griffin, Richardson, and San Antonio something in regard to Capt. Nolan's Co., and asked that help be sent to them. Lt. Morrison says there are sixty men in and about the post who can shoot—they have armed all citizen employees &c.

Mr. Millspaugh [the post trader] agrees to protect the line from his store to our quarters. They have the water wagons filled, and in different places on the edge of the parade ground, and have taken every precaution to have every thing safe, and a feeling of security to pervade the garrison. Mrs. McLaughlen feels quiet enough to stay alone tonight. She hopes the General will be home by or before the 12th.

I will send you news of [unintelligible] Lt. Cooper as soon as possible. Will send postal by way of San Antonio. You may occasionally get one sooner than news of Ft. Worth.

Yours as ever
Alice K. G.

[TGCHS]

The strain of Charlie's illness and the uncertainty of the fate of Company A, along with the reduced security at Fort Concho, placed Alice under great stress. But she drew strength from the recognition that she was not alone in her suffering. Dr. James Buell had not recovered from sunstroke and would soon take a leave of absence from the army. Captain Jacob Paulus suffered seizures that left him paralyzed for weeks, and Lieutenant Gasman's family still mourned the infant who had died shortly after birth. Other families had their problems as well, as the following letter indicates.

Alice had further news regarding the lost expedition. The men of Company A had gone without water for eighty-six hours, and four troopers had died from thirst and exhaustion. The rest finally arrived at Double Lakes, where they found a supply of water and were rescued by fellow troopers from the Tenth Cavalry.[24]

Fort Concho Aug. 7th 1877

Dear Ben

... Dr. Buells sickness is a very tedious, and discouraging one, and their prospective journey ... alone, rather forlorn. Capt. Keyes has been tried by Court Martial, his brother dismissed the service.

The Gasmans had, and still have their own troubles. Capt. Kennedy, was quite awhile on the sick list, Lt. Ward was sick in the hospital the latest news. It is said that Dr. King made that servant, Harriet stop eating dirt, which caused her to become insane, ... and Mrs. King seems rather left alone on account of her having talked so freely of most persons in the garrison. Lt. Smither has lost his father, is troubled about his little boy, and not very well. Capt. Little has been in quite a [lot of trouble], the boy had a dangerous fever, & Mrs. Little had had hemorrhages of the lungs. . . .

Capt. Nolan has lost his wife, has had to leave his motherless children to the care of servants, while he has been on a scout in which there has been great suffering for lack of water. The Dunbars have had no special trouble that I know of except the death of a niece of Mrs. Dunbar. . . . Capt. Paulus sickness is an uncommon one, and although he is so much better now, I suppose he is liable to a return of its severity almost any time. . . .

My inference from all this, is that human beings in general, need the discipline of sorrow, and trouble, and are sure to get it one way or another.

Yesterday Morrison put Nolan's 1st Sergeant, and the other two men who came in with him, into the guardhouse, having found reason to believe them deserters and wilfully guilty of creating false alarm. This morning Nash and Roberts of Co. A came in. . . .

Capt. Nolan gave me his report to read as published in the San Antonio Herald. What I wrote to you in regard to the men drinking their own, and the horses urine is published in the report, also that a liberal amount of sugar was issued to them to make it palatable!!

Helen has taken cold and has a sore throat today so that I sent for Dr. King to give her something for it. I hope she will be better tomorrow. Love to Charlie and all.

Yours affectionately

Alice K. Grierson

[TGCHS]

Ben was relieved to learn that no more than four lives had been lost, and he shared Alice's philosophical view of their troubles. Because Charlie was still unruly, Ben was forced to confine him to the attic of the Old Homestead. He sought to reassure Alice that this caused Charlie no pain or discomfort.

Jacksonville Ill.

Aug. 13th 1877.

Dear Alice,

... John has just brought me your letter of the 7th, also a letter from Lt. Morrison—both of which contained the good news in regard to the safety of Capt. Nolan & Lieut. Cooper. This is the first information I received contradicting former reports. I rejoice & am exceedingly glad & happy to know that Nolan & his command are safe and that the loss is comparatively small, considering that the command was so long without water in such a desert country.

I am well aware that every body or all people in this wide world have their troubles. And your pen pictures of the troubles & afflictions of the different persons & families of those lately constituting the garrison is but a miniature picture of the whole world, or people therein.

I think that Charley will be able to see & read your letter in a few days. I talked with Dr. Jones this day in regard to taking Charley out to walk about the place or out to ride. He said that it is best to wait awhile yet.

You must not suffer yourself to think that Charley suffers by being confined to the attic room. He is in good spirits, a very large proportion of the time. Everything possible that can, is to the best of our ability, being done for him and he is *rapidly* recovering.

We must not suffer ourselves to *become* impatient. A temporary cure is not what is desired but we wish him get *permanently* well, &

we all think that he will recover his health entirely—but this will take time care.

> I must stop & mail this. As Ever
> Yours etc.
> BHG

[TTU]

Alice was concerned about her husband as well as about Charlie. Letters from relatives indicated that Ben was under intense pressure. Not only was he worried about Charlie, but his leave of absence would cost him half his monthly salary when Congress finally appropriated the funds for the army's back pay.

Fort Concho Aug. 16th 1877

Dear Ben

Another tedious three days is drawing to a close. From Monday evening until Thursday evening always seems so long, and the mail comes so late in the evening, that there is very little opportunity of writing after it comes in. I did not write a postal yesterday as there was no news. . . .

It seemed quite pleasant to hear the band again last evening. I believe it has not played since Capt. Cunningham's company went away. . . .

Evening

Your letters of the 9th, 10th, & 11th, have just been read, and it is of course too late to answer them fully. I think a reasonable amount of checkers will be good for you, as I know it is not well to think too much of any one subject, and Charlie's case is too painful to dwell on it, to the exclusion of some healthful recreation. If thinking of him would hasten his recovery we might afford to spend our time in that way, but as we need to keep ourselves in the best possible condition so as to bear patiently with his disease we must have some recreation to preserve our own health.

Capt. Nolan and Lt. Cooper don't like to be congratulated on their safe return or have much said about their scout. They make as light of their sufferings as possible, but the truth is they were simply horrible, and would have been much worse, had not Capt. Lee found, or overtaken them. . . .

Did Charlie see the bars being put on & if so, did he object to it? Does he want to go down stairs & does he have cards, papers, books, or any sort of *thing* to amuse himself with? Helen, Robert and Lt. Tear were out this afternoon. Robert shot six plover and a jack rabbit. . . .

Yours as ever
Alice K. Grierson

[TTU]

While Ben and Charlie remained at Jacksonville, Edie's twelfth birthday was celebrated on August 27. The party included both children and adults.

Fort Concho Aug. 28th 1877

My dear Ben

Edith's birthday teaparty went off at 6 o'clock last evening according to program, and while we were at the tea table, your two letters of the 21st and the one of the 22nd were brought to me. Had it been an ordinary occasion, supper would have been postponed, until after reading the letters. As it was, I did open and look over one at the table, but my fingers felt sticky, and I waited for reading the others until we left the table. . . .

Edith invited to her party Katie & Ned Nolan, Alice and Arthur Dunbar, Harry Cooper, Lillie and Bessie Constable, Frank Morrison, Amy King, Annie Little, and to spend the evening Lt. Smither, and Lt. Tear. Robert and I sat at your end of the table. We had two tables put together and Edith sat at the opposite end with her toy tea set, which kept her busy to refill. The others sat along the sides of the table.

Edith says, tell you she had a splendid time, but woke up sick this morning, and was not able to get off her nightgown or come down stairs until two o'clock this afternoon. She got up earlier than usual yesterday morning, was in a state of excitement all day, and did not get to bed until 11 o'clock, which was an hour or more later than I intended her party to break up. Consequently she had a headache, and sick stomach this morning.

The band omitted playing at retreat, by direction of Lt. Smither, and at tattoo serenaded Edith. Then all the company went out on the parade ground and played games, Capt. Nolan even joining in them, as well as Lt. Smither and Lt. Tear. Mrs. King sent quite a quantity of cake to Edith which Bill Davis made in honor of the occasion, and Capt. Nolan sent a dish of Elpaso grapes, and Mr. Die sent two small paper bags of same, he having just returned from ElPaso. The grapes were of course quite a treat as we have so little fresh fruit here, but Katie Nolan had a sick night from eating so many of them. They played "Consequences," had singing &c. in the house. Lt. Tear and Helen, Robert and I played just one game of whist after the younger fry had gone and Smither played "Simon says up &c." with Edith. Then Robert played backgammon with Edith while Smither and Helen played checkers.

[TGCHS]

At last Charlie recovered sufficiently to make the long trip back to Fort Concho with his father. The two arrived home on September 11, 1877, reuniting the entire family for the first time since Charlie entered West Point three years earlier.

The following year Robert postponed returning to school. Since it was commonly assumed that emotional difficulties in young people often arose from too much mental exertion, the whole family devoted as much energy as possible to the prescribed antidote, a variety of outdoor sports and activities.[25]

Throughout 1878, bands of Apaches plagued west Texas. In addition, the region continued to attract Lipan raiders and Mexican bandits from south of the border, as well as thieves, outlaws, and gamblers. In response to these troubles, the army created the District of the Pecos and placed Colonel Grierson in command.[26]

In May 1878 Ben, accompanied by his two oldest sons, set out on an exploring and mapping expedition of the region. Along the way he stopped at Fort Davis and, in a letter to Alice, noted that there were desirable assignments in west Texas after all. Perhaps with his new appointment they would one day move to this gracious old fort.[27]

Fort Davis, Texas
May 29, 1878

My Dear Alice,

We arrived here at 10 A.M. to-day.... In addition to meeting and seeing people generally to-day, I have attended to some official matters which required immediate attention. I have also inspected the cavalry horses, quartermaster animals and took a look in a general way at all the buildings of the post and [will] give them a closer inspection to-morrow.

Col. Andrews took me through the most of his house or quarters. I was in all the rooms except the dining room and the new kitchen and dining room which are nearly completed. The latter building is detached from the main building and is adobe with tin roof and I judge will be very nice and comfortable. The quarters here have no attics but the rooms are high-ceiling and airy and better than the rooms in the quarters at Concho. The quarters here are similar to those at Stockton, but I judge them to be much better.

The quarters Col. Andrew occupies is a palace compared with our old rat trap at Concho that we live in. On the west side of the building (which is of stone) are three rooms about 18 feet square. Then there is a hall considerably wider than the one in our quarters. Then on the opposite side of the hall is a fine room which is used as a bedroom, and to this is an additional bedroom lately built by Col. Andrews. All the rooms are well furnished and comfortable. The climate is much cooler here than at Concho.

The surrounding mountains make a beautiful picture, look in whatever direction you may. The post is not located as I would have placed it, had I had charge of the matter. It has an appearance of being crowded into or between two hills or mounds and I felt some like taking hold of it and pulling it out and away from a position where Indians or an enemy might with ease take possession of the hilltops and fire down upon the garrison.

Altogether, however, I like the post much better than Stockton or even Concho, although the views are a little restricted or confined, yet the scenery is beautiful. In front, or from the front porch, the view is much more extended, the mountains encircled by the horizon and 10 to 12 miles distant or perhaps, to speak more correctly, the horizon is shut off by the mountains 10 or 15 miles distant. . . .

> Love to all
> As ever
> Affectionately, etc.
> B. H. G.

[TTU]

By July, following Helen Fuller's marriage to Lieutenant Davis, both Charlie and Robert were making plans to return East and resume their studies. Alice received a letter from Louisa Semple offering condolences for the loss of their company and congratulations that all the children were approaching adulthood. Her expressed hope that Alice and Ben would live long enough to see them "breast the waves for themselves" contained a terrible irony, given the event that would soon transpire.

Louisa's letter also referred to a forthcoming Methodist Conference in Jacksonville. In all probability the ministers or bishops would not address the social questions of the era or deal with the continuing hardships that left many homeless. The persistence of such suffering was beginning to test Louisa's faith.

Jacksonville July 31 1878

Dear Alice

Robert's letter of the 20th to his Grandmother came to day. I have read it. I see that Charlie and Robt expect to leave Concho a little sooner than Ben thought when he wrote on the 17th. I suppose they will be here the 8th or 10th of August. No doubt you will miss them very much but mails and telegraphs are comfortable inventions. . . .

The Methodist Episcopal Conference (whether annual or general I can't say) meets here in September, when there will be naturally a stunning fire of great guns. I wish all the tramps in Illinois could be on hand at that time, to be converted into well to-do citizens. That would be a work for the Revds worth meeting for. The tramps are such a body of lost sheep that they will soon compel attention from every quarter. If they could only pay preachers and build churches, their souls would become "precious" immediately. Think if I am well enough I will hear some of the Revds in Sept and if they should touch upon any of the great questions of the day, in any humane or rational way, I will be glad to tell you about it. . . .

I am fortunate enough to have a consoling faith in the "Sum of things." Still there are moments when I feel impelled to ask if this is not a world of orphan children every soul of man "crying in the night!" The Divine Fatherhood seems to be hidden in the case of millions of the race.

You will soon have, not two, but four young men in your family besides one young lady. I hope you and Ben will live to see them able to breast the waves for themselves, and long enough too, to enjoy their prosperity. I will be glad to see Charlie and Robert, and hope they may have a pleasant journey. They may possibly be here about the time you receive this.

Affectionately Yours
Louisa Semple

[TTU]

After her two oldest sons departed, Alice turned her full attention to Edie, Harry, and George. On August 27 Edie, who was not feeling well, celebrated her thirteenth birthday quietly. Several days later the post physician diagnosed her illness as typhoid fever,[28] and Alice began a desperate struggle to save her daughter's life. In the following letter to Robert she described her efforts calmly to avoid alarming her son.

Fort Concho, Sept. 2nd 1878

My dear Robert

Edith is very sick, but has been more comfortable today than any day since Saturday. We do not know whether her fever has reached its highest or not, but in any event it will be several weeks before she is well, as under the most favorable circumstances, Typhoid Fever is very slow, and tedious. She takes no solid food, but lives on wines, brandy, & essence of beef injected into her bowels &c. She takes most of medicines also by injection, as her stomach will retain nothing, except in very small quantities.

Cousin Helen is staying with her this afternoon. I am of course the proper person to take care of her but she gets very tired having me both day and night, and I of course need some rest as well as she.

We have no later news of Charlie yet, than his leaving Jacksonville but hope soon to hear of his arrival at West Point. . . .

The Inspector Gen. Mason, and the Paymaster Major Bates arrived today, and are installed in Capt. Kennedy's quarters. We could not entertain them on account of Edith's sickness, besides papa has not been well for two days, and feels much more like lying down and resting, than having general inspection. Papa found the box of things you sent all right on opening them. I will let you and Charlie know how Edith gets along as often as possible, and you will of course let the other friends know.

Affectionately your Mother
Alice K. Grierson

[TGCHS]

Despite Alice's efforts, Edie died on September 9. A few days later Alice described her daughter's illness and death to a friend, Fanny McLaughlen, wife of Major Napoleon Bonaparte McLaughlen.

Fort Concho Sept. 21st 1878

My dear Mrs. McLaughlen

Your letter dated the 8th and mailed the 12th was received in the afternoon of the 15th.

You remember how eagerly Edith ran home for ink and pen the morning you left Concho so that you and the Gen. might write your names in her Autograph Album—I was quite pleased when she showed them to me to see you had written

Your friend

Fanny R McLaughlen

Believing that it was not entirely compliment, and that you will be interested in hearing *from me* some particulars in reference to her last few weeks with us, I now write. Were you living next door there are a thousand things I would tell you, which would of course be too tedious to write or read, and first I enclose four pictures which the Gen. had taken the day after Edith's death. If you or the Gen. would like either, choose the one you like best. Then Mrs. Esterley can select, and Mamie Beck can have one, and the fourth can be returned to me. If you prefer remembering Edith as you knew her, it will neither hurt nor offend me if you do not accept a picture. The photographs are so unlike her living self, that I don't believe I would recognize them, but *I know* they were taken from her form and features.

You may remember that Edith had some trouble with swollen and inflamed tonsils, and went a number of times to the Hospital to have them touched with caustic, before you left, and while Miss Fuller was sick the last of July & 1st of August, Dr. DeHanne spoke of Edith looking pale, and said some medicine, which had been prepared for Miss Fuller, would be good for Edith, and perhaps she had better take some. Edith scouted the idea, said "catch me taking medicine when I am not sick."

Monday morning, Aug. 19th, her throat was again troubling her and she went to the hospital that morning and the next and had her throat touched. Her head ached a little while she was at the hospital and during the day, but she kept about the house. Wednesday she had, what I then called, a violent sick headache, it continued for four days. She was so opposed to taking medicine, I think I did not send for the Doctor until Friday or perhaps Thursday afternoon. He ordered some very small pills for her of which she took but one. The Dr. said Gastric troubles were very common and that she needed rest, quiet, and milk & lime water for diet. She disliked milk and did not try to take it and took but little of the lime water.

Saturday afternoon, the 24th, the Gen. came in from the spring and beyond, quite ill, having almost had sunstroke while hunting, on the way home. As soon as he saw Edith in bed in our room, he went up stairs and lay down on her bed, and as he seemed so much worse than she, I gave him my undivided attention. Edith had said she was going to get up when papa came home, but we did not know he would come Saturday. When, however, she saw he had come, sick, she felt that she must not keep him out of his own bed, so crept up stairs, dressed herself and after a while came down, was at the table at lunch, and went again up stairs at bed time, lying on the lounges in the meantime.

Sunday, neither the Gen. nor Edith wished me to stay at home, so both Miss Fuller and I went to church. The Gen. went to the office on Monday, but Walker [a striker] took him in the large carriage and went for him, and for a day or two afterwards.

Tuesday, the 27th, was Edith's birthday and when Walker went to bring the Gen. from the office, Edith rode in the carriage and invited Alice [Dunbar], Lillie [Constable], and Bessie [Constable], to come in the evening and eat cake and melons, play games &c. About dark, I sent Walker to ask Lt. Tear and Lt. Hodges to come also, and Lt. Davis was here. I only allowed Edith to ask the girls to stay until taps. At that time they went home, and the officers just after.

On Wednesday, she walked down to the chaplains and sat quite awhile, talking of her birthday presents &c., also went horseback riding about retreat. Lillie was to have gone, but Mrs. Constable had the horses hitched to the Ambulance & went riding, so Lillie could not go, & Edith only rode about the post.

She kept about the house Thursday & Friday but vomiting returned Friday noon and again in the evening. Saturday morning she said she felt so sleepy, she would not get up—nor did she afterward. I thought I ought to send for the Doctor on Saturday, but she begged so hard to have me wait until Sunday, and then I might if she were not better.

Sunday morning, I sent for the Doctor and after seeing her, he told me, before leaving the house, that her disease had assumed a Typhoid character, and in the evening he told Miss Fuller she was very dangerously ill. I took care of her almost constantly day and night, except when eating my meals. Thursday, Miss Fuller was with her through the afternoon, but I was in & out giving medicine, wine &c.

Friday P.M. I slept three or four hours, as I was exhausted from loss of sleep, but when I returned I saw she would die. Saturday night, about 1 o'clock, she had a sinking spell and for two or three hours I thought her dying. The Gen., Miss Fuller and I were up all night, Saturday night, & I had been up all night for three nights previous, and awake all of Tuesday night. I was [so] entirely worn out that the Doctor, Gen. and Miss Fuller insisted on my coming down stairs and resting. We sent for Mrs. Smither who came and stayed until 12 o'clock, Sunday night.

I went up at that time, Mrs. Smither went home, and Miss Fuller to bed. I had been away from her 18 hours. She was more comfortable Sunday night than any night of her last sickness, and lay sleeping quietly next day until 2 o'clock P.M. when a marked change took place in her breathing. The vomiting which had ceased 4 days returned, and she lay dying until 8 o'clock, Monday evening, the 9th of Sept., when all was over.

Her sufferings were very acute. The fever made her a little flighty and the large dose of Quinine, which she retained by injection Wed. evening, made her wild for two or three days. The Gen.

telegraphed to Fort Worth for ice on Sunday. We hoped it would
come Wednesday, but it did not until Thursday. She thought it
never would get here. It was the greatest comfort to her and, to me,
it was music to hear her chew it. It was the only thing she chewed
during her sickness except a few grapes.
[TGCHS]

The death of a child was not an uncommon event on a frontier post.
At such times the entire regiment gathered round the bereaved family
and offered strong support. Edie was given a military funeral and "buried
like a soldier girl" at a site close to the post. Soldiers constructed a stone
wall enclosure, and here Alice began each day, tending the flowers and
carrying on her correspondence.[29]

Alice emerged from her ordeal remarkably well. She recognized that
many others had endured their share of affliction and found in their common sufferings a strengthening of human bonds.

Fort Concho Oct. 18th 1878

My dear Charlie

I have been intending for the last two days to write to you, but
one way and another, the time has slipped by without my doing
so. How do you sleep now? I hope much better than you did while
here. It is very essential to good health to sleep well, and enough.
I suppose you are obliged to study some in the evenings, but as far
as possible, I think it is better to study in day time.

Of course, as you say, we have gotten "into the usual way of
living," pretty much. We have not been forlorn, and gloomy at any
time. The effect of anxiety and fatigue have worn off and for two
or three weeks I have slept very well. I would not be conscious of
being asleep all night long, some nights during the first three or
four weeks after Edith died, but now that I usually sleep quite well,
I feel much better.

Yesterday afternoon, a little before sundown, I started to walk to
the cemetery, and just beyond our yard Parker, the Sergeant Major
came to me and handed me three letters, I put them into my pocket,
and when I got to the cemetery, I took the box (which I have by the
stone wall to climb on) inside the board fence, sat down on it, and
read my letters beside Edith's grave.

The first was a beautiful one from Mrs. Keyes, the Captain's

Mother. She is living near Winchester, Virginia, she had heard about Edith from some friend in St. Louis. It was very kind of her to write—she has had troubles enough of her own to teach her how to sympathize with others. Another letter was from Mrs. McLaughlen, a very good, kind, letter. Gen. McLaughlen and Kitty have both been quite sick. "Sally" left her, and, for more than a week, Mrs. Beck had been very sick, and Mrs. McLaughlen had been helping take care of her, and had Mamie and Paul Beck staying with her, so that she had been pretty well worn out. The other letter was from Ellen and I always like her letters. She enclosed a newspaper slip containing a most vivid description of the fire in Chicago seven years ago, in the fewest possible words.

Sergeant Brenner has just been in, and read and translated a long letter which Robert wrote in German to him on the 12th, Sergeant B. says there are very few mistakes in it. All the friends were well in J——last Saturday.

Affectionately your Mother
Alice K. Grierson

[TGCHS]

In Jacksonville Robert continued to live with Louisa on the second floor of the Old Homestead and boarded with the Greens, the family that currently occupied the first floor. Though he still needed two more years of high school before graduating, he was already thinking of following Charlie to West Point.

Jacksonville Illinois.
Sunday Nov. 24th 1878

Dear Mama

I recd a letter from Charlie Wednesday with a cabinet photograph in it. . . .

We are having beautiful weather for so late in the fall. I had 1 doz tin types taken yesterday for $1.25; they are not very good. I'm going to try and have some good pictures taken before long. I enclose some of the pictures. The one standing is what I call, I don't care a darn picture.

—About West Point—

I'd like to go ever so much and I think it would be the best thing in the world for me if I could start it. Charlie says there's no difficulty about two of the same family going. I'd want to graduate at the High school first, and if I'd go then and get through all right, I'd graduate before I'm 24, and that's soon enough. I like army life and I've seen more of it than any other kind. Tell papa about it and let me know what both of you think. Of course that's in the future, but still, I thought it was well enough to speak of it. I think it is one of the greatest honors a person can have in this country to be a graduate of West Point. I would get such a thorough education and sound drilling that it would be an advantage to me all the days of my life. . . .

Yours affectionately
Robt K. Grierson

[TTU]

Robert's plans inspired little enthusiasm in Alice. Given his moodiness, she doubted that he could withstand the pressures that she believed had contributed to Charlie's illness. Unwilling to tell him this, she evaded the issue. Meeting no response about West Point, Robert next suggested the Naval Academy. Unable to equivocate any longer, Alice made it clear that she did not favor his admission to either school. She also began planning another trip to Jacksonville.

Illness and death were constant companions on the frontier, and so was alcoholism. Officers of the Tenth were not immune, and a number of them were noted tipplers. Lieutenant William Beck was charged with having abused his men while intoxicated on assignment in San Antonio. Several soldiers had almost died when he forced them to march despite heat and exhaustion over broken and rocky terrain.[30]

Not long before, another veteran of the Tenth, Captain Thomas Little, had been cashiered for consorting openly with a prostitute while in uniform and then pressing charges against her, alleging that she had stolen his purse while rendering services. Such activities represented "conduct unbecoming an officer and a gentleman" and reflected poorly on the army in frontier communities.[31]

Fort Concho Jan. 24th 1879

My dear Robert

Yours of the 19th came last evening. I received a letter of the 12th from Charlie, Friday evening 24th, don't know why it was so long coming.

I can't tell what time I will be in Jacksonville. I think I will leave here by or before the 15th of May. Don't set your heart on giving a reception to the graduating class, though I am willing, if it is practicable, that you should have a gathering, neither expensive, nor formal. I presume I will be very tired when I arrive in J and won't feel good for much in the way of work.

I hope you will be as little "spooney" as possible with any of the girls, and let your letters be friendly, without being especially "sweet." I copy a sentence from the printed "Regulations Governing the Admission of Candidates to the Naval Academy."

"Candidates for appointment as midshipmen must be between *fourteen* and *eighteen* years of age when examined for admission."

I never liked the idea of your going to Annapolis, as you know —nor do I think favorably of your going to West Point. We will try and make some satisfactory arrangement for you by the time you graduate at the High School.

... Lt. Beck got drunk after he went to San Antonio and Gen. Ord placed him in close arrest, only gave him the limits of the Menger Hotel where he was staying. . . .

The fishing season is commencing here. I saw some fishing poles going out yesterday, and Harry and George say the Chaplain's family is going fishing today. We scarcely need fire it is so warm. Love to all.

Affectionately your mother
Alice K. Grierson

[ISHL]

Robert failed to understand the true reasons for his mother's concern and instead concluded that she mistrusted him.

Jacksonville Illinois.—
Wednesday Feb. 26th 1879.

Dear Mama.

Your letter of the 19th was received Monday. . . .

I get along pretty well at school and intend to keep on in that way. If I never "fool with the girls" anymore than I have since I've been away this time I'll do mighty well. It is my aim to do nothing while you are away from me, that I wouldn't do before your face. I *mean* this and I *follow it out* the very best I know how. I want you to understand that I'm no coward—what I do I do openly—I don't try to hide it from you. I here make you this promise and if I *ever* break it may I fall dead on the spot:—I never intend to *say* or *do* anything improper with a girl. I'm a "bad egg" and I believe I know it as well as anyone. I'm not nearly as bad as I used to be, and I don't believe I'm as bad by a long shot as most boys of my age would be, if they had the chance of all the bad, as I have. If I were disposed to be bad, no one ever had a better chance to "raise hell" than I have.

There are plenty of boys of my age who do nothing but smoke, drink, swear, stay out late at night, flirt with the girls, and something far worse than all this—viz—go to those bad houses that are in every town.—I do not smoke and I don't intend to. I have drank three or four glasses of beer since I've been here but I would have drank ten times as much if I'd been at Concho—I never intend to drink to amount to anything. Sometimes if I get angry I may say bad words but it is a very bad habit, and I assure you, I do not admire it. I do not go out late at night, but very seldom, and as to "fooling with the girls," I'm nowhere near as "spoony" as I was a year ago. No sir, I'm a better boy than I used to be. The last named (going to those places) is something I *never did* and *never* will do. I'll try to do as well as I can, and will be regular in my habits, and will not get into any scrapes, if I can help it. . . .

Your loving son
Robt K. Grierson.

[TTU]

Separation from Ben was not as much an issue in this trip back East, since he had been ordered to New York City for the double court-martial of Colonels David S. Stanley and William B. Hazen.[32] Afterward, he planned additional explorations of the trans-Pecos region and was not due back at Fort Concho before midsummer.

Robert gave Alice an unusually enthusiastic welcome when she arrived in Jacksonville earlier than originally planned. It was a pleasure to return to familiar surroundings, but her later letters indicated that her hometown was changing. Durfee's had just opened the first five-cent counter (the beginnings of a dime store), a number of Jacksonville homes were supplied with natural gas, and trolley cars provided transportation across town.[33]

Jacksonville Monday A.M.
Apr. 7th 1879

Dear Ben

Robert climbed on the train at the R.R. crossing and came in at
the back of the car, and took each one of us by surprise, as we were
not sitting together. My father, John, Wese [Louisa Fuller, Helen
Fuller Davis's sister], and Marion [Grierson Capps, Ben's niece]
were at the Depot to meet us. I rode up with pa in the shabby old
buggy, with Old Jim, in spite of Robert's protest. . . .

Mrs. Green had fire in the (big) parlor and the room above the
two beds made up for us. Dinner was ready, as soon as we got the
thickest of the dirt washed off our hands, and when it was over,
I assure you it was a pleasure to unpack my Ark of a trunk, and
numerous bundles in a large room with our own empty wardrobe,
bureau, and washstand to receive the contents. The carpets, furniture, and pictures on our side of the hall, and in the halls, look like
old familiar friends. I have not yet been in on Mrs. Green's side of
the hall, though she has invited me to come, but saw through the
windows some nice plants and flowers. . . .

Harry & George commenced school at the 1st Ward, (Miss Toby
Principal) this morning. I am going up to Wese Fuller's this afternoon, also to the Dentist. I was never so glad to get back to J——
before, and it is very fine to have all the good of the house and no
bother of housekeeping.

Robert is bleached in the face, to what he was in Concho, and
his face is thin, but his grip is like yours. He is charmed with his
gun, and went to the river duck hunting and was quite successful.

I found a letter here from Charlie—he was well, and pleased
with the prospect of seeing you.

Yours affectionately,
Alice K. Grierson

[TTU]

While Alice was away from Fort Concho, post matters continued to
concern her. Rachel Beck, whose husband had just been sentenced to
dismissal for one year without pay after his recent court-martial, wrote
Alice entreating her to ask Ben to request clemency for his troublesome
officer.[34]

Joplin Mo. June 1st 1879

Mrs. B. H. Grierson
   Jacksonville
     Morgan County
      Illinois

My dear Mrs. Grierson,

Enclosed please find a letter from Mr. [Congressman William] Springer of Illinois, to myself, attention to Mr. Beck's case, which I wish you would please be kind enough to forward to the General—and ask him to *please, for my sake and the children's,* as well as for Mr. B——'s, for whom I think I owe much in the *future,* to write and recommend Lieut. B. to executive clemency—as he is the Col. of the regiment to which Mr. B. belongs. It would be of great welcome to me.

A majority of the court and the Commanding Gen. of the dept. have already recommended him to mercy—and Senators Davis, Logan and Springer have all been very kind to me and written to the Secretary of war in his behalf, and I have great hopes of his ultimate restoration to duty. The Court found him guilty of *drunkeness and ill treatment of his men,* and sentenced him to "dismissal."

I beg that you will pardon me for bringing my troubles to you but I know that your request, to the Gen. on our behalf, will guarantee his endorsement in our favor. Please ask the Gen. to be kind enough to return me Mr. Springer's letter.

My health is much improved since I came here, in spite of all of my anxiety, about our troubles. Willie is in Jacksonville with his father's aunt. I am *very anxious* to have him with me, as *soon* as *possible.* Perhaps I shall come for him. I hope that you and yours are well. Please remember me to Mrs. Semple also Mrs. Davis. Tell the boys that Jack speaks of them often, and he and Mamie send love to them. I suppose that you will go to West Point to see Charlie graduate. Please remember me to him. With many thanks for all of your past kindness and best wishes for you and yours, and a request that you will kindly pardon this trespass upon your time and kindness, my dear Mrs. Grierson.

       Yours most respectfully
       R. L. Beck

[TTU]

This time Alice, having little patience with drunkenness, was not sympathetic.

Jacksonville July 8th 1879

My dear Ben

I received the enclosed letter from Mrs. Beck yesterday. I have just written to her, that I doubt very much whether you can do any thing for Lt. Beck, and that unless they have relatives who can furnish them money the coming year, I should think they would be compelled to practice a rigid economy, and that if I am correctly informed as to Lt. Beck's finances, that I should think a closer economy than I have ever known either Lt. or Mrs. Beck to practice, would be essential to his keeping out of farther difficulties.

I also told her that if Willie could be put at some work that he would be willing to do, and under the control of a judicious man, it seemed to me to be the best thing for him &tc. &tc. I thought I might just as well tell her some plain truths and she will probably not think it worth while to write to me again. . . .

. . . This is your birthday.

Affectionately yours.
Alice K. Grierson.

[TTU]

Despite Alice's adamant stand, the colonel, along with many others, interceded in Beck's case and his sentence was commuted to eight months.[35]

By late July Ben was still traveling throughout the trans-Pecos region, and Alice remained in Jacksonville "on Robert's account." The Greens, who provided Robert with board and some measure of a homelike environment, had announced their intention of leaving the Old Homestead in September. Once more Alice confronted the question of how best to provide for her second son. Her problem was complicated because Harry, missing the horseback riding, hunting, fishing, and the wide open spaces, longed to return to his father's post.

Jacksonville July 26th 1879

My dear Ben

Harry is very anxious to have me write and ask you to say something about our coming back to Concho. Poor Harry is pretty homesick, and can't see why I want to stay so long. How long do you expect to be out West, and do you expect us to come by stage, all the way from Worth, part of the way, or any of the way?

It was on Robert's account especially that I thought best to stay, and it would not of course be best to go back when you are away. Harry would like being here much better I think if we had the house to ourselves, but is too late now to remedy that matter for this visit. . . .

. . . If the Greens stay here until just after the middle of Sept as they wished to do, it will only be a little over eight months until Robert expects to graduate at the High School, and then he would want to go to Concho or wherever we are. The expense of paying his board and a servant's is of course quite an item, but we did it for almost five months when our family was larger by Helen and Edith, and what Kate wasted would a good deal more than board Louisa. It is a puzzling problem to know what is best to do. It is certainly very forlorn for Louisa to live alone as she does and the idea of living with the Greens or other "drovers" is almost intolerable to her. . . .

Yours as ever
Alice K. Grierson

[TTU]

At the end of September, after obtaining clearances through the yellow-fever quarantines surrounding Saint Louis, Missouri, and Little Rock and Texarkana, Arkansas, Alice, Harry, and George returned to Fort Concho. Alice was delighted to discover definite improvements. Water pumps had been installed outside the officers' quarters, a far greater convenience than the weekly water wagons. Vegetables and fruits, moreover, were available at reasonable prices. Finally, three post schools were in operation, one for the white children of officers, a second for the black children of the enlisted men, and a night school in which the chaplain could continue his assignment to teach the buffalo soldiers to read and write.[36]

Soon after her homecoming Alice began receiving letters from Robert revealing a great deal of inner turmoil.

Jacksonville Illinois.
Sunday, Nov. 13th 1879.—

My dear Mother

Your letter of the 11 just came last Monday. . . .

I have had no trouble or unpleasantness with anybody but I'm not satisfied with myself in a great many respects. My conscience tells me what I am, and my reason what I ought to be and the pictures are far from being alike. In spite of all the blessings I have, I feel unhappy. I have felt this way a good many times, when I've written to you, though I said nothing, and I have concluded that it is not right to act one way and feel just the opposite.

I'm not homesick and I don't believe I have the "blues" exactly, but I feel as though I had no friend on whose bosom I could lay my head. If I could see you I'd not be in this condition—and the next best thing I suppose is to write the way I feel. These two sentences, "There is no rest for the wicked"—and "The way of the transgressor is hard" ring in my ears continually. I wish that I could feel in my heart that there is a Heavenly Father who cares two straws for me. When you feel badly, remember you are not the only one—and I suppose I'd better apply this to myself as well. I believe I'm a rather singular mortal anyhow—there are so many conflicting currents in my nature.

Now, that I've spoken I feel somewhat relieved. What would we do without hope when we get "cross grained and ill natured"? I will make up the lessons I missed by being away Friday so it will be about the same as if I'd been there.—I hope I'll be a little more tranquil the next time I write. I was at Uncle John's this evening and recd. your letter of the 16 and check for $10.00. When the time comes, I think I can leave Jacksonville without the slightest pang of regret.

Affectionately
R. K. G.

I recd a letter from Charlie last Tuesday. I will answer it when I get in a good humor.

[TTU]

Although Robert's letters continued in this vein throughout the winter, he maintained high grades and finished second in his class, a distinction that required him to give a speech. As commencement approached, he again expressed hope that he could enter West Point Military Academy. His brother Charlie, having graduated the previous spring, was serving as a second lieutenant in the Tenth Cavalry.

Jacksonville Illinois
Sunday, March 28th 1880

Dear Mama,

. . . I am very busy thinking, reading, & looking up matter generally for my "Oration." I had a talk with Dr. Jones Thursday morning about my subject. I was up town this morning, stopped at Wese's a few minutes & then was at Mr. Wolcotts & Mr. Kings. Borrowed Bacon's essays from Mr. W. & Guizot's History of Civilization from Mr. King.

My subject is "War & its influence on Civilization." It's a pretty big gun to shoot but if I hold it tight I guess the recoil will not hurt me. Such a subject requires lots of thought & reading. I'll do as well as I can. I'll take a big load of study on *the subject before I* pull the trigger.

The more I think about West Point the more I think it would be a good thing for me to go. I wish Papa would try & get me an appointment for June '81. I feel *in my bones* that if I'd go about it right I could go through. A year in Texas ought to make a *man* of me i.e. as far as being tough is concerned. You see if I went to West Point I would study the very things I like and I'd be "paddling my own canoe" and would be no expense to Papa and I would if I was sent to some Engineering School. I want to go to some school after the High School, and I think West Point is the place.

Though I occasionally give out, I know I'm tough if I give myself half a chance. I speak about this now because the appointments are made a year ahead and *it may get too late*. Well, I must read some article relating to "War" or "Civilization"—

Affectionately Your Son
Robt. K. Grierson

[TGCHS]

Several weeks later Robert was still preparing his address. Undoubtedly, it was painful to both Alice and her son that no member of his immediate family would be present on this occasion.

Jacksonville Illinois.
Tuesday, Apl. 13, 1880.

Dear Mama.

... I'd give anything if you were here—you could read to me &
help me a great deal besides just being here. My head doesn't feel
right—not for studying anyhow, & my eyes hurt most of the time.
Composition or letter writing has generally been easy enough for
me but it seems as if my head was empty when it comes to writing
on such subjects as the one I have—nearly everything I read is on
the opposite side of the question from what I take. I don't intend to
give it up though—it will *have* to wind up right.—

Aunt Louisa had a tramp working here all last week—he worked
yesterday too. I believe I'd rather do any kind of work than try to
write my piece.—We were examined in Shakespeare, Friday—I got
93%—. ...

You'll have to excuse such a letter as this. I'm just sick & tired
of anything that requires any kind of mental effort.

Affectionately Your Son
Robt. K. Grierson.

[TGCHS]

Shortly after commencement Robert rejoined his family at Fort Concho. Colonel Grierson was preparing to lead troops against Victorio, chief
of the Warm Springs Apaches, a tribe that had left its reservation at San
Carlos and was raiding a vast area along the Texas border and deep into
Mexico.[37] Robert was overjoyed when his father agreed to his participation
in the campaign.

Colonel Grierson, his son, and an escort of eight troopers left Fort
Concho on July 10. The small size of the group worried Alice, but she
understood that her husband had dispatched men from various companies
of the Tenth to substations, mountain passes, and water holes, sites that
he knew intimately from his extensive exploring and mapping expeditions.
His plan was to await Victorio at these locations, thereby avoiding the
fruitless pursuits and costly but inconclusive skirmishes that had marked
the Ninth Cavalry's campaign against Victorio under Colonel Edward
Hatch.[38]

Colonel Grierson's strategy succeeded admirably. On July 30 a victory over Victorio at Tinaja de las Palmas, a small but critically located
water hole, drove the Apache chief's forces across the Rio Grande into

Mexico.[39] When Alice received the news she was greatly relieved that so far the campaign had gone well.

Fort Concho Aug. 6th 1880

My dear Ben

Your letter of the 20th July is the latest letter from you, though I had one of the 26th from Robert. I received your dispatch of the 3rd. Lt. Smither has just been in, and shown me a document from Dept. Hd. Qrts. acknowledging the receipt of your "Modest" & satisfactory report of a great success &c. . . .

I think it very fortunate you received notice of the approach of Victorio's band, it is risky business traveling with so small an escort. I hope you will take every honorable precaution for your safety. . . .

. . . Davis is quite elated over your success with the Indians. Love to Robert.

Yours as ever
Alice K. Grierson

[ISHL]

That same day, August 6, Grierson again met and defeated Victorio at Rattlesnake Springs, forcing the now-demoralized Apaches back into Mexico. There, two months later, Mexican troops under Colonel Joaquín Terrazas cornered Victorio in the Tres Castillos Mountains. The ensuing battle claimed the lives of Victorio and most of his band.[40]

Alice described her first news of the final outcome in a letter to Charlie, who was on duty at a substation. With Victorio defeated, life had returned to normal at Fort Concho as the garrison settled down to the usual round of parties. Masquerades were a favorite form of entertainment, and the choice of impersonations reveals how casually prejudice was accepted in that era.

By impersonating Johnson C. Whittaker, Lieutenant Leavell was ridiculing a black cadet who had been found a few months earlier tied to his bedpost at West Point and suffering from severe head injuries. His explanation was that three masked men had assaulted him. A subsequent military investigation, however, concluded that Whittaker's head injuries were self-inflicted, although it was impossible to explain how these events could have transpired. Soon afterward he failed his final exams, and with his dismissal the doors of West Point were closed to blacks for many years.[41]

Fort Concho Oct. 24th 1880

My dear Charlie

Your note of the 15th and postal of the 20th have just come. Papa telegraphed me from Van Horn's Wells, and Eagle Springs. It has been twice published in the Press Dispatches that Victorio, with fifty of his warriors, and 18 women and children, had been killed by the Mexican troops. Papa telegraphs Lt. Smither, that the report lacks confirmation. . . .

. . . Fanny Monroe gave a Masquerade Party last week. Lt. Leavell said he wanted to personate Cadet Whittaker, and wanted to borrow your Cadet Uniform for the purpose. I loaned it to him, and he came in to show us how he looked, which was hideous. He had his face blackened, and then painted red in the most savage style. Lt. Eggleston said he washed it off soon after his arrival at the party. Helen and family are well. You know the Hd Qtrs of the 24th is to be at Camp Supply.

Affectionately
Alice K. Grierson

[ISHL]

Louisa Semple, for one, did not rejoice at Victorio's death, for her sentiments were those of the eastern humanitarian.

Jacksonville, Oct. 31st 1880

Dear Alice,

Your letter of the 18th received about the 25th or 26th—I wrote you on the 17th. . . .

I suppose now that Victorio is dispatched to the "place where he will hunger and thirst no more," the troops will have less to do. I am glad Ben was not at the final scene of butchery. Teraspas [Terrazas] waived [Lieutenant Colonel George] Buell back from sharing the *glory* of the victory over a lot of starved wretches. Centuries of shameful dealings with the Indians of course must ripen into such horrible events. How I wish Ben was rid of the business. . . .

The political excitement here as every where, is intense. Genl. Grant has fired up into a speech-maker. It is amazing to see how he strings several sentences together before he gives out. After the election I suppose he will have a relapse, but now he has shown that he has a small but "precious treasure" of words that fall with no uncertain sound but with a clear ring in them. He is determined that [Democratic candidate for President, General Winfield Scott] Hancock shall not "smile all over" if he can prevent it. . . .

Affectionately Yours,
Louisa Semple

[TTU]

Alice shared many of Louisa's sentiments regarding United States Indian policy, but her perspective at Fort Concho was somewhat different. She was relieved that with the death of Victorio the Indian threat to the peaceful settlement of the trans-Pecos region had ended. Not only was her husband safe from dangerous campaigns for the foreseeable future, but so was her son Charlie.

Only one concern marred Alice's peace of mind. Her brother Thomas had suffered serious financial reverses that, as her father informed her, had left him despondent.

Jacksonville, Oct. 18. 1880

My dear daughter Alice,
    Fort Concho
        Texas,

One week ago this morning I left for Chicago, returned Thursday night, stayed one night with Ellen, the second night with Rufus & the last night with Thomas. I found Thomas much better off financially than I expected, and worse off mentally than I anticipated. All his liabilities are liquidated by giving the new firm's paper to his creditors for the full amount of his indebtedness, and will have his homestead, the Sandy Lake property, all free & paid for and several thousand dollars besides.

I wish his mental condition was in as good condition. He is very low spirited, calls it the blues, fears that his children will have to go to the poorhouse, that he will be like his cousin John Manning, or have softening of the brain like his mother.

Mary and the children are all in good health. At the breakfast table I looked at the children and thought that I never saw a better looking lot of children belonging to one family. Thomas seems to be conscious of his situation, and the danger of his condition, he is on a salary of $3,000 per year. The name of the new firm is "The Kirk Iron and Hardware Company." All in usual health.

Affectionately your father,
John Kirk

[TTU]

On January 14, 1881, Tom Kirk killed himself, leaving behind a wife pregnant with their eleventh child. Instead of collapsing under her grief, Mary Fuller Kirk placed her home in the hands of a real-estate agent and relocated her family in Jacksonville, where she took up residence in the Old Homestead with Louisa Semple.[42] No sooner had she moved in than tragedy struck again, claiming her four-year-old son.

Jacksonville
Thursday Morning Apl. 7th 1881.

Dear Ben & Alice.

Poor little Ralph died this morning ¼ to 7 o'clock. His disease proved to be spinal meningitis. He suffered terribly Tuesday night. And Mary and I thought then he could not live. Yesterday he appeared to be dying but rallied in the afternoon, and we encouraged some hopes. At the last he passed away quietly. Doctor Jones was the physician & of course did all he could. Mary says she gets a blow on one side and is kept from falling by a blow on the other side. She had a special feeling of tenderness and admiration for Ralph, he was so gentle and serene in disposition.

The little clay image is very beautiful lying below in the East back room. Mary requested to have the funeral from Mr. Kirk's as the place here is not yet in order. The porches and yard are still littered with things. The large parlor crammed full and nothing settled. The funeral will be on Saturday. Louisa F. [Wese Fuller] sat up with Ralph last night.

Affectionately Yours
Louisa Semple.

[TTU]

Mary's strength did not desert her.

Jacksonville, May 16th 1881

My dear daughter Alice,
Fort Concho,
Texas.

Your letter of April 18th came duly to hands.

Mary bears up remarkably well under her heavy sorrow. I wonder sometimes that she can be so pleasant and cheerful. But the fact is Mary is a remarkable woman, I think more & more of her as I become better acquainted with her. The children are all very well & seem to enjoy being in Jacksonville very well.

Mr. Ulard, Mary's agent, rented the place whilst I was in Chicago, got $500 in gold down, & pays the other hundred dollars in two monthly payments.

I received, sometime since Bens Report of his military operations. I was very much interested in reading it, and am greatly obliged for it. . . .

Affectionately your father
John Kirk.

[TTU]

Shortly thereafter Mary Kirk had the following announcement to make.

Jacksonville June 3rd 1881

Dear Aunt Alice, Helen, & all

It has fallen out rather oddly that I am first to announce the arrival of a baby girl, here on the 21st of May. Helen [Mary's oldest daughter] was to have written, & Auntie spoke of writing last Sunday, but by some chance did not, & as I am unusually well, I concluded to announce myself. The baby is a very pretty, plump, perfect little creature (as babies go) with fine thick black hair. Aunty insists that she is beautiful but her mother can hardly say so much. She is reasonably good, & growing very fast. In spite of the feelings I have had all along—that I could only cry over this baby—I find that I quite enjoy her & am satisfied that she is a girl.

I am so very strong and well & got by so nicely & quickly with the project that I am inclined to feel gratified with my management, when in reality it was good fortune only. No one was disturbed at night, the baby was born at 10 a.m. Auntie officiated in a very satisfactory manner, & washed the baby a week. Helen was chief nurse of me, & since Auntie retired has washed the baby also. I did not lack for once the care I needed, & on the climactic day with the help of Aunty & Helen, walked out to see the races which was a sight worth seeing & one I wish it was possible for you to see. I must stop or end in being entirely illegible & unintelligible.

With love

Mary N. F. Kirk

[TTU]

For Alice the time had come to return to Illinois to aid and comfort Mary, visit other relatives in Chicago, and investigate with Robert professional programs outside the military. In spite of Robert's importuning she remained convinced that he was incapable of withstanding the strain of a military academy. By late July, as the entire nation awaited news of President Garfield, who lay dying from the twin effects of an assassin's bullet and poor medical care, Alice proposed the following plan to her husband.

Chicago July 24th 1881

My dear Ben

... It is now near the first of August, and Robert wants to go to Michigan University the latter part of September, so I think it is time you decide in regard to the matter. Suspense is hard for most persons to bear, and when a young man is so nearly 21, it is but right there should be something definite regarding his future business, or profession. I think it is the best thing he can do the coming year, and if you go to Europe next year, and think best to take him, no doubt he will be glad to go. . . .

Tell Harry & George that Albert keeps posted in all the news from President Garfield, he was telling us the bad news from him last evening. I am glad you have the superintending the printing of your record to occupy your leisures. Love to Charlie & all.

Affectionately

Alice K. Grierson

[TTU]

Ben responded quickly.

Fort Concho Texas
July 31st 1881

My Dear Alice,

Yours of the 24th inst is received & came by yesterday's mail. I wrote you the day before. . . . Charlie wrote to you yesterday & directed his letter to the same point. Helen has received the things you sent for the baby. I told her not to bother about sending you the money as the matter could be fixed up hereafter. . . .

In regard to Robert going to Ann Arbor Mich. in Medicine, I leave the matter to you and himself to determine. Possibly it will be as good as anything else he can do for the present. If it does not turn out all right, he will be apt to find it out in the course of a year. What will be the expenses for one year, or per year? Give me the figures as near as you can. It will be an expensive business, I presume, and if he goes there, he should not forget this, and make the best possible use of his time, while he remains at the institution. . . .

Affectionately
B. H. G.

[ISHL]

Robert remained in the East and entered the University of Michigan that fall. Alice returned to Fort Concho with Grace Fuller, Helen Fuller Davis's younger sister. Once more Alice hoped that one of Ben's nieces would find a suitable husband among the garrison's officers.

Despite a difficult curriculum, Robert performed well during his first semester. The holidays, however, posed a problem. Originally, he had planned to spend Christmas with the Fitches, old family friends who lived in Detroit. When unexpected company arrived, the Fitches regretfully withdrew Robert's invitation.[43]

Disappointed, Robert returned to Jacksonville. He threw himself into a frantic whirl of parties and tried to convince everyone that he was having a wonderful time. In truth he longed for his family.

Jacksonville Illinois
Tuesday Jan. 3rd 1882.

Dear Mama & all the Family:

Your postal card of the 21st ult. came soon after I wrote to you last Wednesday & your very entertaining Christmas letter of the 27th was rec'd Sunday last Jan. 1st '82. . . .

Grace Fuller Maxon.
Courtesy of the National Park
Service, Fort Davis National
Historic Site.

I'm having a delightful time. I never cut such a swell in Jacksonville before. J'ai fait mon debut dans la societie celebré de cette sage ville.

Saturday evening Prof. Block was here to tea & stayed an hour or more after tea. I showed him my fine album & he (like all who have seen it) admired it very much. Prof. Block played some pretty waltzes on the piano, & Helen [Kirk] and I waltzed. From here Prof. Block and I went to a party at Dr. Prince's. There was quite a large company present mostly young folks, & most of the evening was spent in playing a game called "Thumpe" (which consists in guessing a word that has been chosen—simply by asking questions that can be answered by yes or no). Grace no doubt understands the game. Nice refreshments were passed around, and the party wound up with a hop. I never had danced a waltz quadrille before— they are 'immense.' Charlie ought to have been there to waltz with Helen Ayres & Jennie or Laurie. Charlie was very kindly inquired about. In fact *all* the friends ask about *all* of you. We saw the old year buried & & the new Year born, & were guilty of dancing on Sunday morn'. . . .

. . . You know I am Aunt Louisa's guest, & take my meals in her room. For a few days she & I were at Aunt Mary's table. Supper is just ready, & I'm invited to an 'oyster stew' this eve' at Davenports'.

I went New Years Calling yesterday in grand style in company of Prof. Dwight & Prof. Block. Called on over 200 ladies (from 10 to 20 ladies at each 'open house'), after the calling went to "the grand ball for the callers" at Efler's & had the most glorious time I ever had in my life at a dance. I went to bed at 2 a.m. (today) & slept ten hours—till noon and I feel first rate. I make up the sleep I *lose,* which is the way to do when you do as you choose.

The time I'm having is "too utterly, too, too utter" as they say at Ann Arbor. I shall 'snort to remark' all about New Years in my next letter. I wish Papa would send me an Army Register to Ann Arbor—one of '80 or '81 will do. All of you certainly had a fine Christmas. Happy New Years' to all.

Affectionately your son
R. K. Grierson

[TTU]

Robert intended to complete the holidays by visiting his Aunt Ellen's family in Chicago. He never arrived. Instead Ellen's husband, Harvey B. Fuller, Jr., received word that Robert had been confined to the Harrison Street jail after going berserk and creating a disturbance at the Grand Pacific Hotel.

Ellen Kirk Fuller's letters to Alice described the events leading up to Robert's incarceration. After gaining his release, Harvey Fuller, Sr., brought Robert back to Jacksonville, where the young man was placed in the attic of the Old Homestead under Louisa Semple's care.

Chicago, Jan. 19, 1882

My Dear Sister.

Harvey returned from Jacksonville, Tuesday afternoon, having gone down with Robert. We did not notice the item in Sunday's paper about Robert, and knew nothing of it, till the younger Mr. Cooper came out a little after noon and told us. Harvey went right down town with him, thinking they might bring him out here; but they found that wholly inadmissible. He had been as well treated by every one, as possible under the circumstances, the officials judging him to be respectably connected. Harvey was with him nearly all afternoon. He came home for supper but went down again and stayed till about midnight.

Monday morning hearing nothing from J—— as to any one's coming for Robert, he concluded the best thing to do would be for him to go down with him, which he did with the help of an officer.

Mr. Ripley had been to see Robert before Mr. Cooper was; and saw that he had a good breakfast. Mr. Cooper was very kind.

I know of nothing else necessary to write now. I have delayed this almost too long.

We must just hold perfectly still, and do the best thing that presents itself.

With unbounded love and sympathy

Your sister

Ellen K. Fuller

[TTU]

Chicago, Jan. 27th, 1882.

Dear Sister Alice.

I received yours of the 23d this afternoon. I do hope you will have had a letter from J—— before this reaches you. Charlie Capps [John Grierson's son-in-law] did not come to Chicago at all, but he and Mr. Fuller met Robert and Harvey and Officer Gross at the depot in J—— and they walked right up to your home. Robert was taken into the big room over the parlor and was there till the attic was made ready for him. Two men stayed with Robert that night. I do not know whether they were the same who have been with him since or not. Harvey came home on the Tuesday morning train.

There was a $50 postal order among the papers in Robert's pockets. Harvey gave it and Robert's watch to Mary.

Harvey drew money at the store for all expenses; and Pa returned it to H——, since he came home and a sufficient amount to pay the hotel bill besides. Harvey sent the itemized bill which was receipted, to Pa—the other expenses I can give you.

There was no *damage* done at the Grand Pacific. He had taken the bed to pieces and the bedstead down, and had built a sort of barricade and was then ready for action. He was taken from the Grand Pacific to the Harrison St. Station on the South side and was there Saturday night and till about 9 o'clock Sunday night when he was taken over to the jail on the North side for better and more commodious quarters as they said, but they were about the same. He had no irons or anything of the kind on while at the station or jail—he was kept in his cell most of the time. They gave him a little liberty once or twice, letting him into the corridors, but he became so unmanageable they had to put him back. Harvey stayed with him till about ½ past 11 o'clock Sunday night, but there was nothing he could do. They would not permit him in with Robert then, so after paying some one a dollar to keep a special eye on him that he did not hurt himself, he came home.

Harvey went over about 9 o'clock Monday morning. Robert was asleep then, lying naked on the husks which he had torn from his mattress. Robert had had a pair of gold bowed spectacles Sunday. He told Harvey Monday morning the *remains* of them were over at the Harrison St. Station but Harvey could find no sign of them. Harvey took what cigars were left of those Robert had ordered, with his papers and a couple of books he had, to J——. One of the books was a medical work on Venereal diseases.

When Harvey went over to get Robert ready for starting to J——, he was very determined not to be dressed, and it took several men to accomplish it. He was so violent then that they put the straight jacket on, and as they were starting for the depot they shackled his feet also. He would kick so, he sent Harvey down quite a flight of stairs. He was quite unprepared for the attack but managed to keep on his feet. Robert had struck Harvey once while he was trying to persuade him to get dressed; but not in a vicious manner,—just a nervous get-out-of-the-way, *I* am coming, sort of spirit. He was very noisy all the way down to J——. They took off the shackles from his feet at the depot in J——. The straight jacket was still kept on, that night.

I hope Ben will be in J—— or on the way there, when this reaches you. They were expecting and hoping for his arrival this week, the last we heard.

With much love

Yours most truly,
Ellen K. Fuller.

[TTU]

This time Colonel Grierson did not leave Fort Concho to attend an ailing son. Instead Robert remained in Jacksonville under the care of Louisa Semple. When he failed to improve after a few months, Ellen broached the subject of committing him to an asylum. She also advanced a suggestion regarding Harry and George which strongly influenced the Griersons' thinking on the subject of education.

Chicago, April 3d, '82

Dear Sister Alice

I received yours of Mar. 28 Saturday P.M.—When I was writing about false sentiment I was thinking just then in particular of how bad I felt, when Charlie was sick as Robert is, that Ben should have found him confined as he was at West Point, and I cried more than once about it. But I have not felt at all the same about Robert's being deprived of liberty of hand and foot since he has been so: but I *have* shuddered to think how very dreadful it would have been for us if Harvey had been hurt or killed when he sent him flying down that flight of iron stairs at the jail—of course the difference of feeling may be laid to my selfishness. I know it is the "natures" also of mothers and fathers to endure for and from children more than any one else can be expected to and, I think unless they are being wise there may be mistaken kindness very often. And in cases of insanity I think in the great pity friends feel they may as easily be mistakenly kind.

I think now it was a mistake Tom was not taken to the Asylum when he was so insane about business—I am glad to know, as Rufus told me the last time I was at Wilmette, that Tom himself said, after he began to realize truly what he had done, that he ought to have been taken to the Asylum. If he had been he certainly would not have had so many things to humiliate and mortify him, in deciding the question of life or death.

You ought to know, I think, I am not as conceited as to be suggesting anything to be *acted* upon, only that you might have another view to *think* about. I wish I could *quit* thinking about the subject but there seems no getting away from it, there is so much in the world. . . .

I still think the dreadful—my protest now, and then I will hold my peace, that Harry and George may never be subjected to the same influences Charlie and Robert were in being sent away from home (as little boys)—from their father's & mother's authority and influences—to get an education. I don't believe it is study that hurts so much as other things. I'd have a tutor in the family before I'd do it. . . .

With best wishes always,
Your sister
Ellen K. Fuller

[TTU]

Toward the end of April, Alice, accompanied by her son George and Grace Fuller, arrived in Jacksonville. Grace by now was engaged to Lieutenant Mason M. Maxon of the Tenth Cavalry.

Alice introduced more relaxed procedures, dispensing with the forced feeding of the sedative chloral and ending Robert's confinement to the attic. By giving him increasing amounts of freedom, she incurred disastrous results, as Louisa Semple informed her brother.

Jacksonville June 11th 1882

Dear Ben

I acknowledged the receipt of your letter of May 28th. I have been very ill and, am yet scarcely able to write. I had fever and delirium for days and nights, during part of which time my mind was intensely employed about Robert. My sickness was a general breakdown of the whole system, and has lasted nearly a month, and was not caused by the work done in the previous three months, but much more by the undoing of that work, which was effected in sixteen days—from the morning of Apl. 24th to the evening of May 9th. . . .

I wrote you on the 30th of Apl., that I thought Robt. a *little better,* underscoring the words. *That* was the *first time* and the *last time* after the morning of Apl. 24., that any encouraging word could be truthfully written. All the rest, for the whole sixteen days was a downhill rush to destruction. If all the extravagances and excesses committed by poor Robt from Monday morning Apl. 24th to Tuesday evening May 9th were printed they would fill the Jacksonville Journal. No part of the City was unvisited by him. And the City was astonished and disapproved of an insane man having unbounded liberty. His excursions extended from the City to the country, on the East and the West, and from the day into the night. What wonder the case terminated as it did. . . .

. . . He caused while in my hands no trouble to the City, the neighborhood or the house. While I controlled him, no thought of arresting him ever entered any ones head. And I say positively that if any persons had committed the outrage and the ineffaceable injury on me, of tearing my sick child from his home and thrusting him into an insane asylum against my will—and without good cause —I would punish them to the last extent of the law, if I had to spend my life at it.

That he is there now is a triumph to the wretches who would without love, sympathy or pity, have dispatched him there in the first place!—and that is another bitterness to me. But there was a good cause for what was done,—of two terrible evils it was the least. It was the voices of Jacksonville—all classes—men and women— that the state of Alice's mind was such as to make her as incapable of managing Robt as Robt was of managing himself and that it was absolutely necessary to separate them. I went early on Wednesday morning, May 10th, to try if I could not have him returned to the attic, and could effect nothing, because return to the house would be return to the control of his mother. If Robert is not starved or beaten he is better where he is, than as he was previously to May 9th.

> Yours affectionately and sorrowfully,
> Louisa Semple.

[TTU]

As it was popularly believed in the nineteenth century that intellectual strain was a major cause of insanity in young people, Colonel Grierson reached a conclusion similar to Ellen's that education might prove harmful to the younger boys. He had, however, no stomach for returning to Jacksonville and facing the embarrassment of dealing with a second son afflicted with mental illness.

> Concho
> May 17/82.

Dear A——

Nothing from you by to-day's mail. Hope to get another letter to-morrow.

Enclosed send you a slip, cut from the St. Louis Democrat of the 13th. Only three copies were taken at the post & Lt. Cooper [who] is the only one who saw the notice in regard to Robert, tore out the notice from the other two papers. I presume however that it will be copied into other papers and go the rounds like former notices in his case. What will be the expenses for keeping Robert at Oak Lawn Retreat? My understanding is that it is a private asylum or hospital, but as Robert was committed there, it may be possibly a branch of the State Asylum.

Harrie is so *puny* & miserable looking that I have decided to take him out of school, for the present and when the weather is fine keep him out in the open air as much as possible. We must prepare ourselves to *look* this family tendency to *Insanity* square in the face. It has been developed in the *first two* of our children *now living* & under certain circumstances may or might show itself in the two *younger boys*. It is better that they be *clodhoppers* and go through life with but little education than to be afflicted as Charlie & Robert have been. Therefore I look upon a college education for Harrie or George as a doubtful contingency, which can only *be determined upon* one way or the other *hereafter*.

At present I do not feel much like going to Jacksonville, except in the case of urgent necessity. I think possibly it will be well to sell off whatever property we may have there & establish or look up a home somewhere else. In regard to this, however, I will be guided by your wishes, after the matter has been more fully considered.

The paymasters arrived today. I will, before his return to San Antonio, get checks on New York, for this month's pay accounts.

Major Dodge is here again and accepts with his brother [the] closet & the upper hall room.

Aff.

B. H. G.

[ISHL]

Anger had been building in Alice. Not only was she the one in Jacksonville struggling to cope with the painful situation, but questions had been raised regarding her judgment in dealing with Robert. And though the Grierson family was not without its share of emotional problems, Alice interpreted the reference to a "family tendency to *Insanity*" as meaning

145

her family. After all, it was the Kirks who demonstrated what was commonly referred to then as *dementia praecox* in late adolescence or early youth.[44] Such assignment of blame seemed unfair, and to underscore her unhappiness she returned a promissory note to Ben unsigned.

Alice had inherited a small amount of money from her mother which she considered entirely her own. From time to time she used it to advance small loans to her husband, but she always charged him the current bank rate, never less. This reflected the desire she had expressed earlier for more autonomy and greater financial freedom than commonly given wives in that era. There is no evidence that the colonel objected to this arrangement.[45]

Jacksonville May 26th 1882

My dear Ben

... I want you to send me at once, a draft for a hundred dollars, and I hope you will not very long defer sending some money to Dr. McFarland. His place although nice is small—the parlor is so small beside ours. He does not appear at all as if he had grown rich by taking care of insane people.

From the desperate fear you seem to have that I am in various ways going to injure Robert, I am led to suppose that you have utterly, and entirely forgotten, that you had no hesitation in bringing Charlie to my care, and that I successfully brought him from the lowest depths of the disease, when he had the relapse at Christmas, to such good health that he was able to return to West Point, finish his studies, and graduate above the middle of his class, and all this without either an attendant, or an attic in the business. Now what on earth have I done that you can't trust Robert with me. Most assuredly I don't know, I do know that you have treated me ever since Robert was sick as if I were to blame for it.

I am glad however that you say in your letter of May 17th, "*We must prepare ourselves to look this family tendency to insanity square in the face*" & I am of [the] opinion that if you ever look at it squarely, with a willingness to admit that *possibly* you may be accountable for part of it, you will find it to be the case.

Yours of the 21st enclosing Charlie's with his graphic account of the storm, and Harry's with his good account of killing the two antelope came this morning. I have written a long letter to Lt. Maxon this morning, giving him account of how I spent the

$120.00 with which he commissioned me to buy a diamond ring for Grace, and telling him some truths concerning her, which are true whether they are palatable to him or not.

I enclose the telegrams which I found among Robert's papers after he went to Oak Lawn, you will see by the long one to you how his poor soul was tortured. . . .

. . . I return your note. Please send me in place of it your note for four hundred dollars at 4 per cent interest as that is the rate the banks pay.

Yours as ever
Alice K. Grierson

[TTU]

In addition to keenly feeling her husband's lack of support, Alice found herself largely shunned by Jacksonville friends and acquaintances. Broaching the subject of mental illness was too discomfiting for most. Feeling very much alone, Alice did the best she could to arrange for Robert's care. At the same time, she gave Grace Fuller both practical and financial assistance in preparing for her wedding. Whatever her burdens, Alice never failed to fulfill her duties as she perceived them to the extended family.

Jacksonville May 30th 1882

My dear Ben

I acknowledged by postal the receipt yesterday morning of your letter of the 24th, which enclosed check on N.Y. for $75.00. I was very glad to get the money, as I was so nearly out. I gave Grace the seventy five dollars for her wedding dress soon after receiving that hundred dollars of my own money. I told her in Concho, that you had said you would give her, her wedding dress—that you gave Helen fifty dollars for her dress, and she trimmed it with lace which I gave her, which cost sixteen dollars, and I gave her other laces which all together amounted to twenty five dollars, and that I wanted you to do as much for her. . . .

. . . Mr. and Mrs. Ramsay, and Miss Selby a teacher in the Public Schools, called here yesterday afternoon, and Mr. Ramsay told me two or three times, to give his kind remembrances, and best regards to you. Mrs. Jones called here to see me at once, and has always been very kind to me, but *no other* of our acquaintances, had ever called here until yesterday afternoon, Miss Harriet Reed called here to see Susannah [Fuller] and when the Ramsays went into the parlor I met her there, and had quite a pleasant chat.

Mrs. Wolcott called here to see Mary the day after my arrival, I happened to go in the parlor and talked with her quite a little while before I discovered that I was interrupting a private conversation. Mrs. & Dr. (Professor) Adams, and her daughter, Mrs. Lippincott, called here one day, and left kind remembrances for me. I should have excused myself if they had asked to see me, as I was too busy with the care of Robert to see visitors at that time. Mrs. Dr. Prince who recognized me one day at Catline's has shown more kind sympathy for me than any other acquaintance.

I certainly don't feel much indebted to Jacksonville people for attention or kindness since being here at this time. I am very glad to have the Marguey & blossom and wrote to Mrs. [Anson] Mills this morning acknowledging its receipt. This is Decoration Day, but I feel scarcely energy enough to go over to Elizabeths [John Grierson's wife] to see the production. . . .

Yours truly
Alice K. Grierson

[TTU]

By now Alice was seething, as the following letter makes clear. Much of her anger stemmed from the colonel's continuing refusal to join her in Jacksonville.

Jacksonville May 31st 1882

My dear Ben

Yours of the 26th is just received. You speak of receiving my long letter of the 21st, but not one word as to its contents, or one word in reply. Now my long letters to you, have cost me a great deal, and in my opinion are *everyone worth your careful reading at least three times* over. Until you can truthfully assure me that you have carefully read each letter of mine since May 7th three times, I prefer that you write to me *only every other* day, and devote the time you spend in writing to me each alternate day, to reading and carefully considering the import of my letters to you.

I had a pleasant letter from Dr. George McFarland this morning, dated the 28th, but evidently written the 29th, in which he says Robert is doing well—eating well—sleeping well, and while he was writing, Robert was walking out at the stable. The old Doctor has been away about a week, but was to be at home today. I intend going over soon to see the old Doctor, as it will be two weeks June 2nd since I have been at Oak Lawn.

I can see no good reason why you do not take the four months leave, due you since the 18th of Sept. 1881—at least part of it, you are simply losing part of your just dues and to me it seems a foolish piece of business. . . .

Yours, as ever
Alice K. Grierson

[TTU]

Finally, Alice confided to her husband that she no longer felt assured of his affection. Such a disclosure was highly unusual for her, and the colonel sought to bolster her declining spirits.

Fort Concho Texas
June 13th 1882.

My Dear darling Alice,

Your letter of the 9th with one enclosed from the 4 . . . was received this P.M., the mail coming in late. I will forward the letter to Charlie, which you have seen fit to write to him, altho in my judgment it contains some things which had better have been omitted. "I mean no unkindness" in saying this to you.

And now my dear, in some, yes, many of your views and opinions, I fully concur & have great confidence in your judgment, *generally*. But you might as well tell me that the *moon* is really made of green cheese as to say to me, my honey, that I love thee not, for if there be one single thing I know and feel absolutely certain about, it is that, I have loved you devotedly, since I was *knee high to a toad,* and have been for quite a length of time, whether there be *much or little left of me,* Your *affectionate husband. . . .* Therefore *your opinion* that "there is very little of the *affectionate husband left of me or in me*" *is all wrong* and I *emphatically declare* before God, Man & the devil that I have no confidence or belief in such opinion whatever. Altho possibly I may be slightly tottering towards my grave, I am

149

still a man of sufficiently extensive parts, to feel myself able, if I could only be near enough, to *clasp you in my strong arms, to squeeze all such nonsense out of you,* in less than *two minutes.* Yes Mrs. G—— knowing what I do, to tell me, that I love you *but little,* why—*"damn it, tis too bad."* . . .

As ever *affectionately,*
Your husband in *fact* and to all eternity
BHG

[ISHL]

Shortly thereafter Colonel Grierson informed his wife that he would arrive in Jacksonville sometime after July 1. Their relationship again became relaxed and cordial. Robert's condition also began improving slowly, and by fall he had recovered sufficiently to attend the Fuller-Maxon wedding in Jacksonville.

After the wedding Alice, Colonel Grierson, George, and Robert began preparing to return to the frontier. This time Alice's young cousin, Sarah (Sadie) Morley, would accompany them as their new governess. Their destination, however, was not Fort Concho but Fort Davis, the Tenth Cavalry's new headquarters.[46]

With this transfer another phase in Alice's life in the West came to an end. Her living conditions improved, for Davis and subsequent assignments were more desirable locations than Concho. Moreover, the frontier itself was passing away. Civilization, transported largely by the railroads, was making further inroads each year, bringing with it an array of conveniences and amenities.

Although the future held the promise of greater ease and comfort, old family problems remained unresolved. The Griersons confronted the question of how they could help their three youngest sons gain a foothold in life and simultaneously set aside enough income for retirement. Given these demands the lure of easy money could easily lead the family into dangerous ventures.

Colonel Grierson was particularly vulnerable to the temptations of speculation. Having come of age during the Free Soil movement, before the Civil War, he continued to see the West as the land of boundless opportunity even as he actively participated in the closing of the frontier. Unfortunately, his search for profits was destined to bring not security but fear, uncertainty, and the destruction of Alice's peace of mind in her declining years.

Chapter 3

THE FINAL YEARS

The Griersons had spent seven years at Fort Concho, and despite the tragedies that had befallen them there, Alice had grown fond of the place. She found the transition to a new post disruptive, although she was relieved to be reunited with fifteen-year-old Harry after an absence of almost eight months.

Whatever her reservations about a change of station, she was soon captivated by the rugged beauty of the Fort Davis region. Situated on the eastern edge of the scenic Davis Mountains, it boasted moderate summers and mild winters and offered attractive dwellings on officers' row.

Nonetheless, there was never enough room for all the officers and their families. The Maxons, entitled to only a lieutenant's quarters, were "roughing it." But at least Grace had household help even if she had little space. Her servant, inherited from Major Woodward, was Chinese, a minority that was appearing with increasing frequency on western army posts.[1]

Finally, Alice had good news to share with Charlie, on leave in the East. His brother Robert had obtained employment as the forage master shortly after the family's arrival at Fort Davis.[2]

Fort Davis Dec. 4th 1882

My dear Charlie

... We reached here safely at ½ past 3 o'clock Monday morning Nov. 27th. We were 12 hours at Kansas City, and 24 hours at El

*Fort Davis, Texas. Courtesy of the Western History Collections,
University of Oklahoma Library.*

Paso. It rained nearly all day, and was very muddy at El Paso, and
the Hotel Accommodations were poor. Mr. Schutz and Mr. Crosby
had a street car hitched up specially to take us, and two or three
gentlemen from N.Y. over into old Mexico. The street R.R. was
not quite completed.

We saw that old church, and Mr. Crosby took Sadie and me to
that new Mexican Central Depot, which is a large fine building.

Harry met us at Marfa, with the two ambulances, and wagon,
and you may be sure he was glad to see us, and we to see him.
Harry thought the road over was a long 22 miles, but it seemed
much shorter to him coming back. Moss had five fires burning, and
beds ready for us, and provisions so that we had breakfast at home
the morning of our arrival.

Papa had the new Brussells carpets made and put down before
Thanksgiving—We have front and back parlors, and use the room
next [to] the kitchen for dining room, and Sadie has a cot in it.
Papa is going to have the porch back of our bedroom enclosed for
a room for Sadie this week.

Robert commenced his duties as Forage Master Dec. 1st—he is
glad to be earning something, and I am very glad he has something
to do—so far he likes the work well enough.

Maj. Woodward took dinner with us Thanksgiving day, and
breakfast and dinner with us Friday, and then started on his sick

leave. In honor of Roberts birthday, Grace and Lt. Maxon took supper with us Saturday, and Capt. and Mrs. Keyes came in the evening and played whistle. Mrs. Keyes gave Robert quite a pretty two bottle inkstand, with penrack attached, and Sadie made him a pretty penwiper.

Lt. Maxon has rooms over the Chaplain, and a kitchen on the other side. Grace has to come out front, and go around to the kitchen, she has Maj. Woodwards Chinaman for cook, and keeps house under difficulties.

Sadie is well pleased with Texas so far. I don't like Davis as well as Concho yet, but I may like it better after awhile.

George does not wish to import another dog from Illinois— thinks it is too much bother. Jane Thomas is cooking for us, and Papa hired Lawton the 1st of Dec. We also have Moss. All are well.

Affectionately your Mother
Alice K. Grierson
[ISHL]

At Concho the quarters had been smaller and Alice had invested little in furnishings, so that packing would be easier when the inevitable move came. Perhaps it was the beauty of the surroundings that made her decide otherwise at Davis. At any rate, she began decorating their new quarters with care, incurring considerable expense. Among the acquisitions were a Chickering grand piano, a new sofa, and four upholstered chairs.[3] The Griersons enjoyed greater luxury than before as they settled into a more gracious manner of living.

Fort Davis Dec. 7th 1882

My dear Charlie

I received your letter of Dec. 1st, Tuesday evening the 5th. I am glad you were with some of the relatives for Thanksgiving dinner. We are beginning to feel more at home here, now that we have found a place where we can sit and be comfortable, and have found places for the most necessary of our things. The piano, new curtains, parlor mirror, a hogshead of crockery, and some other things came today from Toyah, but the extension table which we need more than any thing else, has not come, nor the sideboard, and the crockery can't be unpacked until the sideboard comes, as there is no place to put it.

Although it was a hard experience for Harry, and me too, for him to be here alone so long, I think it has done him good. He is much more manly than when I left home, much more thoughtful of me, and willing to do any thing he can to help, and is quite gallant to both Sadie and me. Papa and I called last evening at Dr. Gardner's, Lt. Coopers, and Capt. Smither. I have been into Col. Mills, Capt. Keyes, and Lt. Maxons, several times. . . .

There is one little thing I want you to bring from Jacksonville with you—"and *don't you forget it*"—that little black Japanese matchbox in your room up stairs. I would like very much too, to have the half dozen fancy little sauce plates that I left in the dining room closet. Matchboxes and sauce plates are articles we are quite short of. . . .

If you can find anything in your travels that particularly suits your fancy for ten dollars, you can buy it for a Christmas present for yourself, and I will give you the money.

Lawton is doing firstrate so far, and has but little time to loaf, I assure you. I let him go to school evenings.

Kind regards to Mr. Fitch and family. Sadie and Harry say the Misses Murphy are wishing for your return.

Affectionately your Mother
Alice K. Grierson

[ISHL]

Even before they had settled into their new quarters, Colonel Grierson, an inveterate land speculator with holdings in Iowa, Kansas, and San Angelo, Texas, began acquiring large tracts of land in the Fort Davis area. In the fall of 1882 he purchased six sections (3,840 acres) on which he constructed a house, barn, and other buildings. By the following summer he had acquired additional acreage along Limpia Creek, where he established the Spring Valley ranch and stocked it with shorthorn cattle and later sheep. He then turned its operation over to Robert to give his son a start in life.[4]

Colonel Grierson harbored no doubts regarding the wisdom of investing heavily in the Fort Davis area. With the projected closing of Forts Stockton and McKavett, he was certain that Fort Davis would become the dominant military installation in west Texas and one day would house a full brigade. In this case the surrounding area could not fail to prosper. Moreover, the town of Fort Davis, the seat of Presidio County, was located

*The Griersons' Spring Valley Ranch, Fort Davis, Texas. Courtesy of the
National Park Service, Fort Davis National Historic Site.*

only twenty-two miles from Marfa, a site along the Southern Pacific railroad. The best way to bolster his investments, he believed, was to obtain a
spur connecting Fort Davis with Marfa and thus with the transcontinental
line. Late in 1883 Colonel Grierson was spearheading a local drive to raise
thirty thousand dollars to build this connecting link. He was also buying
lots in the unincorporated town of Valentine, forty miles west of the post
and alongside the Southern Pacific.[5]

Overall, Colonel Grierson worried little about his growing indebtedness, for no investment seemed more secure than ranching. Recent works
such as *The Beef Bonanza*, written by another army officer, Major James
Brisbin, promised returns of 25 percent on cattle and 35 percent on sheep
on the relatively cheap land of the Great Plains and the Southwest. As if
to validate these projections, prices in Chicago stockyards reached twenty
to twenty-five dollars a head, a substantial increase over the 1880 price of
seven dollars a head.[6]

All of this investment worried Alice, for Ben had begun borrowing
from her father against her projected inheritance. Besides, the Griersons
now spent more time at their ranches than at the fort itself. At fifty-five,
Alice found ranching a strenuous activity.[7]

By the fall of 1884 Alice, who had not been back to Illinois for two
years, returned to Jacksonville to place Harry in a city school for a few
months. George was left behind because at fifteen he had little interest
in school and seemed happiest spending his time with the enlisted men.

However, her youngest son missed her sorely, especially when his father was out in the field.

> Fort Davis Texas
> Nov. 8th 1884.

Dear Mamma

I did not know what to do with my self to-day so I thought I would write to you. I think you better come back home for I am geting so lonsome that I dont know what to do. Yesterday— evvening I went over to the school-house with Henry Smither and looked at pictures for a long time. Then I came home and went in the dining-room to the fire and wormed my self, and then I got some lunch. And then I went to bed for it was after taps. ———

Lieut. Davis expects to go hunting in a bout two weeks, and he said I might go with him. Tell Harry that Lieut. Davis is going to let me have a new long tom to hunt with, for I want to kill five more antelope before Harry comes back so that it will make 10 antelope. Tell Harry that I hope he will come back when you come.

Every thing seams to be upsidedown ever since you have bin gon and it is still worse since Papa has gon.———

Robert was not hear to correct the words so I did the best I could. love to all.

> Your Son
> Geo. T. Grierson

[TTU]

Alice and Harry returned to Fort Davis in time for Christmas, the last one they would celebrate at the post. Word had reached them that the headquarters of the Tenth Cavalry would soon be moved elsewhere. Perhaps the colonel's investments were not so secure after all.[8]

Alice regretted this move. Not only had she become attached to the Fort Davis area and the beauty of its surroundings, but it meant leaving Robert behind to manage their two ranches and extensive holdings. With his family gone he would be more vulnerable to depression.

Her relations back East also concerned her. Her sister, Ellen Fuller, had recently given birth to twins, and since four of her seven children still survived, the financial strain was so great that her husband, Harvey, had recently started selling on a commission basis in the hope of augmenting his modest salary.

The situation of other relatives was more distressing. Alice's sister-in-law Julia remained in chronic poor health, making it difficult for her to care adequately for her growing family. Finally, late in February Alice received word from her father that her brother Henry was in critical condition. Two years younger than Alice, he had spent his adult life in and out of asylums, struggling to deal with recurrent and debilitating bouts of depression.[9] Once more she began making plans to return to Jacksonville.

Jacksonville February 23rd 1885

My dear daughter Alice

Yours to wife & myself of the 15th ultmt came duly to hand, and it seems that the "Powers that be" has ordained your removal from Fort Davis, and that Ben thinks that you and the boys had better return home and attend school here. A very wise conclusion I think.

As you say it is indeed sad to think of Henry's condition. I am prepared to hear of his death at any time. What a world of trials and afflictions we have to endure. Your Mother, Mary, Maria, John and last and worst of all Thomas, besides all the little ones, and of my grand children, three of yours, three of Thomas, three of Ellens & two of Rufus, all gone to their long home, and I expect soon to follow them.

The following quotation of the Holy Scripture will close my letter, "For whom the Lord loveth he chasteneth, and scourgeth every son whome he receiveth. If ye endure chastening, God dealeth with you as with sons. . . ." Read the 12th chapter of Hebrews. In deep sorrow & affliction

Your father
John Kirk

[TTU]

The move came in April. Headquarters of the Tenth was assigned to Whipple Barracks in Arizona Territory, and various companies were dispersed to Forts Apache, Verde, Thomas, and Grant. Alice, having departed for Jacksonville, was not on hand for the move. Ben's niece, Helen Fuller Davis, however, wrote "An account of a 10th Cavalry march with Gen. B. H. Grierson from Ft. Davis to Ft. Grant," describing both the difficulties and the pleasures of the trip. It is unlikely that most army wives were as enthusiastic about moving as Helen Davis professed to be.

Our regiment, the 10th Cavalry, was ordered to Arizona in 1884, much to our delight, for army people in these days were always ready for a change. We left Ft. Davis, Texas, in April, and had fine weather during the entire march—not a drop of rain. As I had not been very well, my husband and my uncle, who was in command, thought this trip with the command would be a good thing for me, and so it proved.

The twelve troops of cavalry and long train of wagons for carrying camp equipage etc. made a train—when stretched out—about two miles long; one of the three battalions taking the lead and then falling to the rear next morning. This rotation gave them an equal chance of being first and avoiding the dust. Though we passed over practically unbroken ground the dust was terrible for those in the rear. The soldiers, many of them, fastened their handkerchiefs to their hats to protect their eyes.

I was very comfortably fixed for the trip—had a big carriage or hack with satin curtains which were a great convenience, giving me privacy and protection from the sun. I had a maid and very good driver who sat out in front. Instead of horses there was a huge pair of mules to my fine coach. This my uncle had insisted on and very wisely, though I saw the ladies smiling when we started out, but the first long hill we came to changed their tune. My good strong mules went right up while the horses to the carriages could not make it and had to call on the train master for help. Then *we* did the smiling.

Though the marches were not so very long we were glad when we saw our supply camp on the S.[outhern] P.[acific] track. It was quite a train of cars the Quartermaster had sidetracked for our use —tanks of water and wood and other supplies. All the animals, 1200 horses and nearly as many mules, had to have water as well as the soldiers. The water alone for the trip cost the Government $1200. On the whole trip we never saw running water but once— that was the Rio Grand.

While I had done considerable camping out this was a very different scale and I found it all vastly interesting from first to last. Each morning just at the first peep of day reveille sounded and all must be up. Breakfast was served in our big Sibley tent, and then we hurried out so that when what they called 'the general' sounded our tent would be ready to come down. The whole tent city came down at once—like the blowing off of a dandelion puff and woe to any straggler who delayed the systematic packing up of the wagons. There was one lady who never seemed able to get her furbelows on and herself out of the tent and each morning an officer came galloping up to see what caused the delay in packing. We all wore sensible clothes for travelling but this one lady had trains which soon became a fringe of rags at the bottom. What a fine thing *knickers* would have been!

To avoid the dust my husband had my driver start out before the command and it was grand riding so early in the morning with everything fresh, yourself, the driver, and the poor old mules. 'Nothing like a good government mule' as I found out, my respect for them grew each day. At noon my husband and some of the young officers would gallop up to my carriage for a snack to eat, and a little visit. A number of times during the day the troops were halted and saddles were thrown to the ground so that the horses backs could cool. Woe to the man whose horse had a sore back! He was told to walk and his horse was led.

I had imagined we would have lots of game on the trip. We saw very little and soldiers were not allowed to break ranks and in the evenings all were too tired to hunt. The Regimental band played every evening—as guard mount was at sunset. We all enjoyed the music that rang out over the big prairies, after which we all took a walk, being very particular to notice just where in this big tent city our battalion was situated, so that we could find our place, our home. We had imagined we would play cards in the evenings, but everyone felt like turning in early—getting up so early and the long ride was certainly conducive to slumber, and to hunger too. Such appetites as we had, and soldiers certainly know how to make things taste good. What interested most of all was the system, the ease with which this big body of troops, and all the paraphernalia of camp was handled mornings and evenings, no hitch no delay, unless our lady of the trail made B troop wagons a trifle late. It was astonishing how soon after the train halted—wagons were unloaded and you could smell bacon from the various troop kitchens. My uncle had insisted on my having a fine willow rocker fastened on the back of my carriage so that I could have a comfortable place to rest while the wagons were being unpacked and the tents put up.

On reaching El Paso we found the Rio Grand too high to ford as my uncle had planned. So he telegraphed to Washington for permission to cross the bridge into their domain [Mexico], as an armed force can not enter the territory of another country without consent of the powers that be and it took a week of communicating between Washington and Mexico City before we could stretch our long train out and cross over. The day of travel in old Mexico was the hardest of the whole trip—deep sand and hills too on one of which we came so near going over a great cliff—had a land slide, and but for my strong mules it would have been the last of us.

We had a very good time while waiting in El Paso, which was then a little town. The citizens entertained us right royally, dances, dinners etc. and of course their sales to the troops made it pay them to be [hospitable] and when we finally got the desired permission I think the whole population of the town was present to see us cross the bridge.

Deming, New Mexico was our next town—then Willcox on the S.P. which was only one days march to Fort Grant, Arizona, our destination.[10]

By May, Helen Davis was writing her aunt with news of the frustration of Tenth Cavalry troopers. They were involved in General George Crook's Sierra Madre campaign, a long, exhausting, and seemingly futile effort to recapture Chiricahua and Warm Spring Apaches who had fled the San Carlos Reservation under Geronimo, Nana, and Mangus. Before the campaign was over, three thousand soldiers were involved in patrolling and guarding water holes and mountain passes along the tortuous terrain between Mexico and the territories of New Mexico and Arizona. During this time Crook used Apache scouts, a policy that was effective strategically and psychologically against the fleeing Indians but controversial among the army high command.[11]

As Alice had feared, the recent changes had left Robert depressed. With his parents and most of his Tenth Cavalry friends gone, Fort Davis seemed lonely and isolated. The work of running both ranches exhausted him and, worse yet, neither place produced a profit.

Fort Davis Texas.
Sunday, June 7 1885.

My dear Mother.

I was very glad to receive your letter of the 28 ult. I haven't called on many of the 3rd Cavalry folks yet, because I haven't had time. I work from half past six in the morning till five or six in the evening and after such a strain as that I don't feel either in condition or humor to go visiting. I began taking my meals at the Limpia Hotel on Monday 1st inst. and am very well satisfied. The distance makes no difference, as I go and come "in less time than three shakes of a lamb's tail" on my noiseless two-wheeled steed.

The incessant toil is getting monotonous, and though I intend to keep my place for the present, I intend to keep my eyes open. My work is perfect drudgery and is neither beneficial to mind nor body. I spent the forenoon at the office *today*. I wish I had the means to take a rest for a while. Mr. Sender has told me that he'd give me something to do anytime. It has been awfully hot for about ten days. It was 105 in the Q.M. Office. I never saw it so hot here before. When I start for 'the hot place you read about' I'll have to take an ulster and a whole roll of blankets. . . .

. . . Today at dinner I was taken suddenly sick at the stomach and just had time to get outside when I nearly vomited myself inside out. I have had these illnesses too often lately for my pleasure.

Affectionately Yours,
Robt. K. Grierson.

[TTU]

Ten days later Robert was still feeling low. His mother's report of a recent wedding in Jacksonville reminded him that he was not yet in a position to support a wife of his own.

Fort Davis, Texas.
Wednesday, June 17″ 85.

My dear Mother:

Your letter of the 9″ recd. several days ago & one of the 6th from Papa a short time before. I think it'd be very pleasant for you & the boys to spend the summer at Whipple. . . .

... I don't remember whether Julian Wadsworth went to the High School or not. I met him at the Grace Church Sunday School. I knew Miss Short slightly. They have my best wishes. Sometimes I feel as if I'd like to have 'a girl of my own,' if I could afford it, but at present I am barely able to support myself, with no immediate prospect of improvement. Everything is so expensive, & there is always something unexpected to pay for, so that I never get anything ahead, and I've gotten about disgusted trying to.

Col. Brackett calls me by my first name, so I presume I've made a favorable impression on him. . . .

. . . If it wasn't for having to look after the ranches, I think I could find something to do elsewhere. By this time next year I intend to have a change if possible. It is too wearing on me—I don't get rested. People remark that I don't look well, & I sometimes feel that the life of a wild Indian would be preferable to mine.

Maybe I oughtn't to growl, but when one is neither well nor contented I don't see how he can say he is otherwise. It is just like being in jail—a large jail—but jail nevertheless.

I have bought some nice matting which will improve the looks of my room—but what is a room without some bright sweet face to illuminate it? If it wasn't for Fanny with her intelligent look & happy wag of her tail I'd almost break down under the weight of my feelings.

Affectionately Yours,
Robert K. Grierson.

P.S. Since writing the above I've been down to the ranch. Everything is so fresh & green there, that it refreshed me. How I'd like to lie down in the shade of a cottonwood tree by the side of the rippling brook!

[TTU]

Robert remained dejected despite evidence of renewed interest in construction of the proposed spur between Fort Davis and Marfa. Some action was necessary for, with the removal of the Tenth Cavalry, property values were falling.[12]

Recently, he had received a letter from Henry Flipper, the first black to graduate from West Point. After serving as a lieutenant in the Tenth

Cavalry from 1878 to 1882, Flipper had been dismissed following a court-martial. Although exonerated of the charges of embezzlement of Company A funds, he had been found guilty of "conduct unbecoming an officer and a gentleman." Since no white officer would have been discharged under similar circumstances, the Griersons concluded that personal vendettas and racial prejudice were the real reasons for Flipper's dismissal.[13]

Fort Davis Texas.
Monday, June 22nd, 1885.

My dear Mother.

I recd. your letter of the 15th yesterday—also one of the same date from Papa, and Saturday one of the 14th from Papa. Both of his letters referred principally to business matters. It seems that the Fort Davis and Marfa Narrow Gauge Railway is going to take another start. I hope it may, but the longer I live the less faith I have in anything. . . .

My matting is down in my room now & I have things pretty well arranged. I wish I could afford to have some pretty engravings.

Yesterday the Senders, Caswells, Maxons, a Mrs. Fredericks & I went on a picnic to Maxon's goat ranch in Musquez Canyon. We had a roasted kid & a good time generally. I rested & slept a good deal of the time—seems to me I'd rather sleep than do anything else.

I would like to see all of you.

I had a letter from Lieut. Flipper. He desired to be kindly remembered to the Genl., Mrs. Grierson & Lt. Grierson.

Affectionately Yours.
Robert K. Grierson.

[TTU]

Three days later the Presidio County Commission received a petition from leading citizens to move the county seat from Fort Davis to Marfa. Voters approved the change in the July election, ending forever any hope of a railroad connection to the Southern Pacific. By August, land values had plummeted.[14]

Alice remained in Jacksonville throughout the spring and into the summer of 1885. At one point she wrote her husband complaining of feeling old and of one leg that ached so persistently that she had seen a doctor. In an effort to raise her spirits, Colonel Grierson responded with humor.

Whipple Barracks
12 June 1885.

My Dear Alice,

Yours of the 7th inst. has just been received and altho it is too late for this to go out in tomorrow's mail, will write you tonight & possibly add something before closing the letter, for the mail, which will be taken to Town in the evening, for the next day's mail.

I have no recollection of what I wrote you on the 31st ultimo, & trust I said nothing either unkind or disagreeable & will not believe the contents, or any part thereof made you so sick, as to make it necessary for you to go to the Doctor for Medicine and will take it for granted that you were not well or feeling well before the receipt of this *summons* or whatever it may have been. It was well however, to stir you up enough to start you out after the Medicine which I have no doubt from what you say was needed and I trust that it did you good, and made you well, for surely I have no wish to have you sick or to make you so.

The more vim & the less *limpness* you have about you at all time the better it will suit me, and I earnestly hope you will come to Whipple Barracks, well & in everyway feeling happy & well, and that you will come with the determination to enjoy yourself, *laugh & grow fat*, eat, drink & be merry, and that we will all be as "Merry & free as a *crew* can be," as your old Gipsey song, said it first so nicely. If we do not make ourselves happy & contented, it will not be likely that happiness & contentment will come to us for any other reason. Suppose you jump up and *crack your heels together,* or try to do so, *put your toe in your mouth, anything* to make you *lively* & stir you up to this understanding that you are not yet an *old woman.* . . .

. . . I want you to be a girl again—so brace yourself up—buckle on your armour & fight it out on that line for the balance of your life. . . .

As Ever.
Affectionately,
Yours,
B. H. Grierson.

[ISHL]

Alice joined her husband at Whipple Barracks, close to the mining town of Prescott.[15] Once again the scenery was spectacular, for the post was set on a mesa amid pine-forested, granite mountains "much broken by ravines." The quarters, once ramshackle, had been rebuilt, and she enjoyed for the first time indoor plumbing and the "luxury" of hot and cold running water.

Whipple Barracks July 10th, 85

My dear Charlie

I had not time in J to answer your letter of June 22nd, and as papa wrote informing you of our safe arrival here, I thought I would defer writing for a few days. Papa received your telegram declining the detail to Leavenworth, and last evening received your letter of the 6th.

Our journey here was more comfortable than I had expected, no dust and not too warm, until papa joined us, and as we had his company we did not mind it.

All the post and Dept. people have called on us, and we were at quite an elaborate dinner at Capt. Smither on the 8th in honor of Mabel's [Mrs. Smither's] and the General's [Colonel Grierson's] birthday. Capt. and Mrs. Williams, Mrs. Overby, and little Dick and Lizzie Williams were also there. Mrs. Williams made a birthday cake, which her Chinaman decorated with ornamental frosting, and the words, "Mabel Smither July 8th 1885 from Dick and Lizzie." Around the cake was a handsome wreath of flowers from Mrs. Williams plants, and the cake and flowers formed the centre piece of the table. Mrs. Smither also used her brand new decorated china, which is quite a handsome set.

Papa's "Annex" to the front parlor, and what he calls the "innex" where he had had a couple of closets torn out, one in the front, and one in the back parlor, are making a good deal of work, some of it for me as well as for the carpenters, but will be a great improvement when it is done, and things are all settled. The boys and I like this house very well, although it is frame, and has low ceilings. We are so glad to have Attic rooms again, and the bathroom with hot and cold water is a luxury. . . .

Papa has just invested in 20 chickens at 45 cts. each, our cook

Whipple Barracks, 1893. Courtesy of the Arizona Historical Society.

paid 75 cents for a dozen eggs the day of our arrival, a price we would not like to afford very often.

Kind regards to all who inquire.

Affectionately your Mother
Alice K. Grierson

[ISHL]

By contrast, Helen Davis found Fort Grant increasingly difficult. Not only was the water supply "not adequate," but given the proximity of her neighbors, she found it impossible to obtain the necessary rest in the eighth month of her third pregnancy.

The campaign against the Apaches dragged on. These Indians, expert in guerrilla warfare and capable of living off the land, moved rapidly over vast distances. The army, burdened with supplies and suffering from illness and heat exhaustion, traveled more slowly.[16]

Fort Grant, Arizona T.
Oct. 4th 1885.

Dear Aunt Alice,

Yours of Sept. 21st came in due time. We are still alone.

Will is in the field yet and likely to be for some time. . . . There are no indications of the troops being ordered in, though they do not seem to be accomplishing anything. I recd a letter from Will last night, he was then at a little R.R. Station called Benson but was to leave in the morning on a five day scout. He has been quite sick with dysentery but at last account was some better.

There had been a good deal of sickness here, owing, Dr. [William Corbusier] says to the poor water we get. The water supply at best is not adequate to the demands of the post and at present has almost entirely given out. What we use is brought from a distance and is simply horrible stuff, it tastes so badly. I boil all we use and even then feel afraid to let the children have what they want. The Quartermaster told me he saw no prospect of matters mending until the melting of the snows yet to fall. I do not see why such a large post was ever established with such a limited water supply. It is well the troops are not in, for it seems to be quite as much as the water wagons can do to supply the families and small detachments now here.

If Uncle were here, the first thing he would have to do, would be to make another reservoir or in some way remedy this shortcoming.

Lt. Ward is still on sick report though he says the doctor ought to take him off. I am *so* tired of this family, they annoy me til I feel desperate sometimes. The two girls have company every night so late, till about 1 o'clock and get up such a racket that it is impossible to sleep, it even wakes the children. I wish the whole of them would be ordered to San Carlos or some other place where they will not be a torment. . . .

Yes, I would be very afraid to ask Robert to stay here in November. Anytime after that or before I should be very glad to see him.

I had no idea Nell [Ellen Kirk Fuller] expects to be sick. I do hope it is all well over by this time. It is hard enough even when things go as well as they possibly can. At present I have no one to help me but a little girl, 12 years old. The company going out deprived me of a cook. You can imagine my hands are full with cooking & sewing & all. It is *very* hard for me to move about—even harder than either time before & hope it is not twins.

Etta & Nellie are well and both growing up so fast. There is no school here. I do not know what Mrs. Keyes will do for her youngsters.

I miss Charlie so much—it was very pleasant to have him running in. . . .

Miss Tarring is here from Davis, visiting Mrs. Bigelow, she reports a great deal of sickness at Davis, and several deaths along the officers line. They lay it to the water also. How is Robert now? He was not well some time ago. Mrs. Keyes sends best regards to all. Capt. Keyes was in for three days last week. Mr. Davis hopes to be here in Nov. but can not tell for certain.

Yours as ever,
Helen Davis.

[ISHL]

Alice found her stay at Whipple Barracks pleasant but not without its problems. Ben's assignment as commander of the post was less important than his experience and rank warranted. And once more he was passed over for promotion.[17] However, 1886 brought two more vacancies among the generals, and again Colonel Grierson assiduously sought his star.

That winter Mary Crook, General George Crook's wife, who seldom accompanied her husband to frontier posts, was residing at Whipple Barracks with her sister, Mrs. Reed.

Whipple Bk's Feb. 15th 86

My dear Charlie

Yours of the 9th came yesterday. Papa was too busy writing to congressmen and others, to write to you, he wrote 19 letters yesterday. If writing letters will prevent his being "jumped over" in the promotions to be made by Gen. Hancocks death, and Gen. Pope's retirement he intends to prevent it. If he knew the President would appoint by seniority now and hereafter, he would be satisfied to wait, as his turn would come in Apr. 1887, but there is no certainty that he will do so.

Papa thinks the Dept. Officers are less sanguine of Gen. Crook's promotion than before Gen. Hancock's death. What a severe shock his sudden death must have been to Mrs. Hancock. . . .

The Calico Masquerade that was to have been the 17th is postponed until the 24th on account of Gen. Hancock's death. Major Barber I believe suggested it.

We have had a good many calls lately from Prescott people, some who had never called before. I suppose they come to call on Mrs. Crook and her sister, and then call on the Post people also. . . .

Affectionately your Mother
Alice K. Grierson

[ISHL]

Later that month Alice, feeling the strain of her husband's unceasing efforts to gain advancement, found solace in Robert's arrival for a visit and in the round of social activities at the post. Masquerade balls remained a favorite activity among the officers and ladies of the frontier army, and their choices of costumes indicated that racism was prevalent.

Whipple B'k's Feb. 26th, 86

My dear Charlie

Papa received your letter of the 15th a few days ago. I believe he intends writing to Maj. Volkmar [Sheridan's aide-de-camp] as you suggested, but he is so busy writing to congressmen—and others in regard to promotion that I think he has not yet done so. Like you I hope Col. Merritt will not get promotion until his seniors in rank, and years have their turn, but there is no telling who will be favored. I will be glad when the appointments are made. . . .

The Calico Masquerade came off Wednesday night and was quite a pleasant party. As I had not been at an Officers hop for over a year, I went but not in disguise. Papa, Robert, Harry and George were so well disguised that very few recognized them. Papa wore the black domino that I made for him to wear to the Germania Club in St. Louis, also a black mask. Robert has a nice dark blue bicycle suit which he wore, with a Turkey red calico sash over one shoulder and around his waist. He had quite a number and variety of decorations, stars, crescents, rosettes, bows etc., a black mask, and a funny cap, which he made of a red silk handkerchief and variously ornamented.

Grace fixed up a grey skullcap and mask, with red crest and gills, and a long bill to represent a roosters head, for Harry, and he also wore a long rubber coat and a sash over one shoulder. George wore the calico suit which Mrs. Keyes made for him in Davis, for the minstrels, and one of the most hideously ugly black masks I ever saw.

Maj. Woodward was dressed as a colored woman. Mrs. Drum was also a colored woman and acted the character well. Robert waltzed with Mrs. Drum and neither had the least idea with whom they were dancing. . . . Mrs. Crook was Mother Goose with a small broom to sweep the cobwebs from the sky. A number of gentlemen wore pink dominos, Judge French for one. Lt. Hughes was a boy with short patched pants buttoned on a waist. Maj. Woodward and Mrs. Drum acted the funniest. Mrs. Crook said it was a "Swell Hop," swell dress, and swell supper. It is raining and looks dismal out of doors.

Affectionately your Mother
Alice K. Grierson

[ISHL]

By late March Robert and Harry had left Whipple Barracks to tour the Far West. There was still no news regarding who would be promoted to brigadier general. Word had arrived, however, that Geronimo, having surrendered to General Crook on March 27, had escaped from his captors two days later. With thirty-seven followers he had fled into the mountains of northern Mexico, thereby prolonging the Apache war.[18]

Whipple B'k's Mar. 31st, 86

My dear Charlie

Yours of the 21st came yesterday morning. Papa had a letter from Robert this morning written Sat P.M. at Mojave Cal. Trains had been behind time so much that they could not reach San Francisco until sometime Sunday or possibly not until Monday.

They reached the Grand Canyon soon after noon Tuesday, and remained until ½ past 3 o'clock Thursday P.M. a day longer than they had intended as they "never enjoyed such scenery before. It is grand beyond description. The river is 110 yards wide and 150 feet deep, and is full of rapids and whirlpools."

Harry had a narrow escape from a very serious accident. While climbing down a bluff in Diamond Canyon a rock gave way and he slid and fell, but fortunately lighted on his feet. Robert thinks he was a good deal worse frightened than Harry, says "He was as composed as if he habitually traveled through the air like a sky rocket." His right foot was severely sprained so that he had been quite lame with it, but keeping his foot in cool water for hours, and on returning to Peach Springs putting Arnica on it, the swelling had gone down and the soreness [had] gone out of it considerably.

It is bad enough to have a sprained foot near the beginning of a pleasure trip, but we are very thankful it is no worse, it is frightful to think what it might have been.

No appointments of Brigadiers have been made that we know of at this date. I sincerely hope Gen. Merritt will not be one of them. Papa gets a good many encouraging letters from Washington and won't give up that his chances are good until the appointments are really made. I don't enjoy suspense but am glad I am not in Washington "pulling and hauling" as the enclosed slip says the women there were. . . .

Col. Drum returned from his inspecting tour of near two months Sunday evening. Mrs. Drum has seemed very cheerful during his absence but I am glad for her that he is home.

Reports today say that Geronimo, and 20 other Indians with all their supplies escaped last night from Lt. Maus. Papa has just telegraphed to Willcox to find out if it is true.

Mrs. Reed has been quite ill since she and Mrs. Crook returned from California but sits up part of the time now. Mrs. Crook says she is so restless (herself) that she went away to pass the time but it did not go any faster in California.

George, Brooke Alexander, and Moss went hunting last Friday P.M. and Saturday morning George killed two deer at one shot, he felt quite elated.

Affectionately your Mother
Alice K. Grierson

[ISHL]

Geronimo's most recent escape prompted Sheridan to conclude that the policy of using Apache scouts was a failure. He replaced General Crook with General Nelson Miles.

Whipple B'k's Apr. 8th, 1886

My dear Charlie

Yours of the 28th March came soon after I had written you, and as Papa wrote you Sunday I have waited until now. We have had no letter from Robert or Harry since Papa wrote you, but a San Francisco paper of March 31st in which their names were registered at the Lick Hotel and Robert was spoken of in another part of the paper as one of the *leading* citizens of Fort Davis. We think it quite time to get another letter from them.

Gen. Crook telegraphed Mrs. Crook that he had been relieved

and I hear she and Mrs. Reed are packing up. Papa thinks Gen. Miles will give him some command of his regiment if nothing more. . . .

I had a letter from Helen Davis a few days ago—she had expected Lt. Davis in this week, but feared that the escape of Geronimo and other Indians, might postpone his coming indefinitely. . . .

. . . We all feel in a state of expectation as to what the next military news will be, but of course will have to wait as patiently as possible until time shows us. . . .

. . . I know of no news in the garrison.

Affectionately your Mother
Alice K. Grierson

[ISHL]

Later that spring word of the promotions finally arrived. Once more Colonel Grierson had been passed over, this time in favor of Thomas Ruger and J. H. Potter. Alice found little opportunity to console her husband, however, for soon she was in the throes of moving. Headquarters of the Tenth had been transferred to Fort Grant.

Alice was delighted to be reunited with the Davises and see for the first time Helen's most recent child. Moreover, her new home was attractive. The post was located in a mountainous region whose panoramic views extended into northern Mexico. But the water supply, rather than improving since last fall, had grown worse. That summer a prolonged drought dried up all nearby streams, leaving the parade ground and surrounding yards bare of grass. Any new source of water would have to come from the high mountain streams miles away.[19]

Fort Grant July 19th, 86

My dear Charlie

We did take lunch at Mr. Stewart's and found them pleasant people and their house very nice for this country. It made us a little later getting here, and kept Helen waiting dinner. We had breakfast with her next morning, and since have had our meals at home. We find this house quite a pleasant one to camp in. Nearly all the officers and ladies called Friday evening.

Saturday, papa, Mr. Goring and a soldier went on horseback to the mountains, to investigate the water question and did not get back until midnight. Papa thinks there is no doubt but what the

Fort Grant, 1888. Courtesy of the Arizona Historical Society.

post can be well supplied with water if they will furnish the money, mechanics &'c, and yesterday he made his report accordingly. Papa is moving Post Headquarters to your rooms in the bachelors quarters today, and will move into other rooms in the same building tomorrow, and intends having a better looking fence than this brush one.

Our horses and carriage and Mrs. Smither got in before noon Saturday in good condition, and our bedding and mess outfit and some other things came yesterday. Taylor, the recruit you told us of, waited on the table for us at Helen's and has been here waiting on us ever since and does firstrate.

Mrs. Eggleston went to Willcox Saturday to meet her husband and go with him to camp for a couple of weeks. Capt. Smither will come in for a visit as soon as possible, is Judge Advocate I believe of a Court Martial just now.

We had a little rain yesterday but need much more.

Grant of Co. B. died here of Fever, and was buried this morning.

Lt. Maxon is relieving Lt. Hunt as Quarter Master.

I hope you reached your station safely.

Affectionately your Mother
Alice K. Grierson

[ISHL]

As the Apache campaign continued throughout the summer, General Miles quietly adopted Crook's method of using Apache scouts while maintaining relentless pursuit. Finally, Geronimo and his followers, worn out by their flight, surrendered in Skeleton Canyon, sixty-five miles southeast of Fort Bowie. When Mangus and his band gave themselves up to a detachment of buffalo soldiers in the White Mountains two weeks later, the Indian threat to white settlement in the Southwest had ended.[20]

Harry and George, ages nineteen and seventeen, were becoming young men. For the first time Alice felt that it was safe to place George in a boarding school in Tempe, Arizona, although it was unlikely that the damage done his education by post schools and makeshift arrangements could ever be repaired. Harry's case was more hopeful, and she began making plans to send him to Washington University in Saint Louis despite her misgivings regarding the value or safety of higher education. With Charlie stationed at nearby Jefferson Barracks, a training school for cavalry recruits, the risk seemed more manageable.

Ft. Grant Sunday Sept. 12th, 86

My dear Charlie

Papa wrote you on the 9th and sent it by Harry, and said I would write on the same subject in a few days. I fancy you will not take the responsibility of saying Harry had better go to Jacksonville, as long as he has made up his mind that he prefers St. Louis, unless he changes his mind, which I think he is not likely to do before giving St. Louis a trial. Two letters and three catalogues came this morning from California to Papa. Had they come on Thursday possibly papa might have sent Harry to California but it seems Providence did not intend him to go there this fall.

Dr. Jones says our boys "can't stand the great Educational Mills of the country, neither do they need them, nor did their father before them." As I have great respect for Dr. Jones opinion, and as you got sick at West Point, and Robert at Ann Arbor, I naturally feel that we are running some risk in sending Harry to a University. I hope he will not go to many evening entertainments, as I think late hours would be quite as likely to break him down as studying. I hope too he will be careful to dress warmly enough.

I had a nice letter from George today written on the 9th, the third day after I left him at Tempe. He said he had not been homesick at that time, which I was glad to hear. He said there were not many pupils then, so the school had not gotten well going, but there would be more pupils this week. David Crapo, who is to be George's room mate was to be there today.

The troops out are ordered to remain out for the present, and rations were sent to them yesterday. . . .

Affectionately your Mother
Alice K. Grierson

[ISHL]

At last, after spending a year and a half marking time in terms of his career, Colonel Grierson received an assignment commensurate with his background and experience. Alice was happy for her husband, but she was not enthusiastic about moving again after spending only four months at Fort Grant. Such moves were expensive and usually necessitated the selling of furniture and belongings at a loss, since army regulations allowed officers to transport only one thousand pounds at army expense. Thus Alice found herself disposing of furniture, a carriage, horses, and a flock of chickens to avoid paying extra freight charges.[21]

Finances were of increasing concern. The colonel was expanding his cattle holdings at a time when the range was becoming overstocked and the recent prolonged summer drought had left many herds weakened. Prudent investors were selling, bringing about a decline in the stockyard price of steers from a recent high of thirty dollars down to ten dollars a head and sometimes lower.[22]

Ben's brother, John, now sixty-six, still required constant loans, and other members of the extended family requested and obtained occasional help.

Fort Grant Wednesday Nov. 10th, 1886

My dear Charlie

Yours of the 5th came last evening. Papa received a telegram last evening from Gen. Miles saying papa has been ordered to command the Dist. of New Mexico, and directing him to meet Gen. Miles in Willcox today and go with him to Santa Fe, that he was going there direct and wanted to see papa before he went East. Papa left for Willcox a half an hour ago.

As Col. Bradley is to be retired the 8th of Dec. I suppose we will be moved to Santa Fe by that time. I don't suppose I will like it there as well as I do here. This elevation suits me better than a higher one, and besides being a new and good house, this is a very pleasant one. The quarters at Santa Fe are said to be large and good, but these are *the best* we have had in the army. . . .

You had not written us that you had loaned money to Uncle John. In Uncle J's last letter to papa, he asked him to loan him if he could $150.00 to "tide him over the winter." Uncle J says Charlie Capps had let his house run down so that he has had to repair it inside and out, and has put it in a salable condition. Just now papa can't send him money. He left his pay accounts for Oct. with Maj. Woodward this morning, as the paymaster is to be here this evening, and Maj. Woodward furnished him money for his trip.

Papa has paid out so much money for cattle lately, and to run the Ft. Davis ranch, that he had to borrow $60.00 to settle accounts at the end of Oct. If that Mr. Lyon who bought Robert's Kansas land is only prompt in paying the thousand and odd dollars now due, papa will be ahead in funds again, and I have no doubt will help you out on your Texas land payment.

As you did not get my letter of Oct. 26th in time to hand the $1.68 due me to Harry, buy some book or some other little thing for a Christmas present for yourself. I don't expect to have much money to spend for Christmas this year. . . .

Affectionately your Mother
Alice K. Grierson

[ISHL]

Once she had settled in at her new location, Alice discovered that Santa Fe offered many advantages. Not only were the quarters comfortable and homelike, the environment was more stimulating than that of a frontier post. Santa Fe was the military and civil headquarters of the territory of New Mexico and a thriving commercial center as well. Established in 1610, the city was noted for its many Spanish-style adobe houses, erected around courtyards, as well as a number of attractive new buildings. It was a pleasure to stroll down the narrow, picturesque streets and along the broad plaza with its imposing Governor's Palace. Close by were the military offices.

Alice found the climate "charming," a predictable reaction given Santa Fe's location on a plateau high on the western slope of the Rocky Mountains. The population was as varied as the architecture; Mexicans and Anglos were joined on market days by Navajos, Utes, and Northern Apaches. Pueblo Indians lived nearby but tended to remain in their villages, although their leather goods and baskets were displayed throughout the city.[23]

As the holiday season approached, Alice looked forward to a visit from Robert and George and the opportunity to show them this historic old town.

Santa Fe Sun. Dec. 5th, 1886

My dear Charlie

I was just ready to write to you the other day, when papa told me he had written to you and I had better write to some of the others. I was under the impression I had an unanswered letter from you— if so I have mislaid it, the latest date I find from you is Nov 16th which I answered.

So far I like Santa Fe very well—the weather has been charming and though the house is not new, I like it and the grounds very much better than those at Grant. I enjoy the convenience of gas, and the grounds and outbuildings—stone and brick walks, neat lattice fences &'c make the place seem much more *homelike* than any we have lived in on the frontier. A market too affords a greater variety in the bill of fare—one *can* go *shopping* too, and is not obliged to send away for every article of dress one needs.

There is more government furniture in the house than I ever saw in an Army house except the one in San Antonio.

We brought a roll of carpets, a roll of bedding, our messchest and enough dishes in trunks to set up housekeeping. So to Capt. Clague's surprise we slept in our own quarters the first night, and have had our meals at home ever since. We took breakfast and dinner at Capt. Clague's the first day.

Maj. Woodward arrived yesterday morning—having had private business to attend to in El Paso. He took his meals at the Hotel yesterday, but had his breakfast with us this morning and will take his meals here until he gets his own mess going. Our Chinaman likes his kitchen and the place here better than at Grant—he has found two other Chinamen, one of them he calls his cousin.

Robert wishes it were the 20th so he could start for Santa Fe. Papa returned today passes which we did not use, and asked for passes for Robert and George instead. I wish you and Harry could be here for the holidays too. Harry expects to spend them in J.

He wrote to Helen Kirk that it was awfully lonesome in St. Louis since you left—but has hinted nothing of the kind to me. In a letter to me of Nov. 24th he said he had been at dancing school one evening, and had learned a good deal in one lesson.

George says he has not been homesick at Tempe at all.

Quite a number of citizens have called on us already, as well as Officers and ladies. . . .

. . . Helen felt very sorry to have us leave Grant. It must seem a little dull there without the Band, and only four companies. Capt. Kennedy was in command, he went into the Van Vliet house. I advised him to go into the C.O. and have all the glory he could of being in command.

Affectionately your Mother
Alice K. Grierson

The Band played in the Public Square this P.M. for the first time, there is a good Band Stand.

[ISHL]

Because of the close relationship between the military and civil government, the constant stream of visitors to one or the other, and the large number of tourists, social activity never ceased. Alice enjoyed the whirl of events, and she was even more pleased that both Robert and George would arrive in time to celebrate Christmas. Only financial strain cast a shadow over her seasonal joy.

Santa Fe Sat. Dec. 18th, 1886

My dear Charlie

Yours of the 9th came several days ago. You did not tell me whether you prefer having your letters addressed to the Hotel, to your private room, or the Recruiting Rendezvous. We are getting on very quietly—our things have not yet gotten here, though they are this side of Deming. It is getting a little monotonous washing in a 25 cent tin washbasin, when we have five good ones *somewhere*.

Robert was to leave Davis today, so suppose he is now on the way here, and we expect him Tuesday morning. I hope our things will get here before that, so I can make a bed for him without borrowing. We don't know yet what day George will leave Tempe, but we expect him by or before Christmas.

Last night the first Military hop of the season was given, and papa and I went over and stayed until after 10 o'clock. There were not as many citizens present as were expected as there were some meetings in town that kept some away. Most of the ladies were married. I saw only four unmarried ones. Miss Strong and Miss Councilman of the Post, and a Miss Alice Webbe (who reminds me of Alice Dunbar) and a Miss Irving. Old Mr. "Sol Speigelbert" [Spiegelberg] over 70 was about as lively in dancing as any of the young men.[24]

I think more people have called on us already than ever called from Prescott. The post being *in the town* makes Army people much more accessible than at Whipple Barracks.

Last Sunday was the most lively day I have seen here, an Excursion Party of 625 people being in the town. The Palace Hotel is diagonally across the street from us, hundreds of the tourists came to it, and all day long were passing on foot, in carriages and other vehicles. A Mr. Marcy and his sister of Jacksonville were of the party, on their way to California. Mr. Marcy had a letter of introduction to papa from Marion Capps, so he and his sister called here, and at papa's office. Papa also brought some other Illinois people to call [on] friends of the Marcys'.

There was another Excursion party here of perhaps 150 on Thursday, but as it was so small it did not take the town so completely.

People here seem to like the music of our Band better than that of the 13th Infty. They say, and papa too, that the music is much softer.

Mr. Will Kimball, son of Major Kimball, is in Santa Fe for a short visit, was at the hop last night and we expect him to dinner today. He has a place near Albuquerque, and is in business there.

I wish I had a nice Christmas present for you, but I haven't.

Affectionately your Mother
Alice K. Grierson

The Legislature is to meet here on the 27th in the new Capitol Building which is said to be very fine.

[ISHL]

The pleasurable round of activities continued. It included such outings as a visit to the new penitentiary and social gatherings with new-found friends, including the families of Governor Edmund Ross and Judge Thomas Catron.[25]

Santa Fe Jan. 10th 1887

My dear Charlie

Yours of the 2nd containing "Menu" of the 3rd Annual Supper of the Lexington Union Club, came several days ago. I have been too busy one way and another to answer it, and have not much time now, as Papa, Robert and I are invited to dinner at Judge Catron's at 6 o'clock and I want to make a call at the Hotel on Mr. and Mrs. Ripley who have been in Santa Fe since very early Saturday morning.

The door bell rang Sat. P.M. and when I answered it, a white haired gentleman, and a lady stood there but neither handed me a card, nor spoke—so I said "this is Mrs. Grierson" whereupon the gentleman said "I think I know Mrs. Grierson." I then looked closely at him, and saw that it was Mr. William Ripley of Chicago, and his wife. He was my Mother's second cousin. We had a very pleasant call from them, and I invited them to dinner yesterday.

Papa had an Ambulance hitched up in the afternoon, and we took them driving about the town, went to the Penitentiary, and as Mrs R. had never visited one, went all through it. Saw the dinner of the convicts put on the table, and the convicts file out of their cells with folded arms, and march to the table. They kept their arms folded until all were seated, and the signal given to commence eating. The prison is well lighted, warmed, and ventilated, so the poor wretches seem well cared for. We stopped at the "Plaza" coming home and heard the Band play for awhile. Mr. and Mrs. Ripley stayed until about 7 o'clock, then returned to the Hotel.

George left for Tempe Friday evening, and is I presume in Phoenix by this time, and will reach Tempe by 7 o'clock this evening.

He had quite "a good send off" as papa says, as 13 of the Band came with their instruments and gave him a concert in the dining room, and did not leave until after George went to the train.

We gave them (the band) a good lunch which they seemed to enjoy.

We had Mrs. Arthur Ross, Miss Eddie, and Miss Fanny Ross, Miss Councilman, Maj. Woodward and Mr. Grundsfeldt here Thursday evening. Two band men with their horns, another with a flute, and George with his guitar made music for us, and Mr. Grundsfeldt and Miss Councilman played on the piano. We also had a game of whist, a game of hearts, and a nice lunch. I have dissipated considerably for me in the last two weeks, but do not intend to keep it up to any great extent, now the holidays are over.

Affectionately your Mother
Alice K. Grierson

[ISHL]

Whatever her schedule, Alice conscientiously maintained kinship ties by keeping all family members fully informed of news. Much of it was distressing. The accident that befell Nellie Davis, for example, was only too common, given the difficulty of keeping children away from danger in the cramped living quarters assigned to junior officers.

Nonetheless, the women of the Kirk-Grierson extended family were resilient, and Helen would undoubtedly bear her sorrow as well as her older sister, Mary Fuller Kirk, had borne hers. Following her husband's suicide, Mary had resumed the study of painting and, at age forty-seven, had achieved modest success in Jacksonville as an artist.

Santa Fe Saturday March 5th 1887

My dear Charlie

Yours of Feb. 28th came this morning. Hope you may like your present Rendezvous building better than you did the first one.

Papa, Maj. Woodward and a party of other gentlemen took a couple of ambulances and a buck board Wednesday, and went out thirty miles to some gold mines in which two or three of the gentleman are interested. They also visited silver and lead mines. They returned Thursday evening and had a fine trip. Papa brought lots of *specimens* of course. Papa may start for Davis tonight or tomorrow night—will not be away more than ten days. He continues to receive from Washington encouraging news as to his prospects for promotion....

Helen Davis wrote me that her little Nellie fell into the fire about Feb. 18th, and burned both hands quite badly—one she is afraid will be a good deal scarred, it is burned so deep. Her baby too had been sick with teething—but both were better. . . .

Papa and I went to Mr. Staabs birthday party last Sunday evening, and did not get home until nearly 2 o'clock in the morning—what do you think of that for dissipation? Sunday too. Mr. Staab is a rich Jew, has two young lady daughters, and the family are in the habit each year of celebrating his birthday. They played a "Comedy in one Act," "Boston Dip," seven characters. It was very well played and was quite funny. Then there was dancing a *big supper*, and more dancing. The party did not break up until after 3 o'clock. The Mr. & Mrs. Walz whose names you saw in the paper *live in St. Louis.* The El Paso family remained in Denver for several days returning here Feb. 26th. Mrs. Walz was at Mr. Staabs party—forgetting it was Sunday she danced the first waltz then remembering it, she would not dance again until after 12 o'clock. Some of the Episcopalian Church ladies danced all through.

I enclose a notice of Capt. Lippincott's lecture on Grierson's Raid—though some one may have sent you a paper with the account. Have you heard of their jubilee in Jacksonville over the finding of coal near the R.R.?

The Art Exhibition in J—— this year was considered the best one they have ever had. Aunt Mary said she had no portrait to exhibit, only studies of two or three heads.

She is not very well satisfied with her work at the studio this winter, does not like Prof. Pattison so well as Prof. Van Lear.

Maj. Woodward has lately sold three lots in El Paso for $2,500. I believe papa said he makes two lots clear.

Affectionately your Mother
Alice K. Grierson

[ISHL]

Among the Griersons there was always a great deal of moving. George had never been enamored of schooling, and it surprised no one when he suggested dropping out entirely to join Robert at Fort Davis. Alice's consent left George ecstatic. He loved the outdoors and welcomed the opportunity to work at the ranch and the chance to hunt and fish during his leisure hours. By late March of 1887 he was on his way to begin a new life under Robert's supervision.[26]

Other members of the Grierson-Kirk extended family were also in transit. As Alice's letter to Charlie makes clear, Ellen Fuller and her family had fallen on hard times. The twins Ellen had borne in 1883 had died in infancy, and less than two years later she had given birth to a second set of twins.[27] These events were traumatic, and to make matters worse, Harvey Fuller, Jr., had been sued. Without notice, the family had fled Chicago to live in Saint Paul, Minnesota.

Santa Fe Monday March 28th 1887

My dear Charlie

I received the surprising news on Saturday from my father, that H. B. Fuller and family had moved to Saint Paul Min., that their house on Idaho St., Chicago, is vacant and for rent. This morning I received a letter from Rufus Kirk to my father saying that the first he knew of Ellen going to St. Paul was Saturday the 19th. Eugene [Rufus's son] came in the city to spend the day with Albert Fuller [Ellen's son] and found the house empty and for rent.

Rufus says an English Firm sued Harvey in the U.S. Court for $10,000.00 for cloth, and about the 10th got judgment against him for *Seventy nine hundred and thirty five* dollars. Ellen had gone on Harvey's bond before he could get the cloth, so I fear the homestead will be swept away and leave a debt hanging over them. My father sent Rufus' letter without a word of comment. Rufus says all his information is from the papers. Harry Kirk [Mary Fuller Kirk's son] wrote his mother of the fact of the move to St. Paul—said Ellen and the children left on the 16th. This letter was the first intimation my father or I had received of the move.

My last letter from Ellen was dated Feb. 16th and I have been wondering why I did not hear. She never mentioned to me that Harvey had been sued, but my father did, but I did not know the amount for which he was sued. Harvey seems to inherit his father's bad management, as 99 out of hundred men do, at least it is said that 99 merchants out of a hundred fail in business. I don't know whether as large a proportion fail in other occupations or not. Ellen has certainly worked hard but has had a comfortable home of her own—it will seem hard if she loses it. . . .

Affectionately your Mother
Alice K. G.

[ISHL]

Alice continued to worry about her husband's growing indebtedness. None of the men in her family could resist adding to their landholdings. Nor did she find it easy to live with the constant uncertainty of who the next general would be. Although she was content to remain a colonel's wife, she knew her husband had his heart set on promotion.

Santa Fe Thursday April 7th 1887

My dear Charlie

Yours of the 1st came Tuesday Morning, but as I had written you the day before I waited a few days before answering.

I enclose a letter which I received from my father this morning and which please return in your next.

Robert has closed a purchase of Mr. Cook's ranch adjoining his, and 160 cattle. Papa came very near buying it a month ago while in Davis, but "there's luck in leisure," [Robert] has only agreed to pay three thousand nine hundred and fifty dollars—five hundred and fifty down. Papa *offered* Mr. Cook *four thousand*—one thousand down when there, but Mr. Cook then thought he would not take less than $4,500.00. Papa yesterday sent checks for $550.00 the first payment and his notes at three, six, nine and twelve months for the balance.

As the cattle are to be mostly for you and George, I hope you will if possible save a little towards these payments, as *I can't see* where the money is coming from to meet them. Of course if Uncle John, Mr. Legard, Lt. Davis, and Mr. Lightner could pay papa what they owe, and he could sell some land, the matter would be easy enough. I look on papa's salary however as the *only sure* income, which as you know is but $4,500.00, and if he is promoted our expenses will be increased.

I practice economy more than any one of the family though I don't think Harry or George at all extravagant. I don't spend 25 cents without *considering* whether I can afford it and as to *five dollars* it is a matter for *many* thoughts. I have *felt poor* ever since papa has been buying so much land in Texas. . . .

I send you a roster of troops in Dist. N.M. Papa has been too busy to think of sending one. Secretary [of War William C.] Endicott wrote papa a very friendly letter, says he will take pleasure in presenting his papers and commendatory letters to the President. He *need* not have said anything, so we think he favors papa's promotion. . . .

Affectionately your Mother

Alice K. Grierson

[ISHL]

Colonel Grierson was again passed over, and this time in an especially painful way. The new general, Wesley Merritt, was not only one of Sheridan's favorites but fourteen years Grierson's junior. Alice assumed, as did Charlie, that Merritt's West Point background had been an advantage in gaining promotion.[28]

Santa Fe Monday April 25th 1887

My dear Charlie

I received the Lexington paper you sent me, containing the notice of your order to Atlanta and hoping it might be revoked. Am glad the people would like to have you stay.

So you will accept the position of Reg. Quarter Master with pleasure! If you really want it I hope the Secretary of War will approve your appointment.

As Gen. Merritt got the promotion instead of papa, I suppose you think *you will take* all you can get from this [time] on. I am glad you will get more pay if your appointment is approved. . . .

Robert says Col. Merritt's promotion, "is one of the most infernal outrages ever perpetrated by the Executive of a Civilized Government."

He expresses his opinion strongly doesn't he? If I considered nothing but my own feelings I would be willing to remain a colonel's wife, here in Santa Fe until papa is retired. Of course I think it is injustice to put so *young* a *Col.* over his seniors—but while the law gives the President the power we *have to* submit.

What is the influence all powerful in the Army and Navy of which you spoke? West Point and Annapolis?

After I had sealed my last letter to you, I found one under a pile of magazines which I had written to you some time previous, but had forgotten to send to the P.O.

A few weeks ago I addressed a letter to Grace to *Ft. Davis Texas* —and since I addressed one to Helen to Fort Grant Texas. I am getting old and forgetful and I address so many letters and papers to Texas, it is not very much wonder I address some there that I mean for other places. Grace's letter was delayed quite a while—but Helen's went direct in spite of the address.

If you leave for Atlanta Saturday—this is probably the last letter I will send to Lexington. . . .

Affectionately your Mother

Alice K. Grierson

[ISHL]

Numerous small but not very profitable mines abounded in the Santa Fe area.[29] Ben's niece Louisa (Wese) Fuller had been visiting the Griersons and was now on her way to see her sister, Helen Davis, at Fort Grant. Wese's other sister, Grace Maxon, was en route to join her husband. Lieutenant Maxon had contracted lung disease while on leave in Milwaukee, where he had gone to attend his dying father.

Santa Fe Monday May 2nd 1887

My dear Charlie

Papa received a letter from you this morning but I forget the date. Cousin Wese left for Grant last evening, she enjoyed her visit here very much, and papa and I did also.

We had a fine trip to the mines last week. We left here Tuesday morning and returned Friday afternoon. Papa, Wese and I had one ambulance, and Major and Mrs. Maynadier another, also a baggage wagon and three white soldiers besides the drivers. We camped the first night near the "Cash Entry" silver mine, 18 or 20 [miles] South West of Santa Fe.

This mine is owned by seven gentlemen one of whom is a Millionaire. There is a shaft 400 feet deep—ladders all the way down, also a metal bucket as large as a barrel, attached to a steel rope which is lowered and raised by steam. A steam pump is kept going most of the time, to pump the water out of the mine. None of our party went down the shaft. Wese would have liked to go down if papa had cared to go but he had once been down a shaft six hundred feet deep and did not care to repeat the experience. This firm has spent $180,000, in and on the mine in the last three or four years. There is a large pile of ore "on the dump," said to be worth many thousands of dollars, but that is as near as they have come to getting their money back.

There are two turquoise mines very near the silver mine, and another three or four miles off, which papa, Wese and Mrs. Maynadier visited. I only went to the one nearest camp. We saw scores —I don't know but hundreds of "gold diggins"—and saw gold washed in a stamp mill at San Pedro, and some washed in a pan at Dolores, our last camp. The most wonderful mine of all was the San Pedro Copper mine, high up on a mountain. It has not been worked for six years or more as it is in litigation—but it has miles of tunnels, passages, chambers &c, where it would be very easy to get lost without a guide.

The mountain scenery was fine, and the sunsets in camp lovely. Wese would not have missed the trip for hundreds of dollars. We had the finest weather there was in April, we could not have asked for better. We took a Mr. Crupon with us from the Cash Entry mine, and a Mr. Denton from the little town of Cerillos. We women had a Sibley tent, the first time I ever used one. The four men slept in a wall tent one night, but they said Major Maynadier snored so loud, they had an A tent put up for him the last night.

Wese had never camped out before, and hopes to have more of it while at Grant. Helen is hoping to get a chance to camp out when Wese gets there, says she needs a change very much—is about as thin as she can be and *go*.

Grace wrote her father that Lt. Maxon is improving rapidly, that he commenced getting better as soon as he heard she and the children were on the way from Grant.

Robert and George were well the last news. Harry was having stomachache from eating too many bananas on the 25th so that he was not in school that day. It is quite cold here for May.

Affectionately your Mother
Alice K. Grierson

[ISHL]

Both Colonel Grierson's investments and indebtedness continued to expand.

Santa Fe Friday May 27th 1887

My dear Charlie

The paper you sent me containing a picture of the Kimball Hotel with your rooms marked came several days ago. Your letters to papa of the 19th and 21st and "The Mountain campaigns in Georgia" and the "Constitution" of May 21st to me are also received, and I am much obliged. I think it is just as well it was "impossible" for you to send any money to papa, and am very glad you advised him to sell "some if not the most" of the Texas land, and not to make "any more investments however good they may appear, until you have a good deal less to look out for."

Papa *begins* to realize that *it is necessary* to sell *something* and has written to Dr. Smith in regard to the San Angelo lots, also in regards to the 160 acres in Iowa to someone who once made him an offer. He is going to try and sell lots in an addition to The Town of Ft. Davis, and as it is now really the county seat of Jeff Davis County, and the county officers are elected—he *may* find sale for some, though *where* the Courthouse will be located is not yet known. I hear old Mr. Murphy has finished his two story house, and will try and sell it to the county for a Courthouse.

I was foolish to have said anything about sending you a birthday present. I have decided not to borrow more money of Grandpa at present. I think I told you I asked Grandpa to loan papa $1,000.00 to buy the Ash place which he did. I did not dream however that papa would buy the Cook place and cattle, and $600.00 of fencing wire. The wire & Ash place are paid for, and the first two payments on the Cook ranch and cattle. The third payment comes Oct. 10th and is one thousand dollars. It is to be hoped papa can get money of Mr. Legard before that, and at least interest from Lieut. Davis —also sell *something*.

Papa made a mistake in counting *too certainly* on his promotion, and incurred some expenses that he would not, could he have *known* Gen. Merritt was to be appointed. I do not think you are extravagant, and if you come out even—or nearly so from your recruiting detail, I think you will do remarkably well and I hope sincerely you will not be much behind.

With Aunt Louisa, and the Jacksonville Homestead on his hands,

I *can't see how papa is to go on carrying* Uncle John. He owes him now twelve hundred dollars I think, besides the $150.00 to you. He has no income (Uncle J) and not a brilliant prospect (in my opinion) of selling either his Rico [Colorado] or J—— property.

Papa has heretofore been pretty good in getting out of tight places, and I feel more hopeful *now* than I have since the Cook purchase was made.

I had pleasant letters from Aunt Mary Kirk and my sister Ellen this morning. . . .

Affectionately your Mother
Alice K. G.

[ISHL]

The post–Civil War army frustrated many excellent soldiers. Until 1890, when Congress passed reform legislation, promotion depended not only upon the creation of a vacancy through death or retirement, but also upon favoritism and political influence. For men and their families who had given their lives to the military, it could only be described as a blatantly unjust system.[30]

Santa Fe Thursday June 16th 1887

My dear Charlie

. . . Congressman Springer spent three days in Santa Fe this week—he took dinner with us Tuesday. Maj. Clague and Maj. Woodward were the only other guests. He seems very agreeable socially. Mr. Springer says it was the Washington, New York and West Point, *social influence* which promoted Gen. Merritt—and that we can scarcely estimate the power of *women* and *social influence* in Washington.

I am glad we had the visit from him—and if he is as familiar with the President as I should judge from his talk, I hope he will be able to do something for papa, Maj. Woodward and other officers who attend to their duties *on the frontier*. Mr. Springer says papa's recommendations were stronger than any one's, and that his friends stood firmly by him—but their power was not so great as the social power that was brought to bear for Gen. Merritt. He also says he never "saw so great a struggle for *any position* in his life. . . ."

Helen Davis has had quite a sick turn but was apparently all right June 10th. Wese calls Col. [Anson] Mills the "Constricting

Officer," says it seems as if he does every thing he can to hamper Lt. Davis and family. They have asked for an Ambulance three times since Wese has been there, were promised it the third time, and were ready, sitting on the porch waiting for it to drive up, but were told the C.O. wants *his* ambulance *himself.* They managed to go in a spring wagon which Lt. Davis has the use of. I think it belongs to Dr. Servis. They think they will not ask for one very soon again.

Affectionately your Mother
Alice K. Grierson

[ISHL]

Anson Mills, who had spent some time at West Point, looked down on Grierson as a "big-hearted man ... with no experience in the regular army," incapable of applying the "required discipline" and prone to displaying favoritism.[31] Thus tension was inevitable between the Davises and Colonel Mills. Whatever Helen Davis's frustrations, however, they were mild compared to the hardships endured by Alice's sister, Ellen. Because of the Fullers' rapidly declining fortunes, Ellen sought to assist her husband by contributing something to the family income. Since she had been a schoolteacher before her marriage, she decided to return to the classroom if she could obtain a position.

Ellen, like her older sister, tended to rely on philosophy and religion in times of trouble. At the same time, she reminded herself that others had their problems and also required comforting. This included Alice, whose leg had grown progressively more painful and disabled, and Ellen's father-in-law, Harvey B. Fuller, Sr., who had recently been paralyzed.

St. Paul, Sep. 4, 1887

Dear Sister Alice:

Yours written last Sunday came Friday morning—which was one day longer than it usually takes to come. . . .

To be helpless and to seem to be useless is indeed a condition hard to contemplate or bear. But I read in Emerson's essay on Success, "Self trust is the first secret of success, the belief that, if you are here, the authorities of the Universe put you here and for cause—," and if we find ourselves here, and kept here, helpless and seemingly useless "The Lord's prisoner"—we may presume it is "for cause," whether we or others can see the *why.* I don't doubt Ma was kept here—"for cause"—in all the sadness of her condition, and I hope *we* at least may have learned a deeper sympathy for helplessness than to merely say 'how sad' or 'how pitiable' or "what a happy release death would be." "He also serves who stands and waits," and he who "stands and waits" in patience and humility and loving kindness surely is helping through character as much as one who simply does work.

I am sorry the rheumatic or nervous symptoms in your case were no better. . . .

The schools open tomorrow and we will have Roger go. Maybe after a while if I do not get anything to do Gertrude will start also. I have not anticipated anything in the way of teaching at the beginning of the school year but I see several of the new schools and additions are expected to be ready by the 1st of Jan. when there may be more chance than I could suppose,—from what the Supt. told me,—would be likely the first of Sep.

For many reasons teaching would seem the most admirable thing to undertake, and I would be satisfied to wait two or three month's for the chance there might be then. . . .

With love as ever
Ellen K. Fuller

[TTU]

Unfortunately, Ellen soon discovered that the Saint Paul School Board preferred unmarried women in the classroom. So instead of teaching, she was obliged to open her home to boarders and take in sewing to augment the family income. Meanwhile, Alice's leg had become much worse. A large growth appeared above her knee, and a physician she consulted in Santa Fe advised amputation.[32]

St. Paul Oct. 18, 1887

Dear Sister Alice

Yours of the 14th came this morning. We think it is *very shocking* —that which Dr. Strong said to you about your leg—both that such may be the fact, and his manner of announcing it. It distresses me that your case should be principally in the care of such a physician as Dr. Strong seems to be. It is a perfect shame that you should have suffered from such a swollen leg so long, and till it was nearly bursting, when so simple an appliance as you tell of, should give relief so soon. Does Dr. Strong leave you sitting with your leg up now, expecting gravity to effect everything? or has he collected wits enough to doctor you for the *cause* of the swelling. Does he consider it dropsical or has he any cause to assign?

I think his statement should make you all feel—himself as well— that you should have the very best opinion and treatment possible and *immediately*. A leg is not so easily replaced that one can afford to let it be "cut off" without every effort to save it. Even then what ever the disease may be which has attacked you in this way, may seize upon the other leg, and then there will not be *many left*. I wish it were so I could help you in some way. But this I think you *must see to,* that you have a better physician and that you all realize how very serious your condition must be to warrant such a remark. . . .

. . . I feel as if you had "put your foot" into the matter so little that I have not at all realized how dreadful your condition may be, and it has oppressed me ever since I received your letter and I do hope you will not allow your leg to become so swelled again without calling in competent assistance.

With love As Ever
E. K. F.

[TTU]

Alice delayed taking any further action until the following June, when the pain became excruciating. Then she and Ben traveled to Jacksonville, where she conferred with her longtime friend and physician, Dr. Horace Jones. Baffled by the case, he sought a second opinion, and again amputation was advised.

Jacksonville June 10th 1888. Sunday

My dear Charlie

I have not been well enough to answer your letter without date nor note of the 28th saying George had gotten off all right. . . .

I am not as well as when I left Santa Fe and have not been at any time. I am not as strong, have not as good an appetite, have had dreadful pain and soreness from my hip to my toes especially from above the knee down. The leg has gotten to feel so very heavy and being so sore is hard to move without hurting it or me. I have written one letter and a postal to my sister Ellen, and a letter to Robert since my arrival which is all and I owed each of them two letters.

Grandpa came in the morning of our arrival and asked if there was any thing he could do for me as he was going down town in his buggy. I asked him to go to Dr. Jones and tell him I would like him to come and see me as soon as convenient. Papa in his gushing headlong manner, put my case entirely in his hands, to my great satisfaction in this instance. Dr. Jones brought Dr. Prince to see me Tuesday P.M. After looking at my leg and talking two or three minutes he said a wooden leg would be better than that one and later told Dr. Jones that if I were in his hands he would cut off my leg the next morning—the third morning after our arrival, when I had not commenced getting rested from the journey in which case *I think* I would have had a good chance of being buried within a week of leaving Santa Fe. Dr. Jones says my tumor is not necessarily malignant or cancerous, but is on the borderline between the malignant and non malignant and *may* become malignant. He is going to do all that is in his power to try and save my leg.

I have seen all the relatives except Uncle Harvey and Charlie and Marion Capps, and Charlie and Marion I saw passing in a buggy. Marion is in miserable health. Mrs. Smalley from Michigan is visiting her and Marion intends going home with her. Mrs. Newhall sent me a couple of New Mexicans. One had a description of the doings Decoration day.

I have to write on a book sitting in the rolling chair, and it makes me very tired. My regards to any who take the trouble to inquire.

Aff your Mother

Alice K. Grierson

[TTU]

Her leg was not amputated. By July Alice's condition had deteriorated to the point where she could neither sit up nor carry on a conversation. Soon thereafter Dr. Jones sent Colonel Grierson in Santa Fe a cryptic telegraph instructing him to "Finish your business." On August 10 Ben arrived in Jacksonville. Although she was failing rapidly, Alice recognized his footsteps on the walk and was comforted by his appearance. When she received a letter from Charlie proposing a visit, however, she asked her cousin, Sadie Morley, to write to him requesting that he stay away.

Jacksonville, Illinois
August 13, 88

Dear Charlie,

Your mother asked me to write you this morning and say she would like so much to see and speak to you each day, but the odor from her limb is so offensive that she imagines she is disgusting and says she prefers you do not come to see her. Her mind is much better the past few days and she does not suffer the pain she did but is very weak indeed. Your father found her better than he expected and I was glad to hear him say so for I feared he would blame some one for her being no better.

Uncle John Kirk found a nurse one day last week. She was to have been here this morning, but Saturday your mother said she would not have her in the house, and asked me not to leave her again and I promised not to. I had five days and nights of rest week before last which helped me out and if this cool weather continues and she is no harder to take care of than at present, I can get along with the help of the girl in the kitchen—and knowing that you appreciate what I do is a comfort and strengthens me to go on doing.

Hastily
Sarah

[TTU]

Three days later Alice died. On the following day she was buried in the family plot in Jacksonville's East Cemetery. Colonel Grierson remained at the Old Homestead for two months, recovering from his grief and putting his affairs in order before resuming military duties in Santa Fe. Shortly after his return to the post, he was ordered to Los Angeles to assume command of the Department of Arizona, a welcome promotion. In his spare time he resumed work on a genealogical history of his family as well as an autobiography, which was based not only on his memories of childhood and youth, but on the extensive correspondence between himself and Alice over a period of thirty-five years.[33]

While Ben became more introspective, reflecting on his family's past and his marriage to Alice, his sons and relatives faced the future without her. Her death was more than a personal loss to her husband and surviving sons; it was a shattering blow to the cohesion of the Grierson and Kirk families. It had been Alice who, through her strength of character, her concern for others, and her ready willingness to provide assistance, had held the extended families together. Without her there was a void that would never be filled.

Robert felt the emptiness when he wrote his brother Charlie shortly after Alice's death: "The last time I saw my mother was when she and Papa bid me goodby at the depot in Sante Fe on the night of Feb. 1, 87. She was perfectly well then & looked as if she would live for many years. That goodby, though the last will always be a happy remembrance. . . . May God help us bear our grief." [34]

Charlie at first seemed to cope well. Having achieved the rank of first lieutenant, he married, fathered three children, and enjoyed a successful army career as he rose to the rank of lieutenant colonel. But in 1915, while stationed at Fort Huachuca, Arizona, he succumbed to mental illness once more and spent the rest of his life in institutions. He died in St. Elizabeth's Hospital in Washington, D.C., in 1928. Before his death he wrote his wife a number of letters in which he painfully recalled the last years of his mother's life, thereby indicating that he had never really come to terms with his bereavement.[35]

Robert's fate was even more tragic. He never recovered from his mother's death, nor was he able to adjust to the loneliness and hardships of cattle ranching at Fort Davis. In 1890, while he was serving as a county commissioner, the treasurer absconded with public funds. When Robert and the other commissioners were ordered to reimburse Davis County, he became extremely agitated. Soon afterward he was placed in Oak Lawn Retreat in Jacksonville. Failing to improve, he was transferred to the state mental hospital, where he remained until his death in 1922.

Harry, having performed poorly at Washington University, had returned to the Spring Valley ranch at Fort Davis prior to his mother's death. After Robert was hospitalized, he and George maintained the ranch together. But since their father's heavily mortgaged real-estate investments did not increase in value and their expenses for maintenance remained high, they found it hard to make a comfortable living.[36] As the years passed, they became more and more estranged from their father, especially after he married a Jacksonville widow, Lillian King, in 1897. When Ben Grierson suffered a stroke in 1911, neither Harry nor George visited him during his illness and only Charlie attended the funeral. Harry died in 1934, but George, known as an eccentric by the townspeople of Fort Davis, survived until 1950.

All of this lay in the future when Ben Grierson received his promotion to brigadier general in 1890, following the death of General George Crook. After all the years of striving, all the letters requesting support from congressmen and others in high places, the attainment of this goal was anticlimactic. He reached the mandatory retirement age three months later. Nonetheless, achieving the rank of brigadier general was a fitting end to a career that had been productive—not as measured by killing Indians but in terms of exploring, mapping, and building on the western frontier.[37]

This career was based upon the efforts of two people, but only one received public acknowledgment. As the commanding officer of western posts, Ben depended heavily upon Alice's managerial skills, her knowledge of military protocol, her sensitivity to the needs and feelings of others, and most of all, her unflagging commitment to him and their children. Under the most trying circumstances, she consistently sought to balance the often-conflicting needs of husband and children of varying ages. Her task was made more difficult because of the public scrutiny she was subjected to as the colonel's wife.

At the same time, many of Alice's contributions were made within the home, away from the public eye. Her upbringing in a family with a keen sense of social responsibility was the basis of her strong support for her husband's liberal attitude toward blacks and Indians. This encouragement was a factor in his continuing role as one of the humanitarian generals in the United States Army and a vital element in his numerous accomplishments as peacemaker and builder.

The nature of Alice's efforts underscores the fact that as a nineteenth-century woman her roles were circumscribed. Alice Grierson saw herself as society saw her: primarily as mother, wife, daughter, and sister. She exemplified, to the best of her ability, the socially prescribed virtues of piety, purity, and domesticity. She tried to develop submissiveness, the other important virtue for women, as well. She followed her husband wherever his military career took them, and she worked unstintingly for his advancement. She even borrowed against her future inheritance in order to help him make investments that she considered ill-advised and overreaching. Nonetheless, when it came to speaking her own mind she deferred to no one.

In her correspondence Alice stated her opinions, whatever the cost. She never attempted to evade facts, however painful, and she seldom equivocated. At times her bluntness must have seemed harsh, but the recipient knew that the woman who wrote was unflinchingly honest. The direct way in which she voiced her sentiments gave her personality a distinctive forcefulness that would be extraordinary even today.

With her husband Alice Grierson faced the hardships, frustrations, and uncertainties that were the common lot of frontier soldiers and their families in the post–Civil War army. In a very real way she too contributed to the opening of the trans-Mississippi West to white settlement. Expecting neither gratitude nor public praise, she performed her assignment with courage, fortitude, and above all, a minimum of complaint, a splendid example of the strong characters found among nineteenth-century women despite the limitations under which they lived and worked.

Appendix

BIOGRAPHICAL
SKETCHES

Unless otherwise noted, the following information is drawn from Francis B. Heitman, *Historical Register and Dictionary of the United States Army from Its Organization, September 19, 1789, to March 2, 1903* (2 vols., Washington, D.C.: Government Printing Office, 1899). Volume and page numbers refer to the exact citation.

ALVORD, HENRY ELIJAH, from Massachusetts. After serving in the Civil War, Alvord joined the Tenth Cavalry as a first lieutenant and was Colonel Grierson's adjutant for one year. He was promoted to captain in 1867 and was unassigned until reassigned to the Ninth Cavalry in 1871. Less than a year later he resigned from the army. (1:161)

ANDREWS, GEORGE LIPPITT, from Rhode Island. A volunteer officer in the Civil War, Andrews attained the rank of lieutenant colonel. Assigned to the Twenty-Fifth Infantry in 1870, he became its commanding officer in 1871. He saw long service in Texas and at one time had his headquarters at Fort Davis.

ARMES, GEORGE A., from Virginia. During the Civil War Armes rose through the ranks and achieved grade of brevet major of volunteers. He joined the Tenth Cavalry as a captain in 1866 but was honorably discharged in 1870. He returned to the Tenth in 1878 and retired in 1883. One of the most controversial officers in the Tenth, Armes chronicled his career in *Ups and Downs of an Army Officer* (Washington, D.C., 1900).

ATWOOD, EDWIN BYRON, from Ohio. A veteran of the Civil War,

Atwood served with the Sixth Infantry for thirty years, from 1870 until his retirement in 1900. (1:174–75)

BADGER, NORMAN, from Massachusetts. Badger began his career as a hospital chaplain for volunteers in 1864. He was honorably mustered out of the army in 1865 but was made chaplain of the Louisville, Kentucky, post that same year. In 1867 he became a post chaplain and served in that position until his death at Fort Concho in 1876. (1:180)

BARBER, MERRITT, from Vermont. Barber entered the army during the Civil War as a private and achieved the rank of captain by 1864. Mustered out in 1865, he reentered the army as a second lieutenant in the Sixteenth Infantry and advanced quickly to first lieutenant. In 1866 he transferred to the Thirty-Fourth Infantry, where he served as regimental adjutant from 1868 to 1869, then to the Sixteenth Infantry, where he served as regimental adjutant until 1872. He was promoted to captain in 1879 and major acting adjutant general three years later. In 1890 he became a lieutenant colonel and in 1896 achieved the rank of colonel. In 1901 he advanced to brigadier general of volunteers and retired. (1:190)

BATES, ALFRED ELLIOTT, from Michigan. West Point, class of 1861. Bates entered the Second Cavalry as a second lieutenant in 1865 and in four months was promoted to first lieutenant. A year later he became regimental quartermaster and in 1867 regimental adjutant. In 1875 he became major paymaster, advancing to colonel acting paymaster in 1899 and shortly thereafter brigadier general paymaster general. (1:198)

BECK, WILLIAM HENRY, from Pennsylvania and Illinois. Although at times an embarrassment to the Griersons because of his alcoholism, Beck was a long-time associate of Colonel Grierson, and his wife, Rachel, was a friend of Alice. Beck enlisted in an Illinois infantry regiment shortly after the outbreak of the Civil War but transferred to the Sixth Illinois Cavalry. After serving as quartermaster sergeant for a year, he was promoted to first lieutenant. He resigned from the service in 1863 for reasons that are unclear. He applied for and received appointment to the Tenth Cavalry in June 1867 as a second lieutenant and won promotion to first lieutenant six months later. From 1867 to 1874 he served as regimental quartermaster of the Tenth. In 1887 he was promoted to captain and in 1903 retired as lieutenant colonel, Third Cavalry. (1:204)

BEDAL, SYLVESTER SHERWOOD, from Minnesota. Bedal served as assistant surgeon for the army from 1874 until his dismissal in 1877. (1:205)

BIG TREE, Kiowa warrior. Arrested along with Satanta and Satank for his part in the Warren Wagon Train massacre near Jacksboro, Texas, in May 1871, Big Tree was sentenced to life in prison. He was released in 1873 and caused no further difficulties. (See Leckie, *Buffalo Soldiers*, 59, 61–63, 67, 70, 74, 76–77, 135 n)

BRACKETT, ALBERT GALLATIN, from New York. Brackett entered the army as a second lieutenant in the Fourth Indiana Infantry in 1847. At the conclusion of the Mexican War he was honorably mustered out but in 1855 reentered as a captain in the Second Cavalry. He served in the Fifth Cavalry and the Ninth Illinois Cavalry during the Civil War. In June 1868 he became lieutenant colonel of the Second Cavalry and eleven years later colonel of the Third Cavalry. He retired in 1891 and died five years later. (1:327)

BRYANT, MONTGOMERY, from Kansas and Missouri. Bryant rose in the ranks of the regular army from lieutenant in the Sixth Infantry in 1857 to captain at the end of the Civil War. He won the brevet rank of major for his service during the battle of Fredericksburg. In 1874 he transferred to the Fourteenth Infantry and later served in the Eighth and Thirteenth infantries, becoming colonel of the latter in 1888. He retired from the army in 1894. (1:254)

BUELL, GEORGE P., from Indiana. Buell entered the Civil War as a lieutenant colonel of the Fifty-Eighth Infantry in 1861 and advanced quickly to colonel. He was breveted brigadier general of volunteers in 1865 for "able management of pontoon trains." In 1866 he accepted the position of lieutenant colonel of the Twenty-Ninth Infantry and three years later transferred to the Eleventh Infantry. He became colonel of the Fifteenth Infantry in 1879 and died in that position four years later. (1:260)

BUELL, JAMES W., from New York. Dr. Buell began his military career as a private in the Second Battalion of the Seventeenth Infantry in 1862 and in 1864 transferred to the U.S. Navy, where he served as an assistant engineer until the end of the Civil War. In 1872 he reentered the navy as an assistant surgeon, but four years later he resigned and shortly thereafter entered the army with the same rank. Despite his health problems following sunstroke while at Fort Concho in 1877, he remained in the army until his retirement in 1891. He died six years later. (1:260)

BYRNE, EDWARD, from Ireland. Byrne served as an officer during the Civil War, rising to lieutenant colonel, Eighteenth New York Cavalry. After the war he joined the reorganized army as a captain in the Tenth Cavalry in 1866. Five years later he was honorably mustered out. (1:271)

CARLTON, CALEB H., from Ohio. West Point, class of 1854. Carlton entered the Seventh Infantry as a second lieutenant in 1859 and transferred to the Fourth Infantry, where he rose to the rank of captain during the Civil War. He was assigned to the Tenth Cavalry in late 1870 and became major in the Third Cavalry six years later. By 1889 he had attained the rank of lieutenant colonel in the Seventh Cavalry and three years later rose to colonel of the Eighth Cavalry. In 1897 he became brigadier general and retired soon afterward. (1:282–83)

CARPENTER, LOUIS H., from New Jersey. A close friend of Ben and Alice Grierson, Carpenter joined the Tenth Cavalry as a company commander after compiling an outstanding record in the Civil War. He and his Company "H" distinguished themselves at the Battle of Beecher's Island in 1868, in the Red River War of 1874–75, and in the Victorio War of 1879–80. Carpenter's long career ended in October 1899, when he retired as a brigadier general. (1:284; see also Leckie, *Buffalo Soldiers*, 12, 33–34, 43, 53, 65, 74, 131, 149 n, 169–70, 217, 223, 226–27)

CLAGUE, JOHN JAMES, from England. Clague entered the army during the Civil War as a private in the Sixth Minnesota Infantry and became a captain in the Eighteenth U.S. Infantry, a black unit, in 1864. Following the war he joined the Fortieth Infantry, also a black unit, as a second lieutenant. In 1870 he was assigned to the Twelfth Infantry and rose to first lieutenant three years later. He was promoted to captain commissary of subsistence in 1880 and to major in 1894. Clague became lieutenant colonel acting commissary general subsistence in 1898 and colonel acting commissary general subsistence in 1900. He retired a year later. (1:302)

COLLADAY, SAMUEL R., from Pennsylvania. Rising through the ranks in the Sixth Pennsylvania Cavalry during the Civil War, Colladay was a captain when the war ended. He joined the Tenth Cavalry as a second lieutenant in January 1871 and died in 1884. (1:317)

CONSTABLE, NATHANIEL S., from England. Constable entered the Nineteenth Missouri Infantry as a first lieutenant in 1861. A year later he became captain assistant quartermaster of volunteers. At the conclusion of the Civil War he received brevets as major and lieutenant colonel of volunteers and was honorably mustered out in August 1865. Two years later he rejoined the army as captain assistant quartermaster and served in that position until his death in 1880. (1:322)

COOPER, CHARLES L., from New York and Pennsylvania. Cooper enlisted as a private in 1862 and by the end of the Civil War had won promotion to first lieutenant in the 127th U.S. Infantry. In July 1866 he was assigned to the Thirty-Ninth Infantry, a black regiment, as second lieutenant and advanced to first lieutenant in 1870. He served as regimental adjutant from 1882 to 1883, when he was made a captain. In 1898 he became a major in the Fifth Cavalry and three years later joined the Fifteenth Cavalry as lieutenant colonel. Shortly thereafter he transferred to the Fourteenth Cavalry and in 1903 was appointed colonel of the Fifth Cavalry. (1:325)

CORBUSIER, WILLIAM H., from New York. Dr. Corbusier entered the army as an assistant surgeon in 1876 and advanced to major surgeon by 1895. His reminiscences and those of his wife, Fanny, are found in Fanny Corbusier, *From Verde to San Carlos*. (1:327)

CRAREY, ——. Dr. Crarey was probably a contract physician with the rank of acting assistant surgeon. Heitman's *Historical Register* has no reference to him.

CROOK, GEORGE, from Ohio. West Point, class of 1848. Crook compiled a brilliant record in the Civil War and was mustered out as a major general of volunteers. As an Indian fighter he was known for his innovations, which included the use of Indian scouts and the substitution of mules for unwieldy transport systems. He was promoted to brigadier in the regular army in 1873 and became major general in 1888. He died of a heart attack in March 1890. (1:340)

CUNNINGHAM, CHARLES N. W., from Ohio and Massachusetts. Cunningham enlisted as a private in the Thirteenth Massachusetts Infantry in 1861 and achieved the rank of captain in the Thirty-Eighth Infantry, a black regiment, by the end of the Civil War. He transferred to the Twenty-Fourth Infantry in 1869 and was dismissed from the service in 1878. (1:344-45)

CUSTER, GEORGE A., from Ohio. After graduating last in his West Point class of 1861, Custer entered the Second Cavalry as a second lieutenant at the beginning of the Civil War and rose rapidly in rank to brevet brigadier general in the regular army and brevet major general of volunteers by the close of the war. Appointed lieutenant colonel in the Seventh Cavalry in 1866, he remained in that rank and regiment until his death at the Battle of the Little Bighorn in 1876. His career was marked by controversy. To some he was a heroic Indian fighter and to others, such as Albert Barnitz and Frederick Benteen, both captains in the Seventh Cavalry, he was a self-promoting glory seeker who casually disregarded the safety of the men he commanded. Understandably, Colonel Grierson was no fan of Custer's. (1:348; see also Barnitz, *In Custer's Cavalry*; Charles K. Mills, *Harvest of Barren Regrets: The Army Career of Frederick William Benteen, 1834–98* [Glendale, California: Arthur H. Clark Co., 1985]; and Leckie and Leckie, *Unlikely Warriors*, 150–51, 159)

DAVIDSON, JOHN W., from Virginia. West Point, class of 1845. Davidson compiled an excellent record as a cavalry officer during the Civil War and emerged as a brevet major general of volunteers. He accepted an appointment as lieutenant colonel, Tenth Cavalry, in 1866. Somewhat of an eccentric, he was never popular with many of the officers of the Tenth nor was his relationship with Grierson close. He died in June 1881. (1:355–56)

DAVIS, NELSON HENRY, from Massachusetts. West Point, class of 1841. Davis served in the regular army and participated in the Mexican War. He was colonel of the Seventh Massachusetts Infantry briefly before becoming major assistant inspector general in 1861. Six years later he was promoted to lieutenant colonel assistant inspector general, and in 1872 he achieved the rank of colonel inspector general. (1:359)

DAVIS, WILLIAM, JR., from Indiana. Brother of Civil War hero

General Jefferson C. Davis, William Davis served in the First Missouri Cavalry as first lieutenant during the Civil War. In 1867 he joined the Tenth Cavalry as a second lieutenant, rising to first lieutenant in 1873. He was regimental quartermaster from 1878 to 1881. Seven years later he was promoted to captain, due in some measure to his marriage to Colonel Grierson's niece, Helen Fuller. He was still a captain when he retired in 1897. (1:360; see also Leckie and Leckie, *Unlikely Warriors*, 252, 297, 339 n.8)

DEHANNE, JEAN VICTOR, from New York. DeHanne entered the army as a private in the 176th New York Infantry in 1862. He was honorably discharged in 1863 and became an assistant surgeon, U.S. Volunteers, in 1864 through 1867. He then entered the U.S. Army as an assistant surgeon, a position he held until his retirement in 1891. (1:364)

DELANEY, MATTHEW AUGUSTUS, from Pennsylvania. Dr. DeLaney may have been a contract surgeon earlier and thus not formally a part of the army until he received an official appointment as assistant surgeon in 1901. (1:365)

DODGE, FRANCIS SAFFORD, from Massachusetts. Dodge entered the Twenty-Third Massachusetts Infantry as an enlisted man in 1861 and two years later was promoted to first lieutenant in the Second U.S. Cavalry, in which he rose to captain in 1865. Honorably mustered out in 1866, he joined the Ninth Cavalry, one of two black cavalry units, as first lieutenant that same year. A year later he was promoted to captain and three years later to major paymaster. In 1901 Dodge became lieutenant colonel deputy paymaster general. (1:376)

DOUGLASS, HENRY, from New York. West Point, class of 1847. Douglass was a major in the Third Infantry at the close of the Civil War. Assigned to the Eleventh Infantry in December 1870, he served in that capacity until 1876, when he was promoted to lieutenant colonel of the Fourteenth Infantry. He was colonel of the Tenth Infantry from 1885 until his retirement in 1891. (1:380–81)

DRUM, RICHARD C., from Pennsylvania. Drum rose through the ranks during the Mexican War and joined the Adjutant General's Office in March 1861. He became adjutant general in 1880. Nine years later he retired from the army after forty-three years of service. (1:384)

DUNBAR, GEORGE WARD, from New York. Dunbar was post chaplain at Fort Concho in 1876. He retired from the army in 1897. (1:387)

EGGLESTON, MILLARD FILLMORE, from Indiana. West Point, class of 1873. Eggleston joined the Tenth Cavalry as a second lieutenant in 1885. His career was blighted by overindulgence in alcohol. The army allowed him to resign in 1890 rather than face dismissal, following charges that he had committed arson by setting fire to Samuel Woodward's possessions in a bizarre incident. (1:400; see also M. F. Eggleston, Appointment,

Commission, and Promotion File, ACP1890, Adjutant General's Office, Record Group 94, National Archives and Records Service, Washington, D.C.)

ESTERLY, CALVIN, from Ohio. West Point, class of 1873. Esterly entered the Tenth Cavalry as a second lieutenant in 1877 and resigned in 1883. (1:408)

FLIPPER, HENRY O., from Georgia. West Point, class of 1877. Flipper was the first black to graduate from West Point. In 1877 he joined the Tenth Cavalry and performed well in the Victorio War of 1880. Racial prejudice remained strong, however, and he aroused the enmity of some white officers when he befriended Mollie Dwyer, sister-in-law of Nicholas Nolan, his company commander. Flipper was at Fort Davis at the time and had been appointed post quartermaster. Soon thereafter he was arrested and charged with embezzlement and "conduct unbecoming an officer"; he was cleared of the charge of embezzlement. After his dishonorable discharge he worked as an engineer in Mexico and sought unsuccessfully to clear his name. He died in Atlanta, Georgia, in 1944. In 1976 he was cleared posthumously of all charges, and the blot was erased from his record. (1:425; see also Dinges, "The Court-Martial of Lieutenant Henry O. Flipper," 12–17, 59–61)

FLOYD-JONES, D.L., from New York. West Point, class of 1845. Floyd-Jones received brevets for gallantry in both the Mexican and Civil wars. In 1867 he became the colonel commanding the Sixth Infantry, a position he held until 1869. Two years later he was assigned to the Third Infantry, and he retired in 1879. (1:426)

FORSYTH, JAMES W., from Ohio. West Point, class of 1851. Forsyth began his army career as a second lieutenant in the Ninth Infantry and at the onset of the Civil War rose to captain in the Eighteenth Infantry. By the war's end he had earned a brevet rank of brigadier general. He entered the Tenth Cavalry as a major in 1866. Three years later he became General Sheridan's aide-de-camp and four years later rose to lieutenant colonel and military secretary on Sheridan's staff. In 1878 he became lieutenant colonel of the First Cavalry and by 1886 was the Seventh Cavalry's colonel. Promoted to brigadier in 1894 and major general three years later, he retired in 1897. (1:430)

FORSYTH, LEWIS CASS, from Michigan. In the Civil War Forsyth began his military career as an assistant quartermaster of volunteers. He entered the regular army as captain assistant quartermaster in 1867 and rose to the rank of lieutenant colonel deputy quartermaster by 1896. He resigned the following year and died in 1902. (1:430)

GARDNER, WILLIAM F., from Pennsylvania. Gardner achieved the rank of first lieutenant during the Civil War and in 1867 was appointed lieutenant in the Thirty-Eighth Infantry, a black regiment. Two years later he was transferred to the Twenty-Fourth Infantry, also black. He died in 1872. (1:446)

GARDNER, WILLIAM H., from the District of Columbia. Gardner served as medical cadet for a year before becoming an assistant surgeon in 1862. He was promoted to major surgeon in 1882 and to lieutenant colonel deputy surgeon general in 1896. He retired two years later. (1:446)

GASMAN, HANS J., from Wisconsin. For two years he was a cadet at West Point but failed to graduate. He joined the Tenth Cavalry as a second lieutenant in 1873 and died six years later. (1:448)

GERONIMO, Chiricachua Indian leader born about 1829. Geronimo became an inveterate raider on both sides of the United States-Mexican border. Campaigns by General George Crook brought a measure of peace in 1873, but a government policy of Apache concentration inaugurated in 1875 led to renewed outbreaks and Geronimo led raids into Arizona and Mexico. He surrendered to General Crook in 1884 and was placed on the San Carlos Indian Reservation. He remained there until May 1885, when he led another outbreak. He agreed to surrender to General Crook in Canyon de los Embudos in northern Mexico in March 1886 but slipped away before troops could escort him and his followers to the reservations. Ultimately, Geronimo surrendered to General Nelson A. Miles in August 1886. The old chief was imprisoned at Fort Pickens, Florida. In 1894 Geronimo and survivors of his band were sent to Fort Sill, Indian Territory, where he died in 1909, still a prisoner of war. (See Joseph A. Stout, Jr., "Geronimo," *Dictionary of American Military Biography*, 3 vols., Roger J. Spiller et al., eds. [Westport, Connecticut: Greenwood Press, 1984]; 1:377–80)

GILLMORE, QUINCY O'MAHER, from New York. West Point, class of 1869. Gillmore joined the Tenth Cavalry as a second lieutenant in June 1873 and resigned on November 12, 1874. Six months later he was appointed second lieutenant in the Eighth Cavalry. He retired in 1896 but returned to the service as lieutenant colonel of the Fourth New Jersey Cavalry in June 1898 and became colonel of that regiment four months later. He was honorably mustered out of volunteers in 1899. (1:458)

GRAHAM, GEORGE W., from New York. Graham rose to the rank of captain during the Civil War. Appointed first lieutenant in the Tenth Cavalry in 1866, he was promoted to captain months later. He showed great promise as a combat officer but was cashiered in 1870. (1:467)

HATCH, EDWARD, from Maine and Iowa. An Iowa businessman who rose from captain to colonel in the Second Iowa Cavalry, Hatch participated in Grierson's raid through Mississippi in 1863. By the conclusion of the Civil War he was a brevet major general and won appointment as colonel of the Ninth Cavalry, a black regiment. A friend of Colonel Grierson, he cooperated with him in the Victorio War of 1878–79. He died in

1889. (1:510; see also Leckie and Leckie, *Unlikely Warriors*, 86–87, 89, 109, 258–60, 325 n.4)

HAZEN, WILLIAM B., from Vermont. West Point, class of 1855. Hazen saw extensive service in the West prior to the Civil War. He achieved national prominence for his service during the war and at its close was a major general of volunteers and commander of the Fifteenth Corps, Army of Tennessee. In March 1867, while commanding the Thirty-Eighth Infantry, a black regiment, Hazen was appointed by General Sherman to head the newly created Southern Indian Military District to administer affairs in Indian Territory. It was in this role that he first met Colonel Grierson, and both men worked to feed, clothe, and control the southern plains Indians after these tribes had been driven onto reservations in Indian Territory. Hazen, however, was soon ordered to other duties. For the next eighteen years (1869–87) he was constantly embroiled in quarrels and court battles. He died suddenly in January 1887 of natural causes. (1:517; see also Kroeker, "William B. Hazen," *Soldiers West*, 193–211)

HOFFMAN, WILLIAM, from New York. West Point, class of 1825. Hoffman won brevets in the Mexican War and was twice breveted during the Civil War, at the end of which he emerged a brevet major general. At the time of his service at Fort Leavenworth he was colonel of the Third Infantry. He retired in 1870. (1:535)

HUGHES, JAMES B., from North Carolina. West Point, class of 1880. Hughes was appointed second lieutenant in the Tenth Cavalry in 1884 and promoted to first lieutenant in 1891. (1:552)

HUNT, LEVI P., from Missouri. West Point, class of 1866. Hunt was assigned as a second lieutenant to the Tenth Cavalry in 1870. Five years later he was promoted to first lieutenant and in 1890 became a captain. He rose to major in the Thirteenth Cavalry in 1901. (1:556)

IRWIN, BERNARD J. D., from Ireland. Dr. Irwin began his medical career in the military as an assistant surgeon in 1856. He rose to major surgeon in 1862, and in 1885 he became lieutenant colonel, assistant medical purveyor. Five years later he achieved the rank of colonel surgeon. He retired in 1894. (1:564)

KELTON, DWIGHT H., from Vermont. Kelton enlisted as a private in the Ninety-Eighth New York Infantry regiment in 1864 and was a captain in the 115th U.S. Colored Infantry at the close of the Civil War. After the war he served in the Tenth Infantry for twenty-two years, retiring as a captain in 1888. (1:590)

KENNEDY, WILLIAM B., from Ireland. At the end of the Civil War Kennedy had achieved the rank of captain in the First California Cavalry. In 1867 he was appointed first lieutenant in the Tenth Cavalry and three years later was promoted to captain. He transferred to the Fourth Cavalry as a major in 1892 and retired with that rank in 1897. (1:592)

KEYES, ALEXANDER SCAMMEL BROOKS, from Massachusetts. Keyes rose through the ranks during the Civil War and received a commission in the regular army at the close of that conflict. He served in the infantry until 1870, when he joined the Tenth Cavalry. He was promoted to captain in 1873 and remained with the Tenth until 1892, when he was transferred to the Third Cavalry. He retired with the rank of major in 1896. (1:595)

KICKING BIRD, Kiowa chieftain. A chief of ability and foresight, Kicking Bird became the principal spokesman and leader of the Kiowa peace faction. After the great outbreak of 1874 he persuaded most of his people to return to the reservation. When he died under mysterious circumstances in 1875, it was commonly believed that he had been poisoned by a member of the war faction. (See Nye, *Carbine and Lance*, 164, 167, 179, 180, 192, 213, 218, 231, 233)

KIDD, MEREDITH H., from Indiana. Kidd held the rank of lieutenant colonel in the Eleventh Indiana Cavalry at the end of the Civil War. He was appointed major in the Tenth Cavalry in March 1867. Because of his heavy drinking, Kidd was not considered an effective officer by Colonel Grierson. Kidd received an honorable discharge at his own request at the end of 1870. (1:596)

KILBOURNE, HENRY SAYLES, from New York. In 1870 Kilbourne was acting assistant surgeon in the U.S. Army and supplied part of the information for Fort Sill in the War Department's *Circular No. 4: A Report on Barracks and Hospitals with Descriptions of Military Posts* (1870). In 1875 he became an assistant surgeon and by 1894 had been promoted to major surgeon. (1:597)

KIMBALL, AMOS S., from New York. For most of his long career Kimball served in the Quartermaster Corps. After the Civil War he was assigned as captain in that unit and was promoted to major in 1883. He retired in 1902 as a brigadier general. (1:597)

KING, WILLIAM H., from Pennsylvania. Dr. King entered the military as an assistant surgeon of the 149th Pennsylvania Infantry in 1863. After he was honorably mustered out a few months later, he joined the Twenty-First Pennsylvania Cavalry as surgeon. He was honorably mustered out of the army again in 1865 but three years later reentered as an assistant surgeon. He died in 1883. (1:600)

KISLINGBURY, FREDERICK F., from England. After nine years in enlisted ranks, Kislingbury was promoted to second lieutenant in the Eleventh Infantry in 1873. Eleven years later he died while on an Arctic expedition under Lieutenant A. W. Greely. (1:604)

LACEY, FRANCIS E., from Ireland. A professional soldier, Lacey enlisted in the army in 1858 and by 1866 had achieved the rank of captain in the Second U.S. Infantry Regiment. He was assigned to the Tenth

Infantry in 1870. At the close of his career in 1897 he was a lieutenant colonel in the Third Infantry. (1:610)

LEAVELL, BENJAMIN W., from Ohio. West Point, class of 1875. Leavell entered the Twenty-Fourth Infantry as a second lieutenant in 1879 and was promoted to first lieutenant in 1884. He advanced to captain in 1897 and retired with the rank of major in 1902. (1:622)

LEBO, THOMAS C., from Pennsylvania. Lebo served throughout the Civil War with the First Pennsylvania Cavalry and was promoted to captain late in 1864. In the postwar period he joined the Tenth Cavalry as a first lieutenant in 1867. Nine years later he advanced to captain. He transferred to the Sixth Cavalry as a major in 1893 and ended his career as colonel of the Fourteenth Cavalry in 1901. (1:622)

LEE, ARTHUR TRACY, from Pennsylvania. Lee entered the army as a second lieutenant in the Fifth Infantry in 1838 and shortly thereafter transferred to the Eighth Infantry. He advanced to first lieutenant in 1845 and to major with the Second Infantry in 1861. Following the Battle of Gettysburg, which cost him his arm, he was breveted lieutenant colonel, and by the time he retired from the army, he had achieved the rank of colonel. He died in 1879. (1:623)

LEE, PHILLIP L., from Virginia. Lee enlisted as a private in a New York cavalry regiment in 1862 and had achieved the rank of first lieutenant by the close of the Civil War. He was appointed first lieutenant in the Tenth Cavalry in 1866 and was promoted to captain in 1869. (1:625)

LIPPINCOTT, CHARLES E., from Illinois. Lippincott rose during the Civil War from captain of an Illinois infantry regiment to brevet brigadier general of volunteers. He was mustered out of the service and remained in civilian life until his death in 1887. (1:634)

LITTLE, THOMAS, from Ireland. He rose through the ranks during the Civil War and was a first lieutenant at war's end. In 1866 he was assigned to the Thirty-First Infantry and a year later was promoted to captain. In 1871 he joined the Tenth Cavalry as a captain and company commander. He was dismissed from the service in 1877 following a court-martial in which he was found guilty of "conduct unbecoming." (1:635)

MACKENZIE, RANALD SLIDELL, from New York. West Point, class of 1862. Mackenzie graduated first in his class and was commissioned a second lieutenant. He participated in all the major engagements in the eastern theater of the Civil War and earned rapid promotion. By the close of the war he was a brevet major general of volunteers and a brevet brigadier general in the regular army. He was appointed colonel of the Forty-First Infantry, a black regiment, and assigned to the Texas frontier. Late in 1870 he transferred to the Fourth Cavalry as its colonel. With this command he earned a reputation as one of the foremost Indian fighters in the army. Later, in campaigns on the northern plains, he achieved additional distinction. He retired as a brigadier general in 1884 and died five years later. (1:672)

MCLAUGLEN, NAPOLEON B., from Vermont. A lifelong professional soldier, McLauglen joined the army as a private in 1850. He was promoted to second lieutenant in the First Cavalry in 1861. He fought at Chancellorsville and Gettysburg and was cited many times for gallant and meritorious service. By 1864 he was colonel of the Fifty-Seventh Massachusetts Infantry and was mustered out at that rank. He was appointed major in the Tenth Cavalry in 1876 and retired in 1882. (1:674–75)

MARKLEY, ALFRED COLLINS, from Pennsylvania. Markley rose through the ranks during the Civil War and emerged as first lieutenant of the 127th U.S. Infantry in 1865. After mustering out, he rejoined the army as a second lieutenant in the Fifty-First Infantry in 1866. He advanced to first lieutenant a year later and in 1868 transferred to the Twenty-Fourth Infantry. He ended his long military career as colonel of the Thirteenth Infantry in 1901. (1:689)

MAXON, MASON M., from Wisconsin. West Point, class of 1864. Maxon joined the Tenth Cavalry in 1869 as a second lieutenant. He was promoted to first lieutenant in 1875 and to captain later in 1889. From 1881 to 1887 he served as regimental quartermaster, in part because he had married one of Colonel Grierson's nieces, Grace Fuller. (1:698)

MAYNADIER, WILLIAM M., from Maryland. Maynadier achieved the rank of major in field artillery during the Civil War and was appointed major paymaster in 1875. Twenty years later he retired. (1:699)

MERRITT, WESLEY, from New York. West Point, class of 1855. One of the "boy generals" of the Civil War, Merritt achieved the rank of major general of volunteers at war's end. Appointed lieutenant colonel of the Ninth Cavalry in 1866, he served in that capacity until his promotion to colonel of the Fifth Cavalry in 1876. He held the rank of brigadier general in the regular army by 1887 and major general by 1895. (1:706)

MILLS, ANSON, from Indiana. Mills attended West Point but failed to graduate. He saw long service as an infantry officer before joining the Tenth Cavalry as a major. A strict disciplinarian, he deplored Colonel Grierson's disregard for military regulations. Mills became a leader of the anti-Grierson faction at Fort Davis but seems to have had little influence on the regiment's colonel. He retired in 1897 with the rank of brigadier general. Mills's career is detailed in his book, *My Story*. (1:713)

MOORE, ORLANDO H., from Pennsylvania. Moore entered the Sixth Infantry as a second lieutenant in 1856 and was promoted to first lieutenant and then captain in 1861. In 1862 he became lieutenant colonel of the Thirteenth Michigan Infantry, and after resigning from volunteer service several months later, he became colonel of the Twenty-Fifth Michigan Infantry in 1862. He was honorably mustered out of volunteer service again in 1865. Heitman makes no mention of further military service until noting that Moore became a major in the Sixth Infantry in 1874. However, since Alice Grierson wrote of Captain Moore as the "senior captain" of the Sixth Infantry in 1869 and also occasionally referred to him by his volunteer title of colonel, it is clear that he had reentered the Sixth soon after the conclusion of the Civil War. (1:723)

MORRISON, JOHN T., from New York. Morrison enlisted as a private in the infantry in 1861 and rose to the rank of first lieutenant in the Second Minnesota Cavalry. In 1867 he was appointed second lieutenant in the Tenth Cavalry and four months later was promoted to first lieutenant. After serving as both regimental quartermaster and regimental adjutant, he became captain in 1882. Five years later he retired. (1:729)

MUNSON, JACOB F., from New York. Munson enlisted as a private in 1861 and rose through the ranks to a brevet captain of volunteers at the end of the war. In 1866 he was appointed second lieutenant in the Sixth Infantry. He remained with that regiment until his retirement in 1896 with the rank of captain. (1:736)

MURDOCH, DANIEL H., from Pennsylvania. Murdoch served as an enlisted man from 1862 to 1864, when he was promoted to second lieutenant in the 122nd Infantry, a black unit. He held the rank of first lieutenant at the end of the war. Appointed as a second lieutenant in the Sixth Infantry in 1866, he had reached the rank of captain in that regiment when he drowned in 1886. (1:736)

MYERS, JAMES W., from Virginia. Myers enlisted as a private in a West Virginia cavalry unit and by the end of the Civil War was a second lieutenant in the Fifth West Virginia Cavalry. He was appointed second lieutenant in the Tenth Cavalry in 1867. A heavy drinker, he was cashiered in 1875. An innocent victim of a saloon brawl in Fort Griffin, Texas, he died while seeking reinstatement in the army. (1:740; Dinges, "Scandal in The Tenth Cavalry," 39–40)

NOLAN, NICHOLAS, from Ireland. A professional soldier, Nolan joined the army as a private in 1852 and remained an enlisted man until 1862, when he was promoted to second lieutenant, Sixth Cavalry. He was a first lieutenant at the end of the war. In 1866 he joined the Tenth Cavalry as a captain. He transferred to the Third Cavalry as a major in 1882 and died one year later. (1:750)

NORVELL, STEVENS T., from Michigan. Norvell, a professional soldier, enlisted as a private in the Fifth Infantry in 1858. By the end of the Civil War he was a first lieutenant. He joined the Tenth Cavalry as a captain in 1870 and was promoted to major in 1890. In 1898 he became lieutenant colonel of the Ninth Cavalry and retired one year later. (1:753)

ORD, EDWARD O. C., from Maryland. West Point, class of 1835. Ord made his reputation for the most part in the western theater of the

Civil War and at war's end was a major general of volunteers and regular army brigadier general. He retired with the rank of major general in 1881. (1:759)

ORLEMAN, LOUIS HENRY, from Germany. Orleman served as an enlisted man in a New York infantry regiment until 1862, when he was promoted to first lieutenant. At the war's end he was a captain. He joined the Tenth Cavalry as a second lieutenant in 1867 and was promoted to first lieutenant in 1874. Five years later he retired. (1:760)

PAULUS, JACOB, from Prussia. Paulus served as an enlisted man and advanced to captain in the Fiftieth Pennsylvania Infantry by the end of the Civil War. In 1869 he was assigned as a first lieutenant in the Twenty-Fifth Infantry, a black regiment stationed on the Texas frontier for many years. He was promoted to captain in 1873, retired from the service in 1879, and died two years later. (1:776–77)

REES, RICHARD, from Wales. Rees rose from enlisted man to captain in the Twenty-First Missouri Infantry during the Civil War. Appointed a second lieutenant in the Sixth Infantry in 1867, he was mustered out of the service in 1870. (1:821)

ROCKWELL, ALMON F., from New York. Commonly referred to as *colonel* because of his brevet rank of lieutenant colonel, Rockwell was actually a captain in the quartermaster corps. He was assigned to Fort Sill in 1870 as quartermaster constructor. In later years he served as colonel and superintendent of public buildings. He retired in 1897. (1:840)

SATANK, one of the principal and most militant chiefs of the Kiowas. In 1871 Satank was arrested for his role in the Warren Wagon Train massacre in Texas. Manacled and chained, he was placed in a wagon for transport to Jacksboro, Texas, for trial. He managed to slip the manacles and seize the carbine of a guard but was shot and killed and his body thrown beside the road. (See Leckie and Leckie, *Unlikely Warriors*, 177, 180, 187–90)

SATANTA, one of the best-known warriors and spokesmen of the Kiowas. In 1871 he was a leader in the massacre of the Warren Wagon Train west of Fort Richardson, Texas. Along with Satank and Big Tree he was arrested for his part in this depredation, tried in civil court in Jacksboro, Texas, and imprisoned. He was released in 1873 but was returned to the Huntsville, Texas, penitentiary in 1875 for his role in the Red River War of 1874–75. Three years later he committed suicide. (See Leckie and Leckie, *Unlikely Warriors*, 158, 161, 171, 179, 187–90, 206–7, 217, 219)

SCHOFIELD, GEORGE WHEELER, from New York. A veteran of the Civil War and a brevet brigadier general, Schofield joined the Tenth Cavalry as a major in 1870. He committed suicide in 1882. (1:865)

SCHOFIELD, JOHN M., from New York. West Point, class of 1849. At the close of the Civil War Schofield was brigadier general in the regular army. He served as secretary of war from May 1868 to March 1869, when he was promoted to major general. He was commander-in-chief of the army from 1888 to 1895 and retired in that year as a lieutenant general. (1:865)

SHAFTER, WILLIAM RUFUS, from Michigan. Shafter entered the Seventh Michigan Infantry as a first lieutenant in 1861, rose rapidly during the war, and emerged as a colonel of the Seventeenth U.S. Infantry, a black unit, and a brevet brigadier general of volunteers. After being honorably mustered out in 1866, he reentered the army as a lieutenant colonel of the Forty-First Infantry that same year. In 1869 he was assigned to the Twenty-Fourth Infantry, a black unit, and ten years later became colonel of the First Infantry. Shafter was promoted to brigadier general in 1897 and a year later, during the Spanish American War, became major general of volunteers. He retired from the regular army in 1899. (1:876)

SHERIDAN, PHILIP H., from Ohio. West Point, class of 1853. Sheridan first served in the West, but it was the Civil War that brought him distinction. As a cavalry officer he rose rapidly in rank and responsibility, and at the close of the war he emerged as a major general, second only to Grant and Sherman in the nation's esteem. In 1867 he was assigned to command the Department of the Missouri and two years later succeeded General Sherman as head of the vast Military Division of the Missouri. Sheridan became commander-in-chief of the army in 1883 and served in that capacity until his death in 1888. (1:881)

SMART, CHARLES, from Scotland. Dr. Smart joined the army as assistant surgeon for the Sixty-Third New York Infantry in 1862 and shortly thereafter became assistant surgeon for the U.S. Army. In 1882 he achieved the rank of major surgeon. He advanced to lieutenant colonel deputy surgeon general in 1897 and four years later was appointed colonel assistant surgeon general. (1:893)

SMITHER, ROBERT G., from Indiana. Smither advanced from enlisted man to first lieutenant during the Civil War. He joined the Tenth Cavalry as a first lieutenant in 1867 and served as regimental adjutant from 1877 to late 1881. That same year he was promoted to captain. He retired in 1888. (1:905)

SPENCER, THOMAS J., from Michigan. Spencer rose through the ranks from enlisted man to second lieutenant in a cavalry regiment during the Civil War. In 1866 he was appointed a second lieutenant in the Tenth Cavalry and thus was one of its original officers. A year later he was promoted to first lieutenant but in 1875 was dismissed from the service. Two years later he was reinstated. He was promoted to captain in March 1879 but was dismissed again in 1881. (1:911)

STANLEY, DAVID S., from Ohio. West Point, class of 1848. Stanley compiled a distinguished Civil War record as he rose from the rank of captain to major general of volunteers. Most of his service was in the western theater of the war and included such battles as Stone River and Franklin. Following the war he became a colonel in the Twenty-Second Infantry, rising to brigadier general in 1884. He retired eight years later. (1:915)

TEAR, WALLACE, from Ohio. Tear entered the army as an enlisted man in the Ninety-Sixth Illinois Infantry in 1862. By the end of the war he had risen to first lieutenant in the Fourteenth U.S. Colored Infantry. In 1867 he reentered the military as a second lieutenant in the Fortieth Infantry, a black unit. Two years later he transferred to the Twenty-Fifth Infantry, also a black unit, and by 1873 was promoted to first lieutenant. He resigned in 1883. (1:950)

TERRAZAS, JOAQUIN, from Chihuahua, Mexico. A veteran Indian fighter and a follower of Benito Juárez, Terrazas was also prominent in the struggle against French intervention. (See Thrapp, *Victorio and the Mimbres Apaches*, 293, 300, 373 n)

THOMPSON, JOHN M., from New Hampshire. Thompson enlisted in 1861 in a New Hampshire infantry unit and rose through the ranks during the war to become captain of the Thirty-Third U.S. Infantry, a black regiment. He was appointed a second lieutenant in the Thirty-Eighth Infantry, also a black regiment, in 1866. Three years later he transferred to the Twenty-Fourth Infantry, again a black unit, as a first lieutenant. He was promoted to captain in 1878 and to major twenty years later. By the time of his retirement in 1901 he was colonel of the Twenty-Third Infantry. (1:957)

TURNER, EDWARD P., from Pennsylvania. Turner was appointed a second lieutenant in the Tenth Cavalry late in 1871. He resigned in 1878. (1:974)

VANDE WIELE, JOHN B., from New York. Vande Wiele enlisted at the outbreak of the Civil War and rose to the rank of brevet major. He joined the Tenth Cavalry as a captain and company commander in 1867. Although an able officer, he was accused of brutality toward the enlisted men of his company. He failed to achieve promotion and retired as a captain in 1879. (1:982)

VAN VLIET, FREDERICK, from New York. He entered the Third Cavalry as a second lieutenant in 1861 and advanced to first lieutenant a year later. In 1866 he was promoted to captain and entered the Tenth Cavalry as a major in 1882. Van Vliet held a number of brevet ranks, including that of lieutenant colonel for meritorious service during the Civil War. (1:984)

VICTORIO, a Mimbres Apache chieftain of great ability. In 1879 Victorio led his people and a few Mescaleros in a breakout from the Fort Stanton Reservation, New Mexico, because he feared he and his band would be forced to live on the San Carlos Reservation in Arizona. For more than a year Victorio either fought off or eluded all efforts by U.S. forces to capture him. After a brief respite in the mountains of northern Mexico, he entered west Texas intent on making his way to the Mescalero (or Fort Stanton) Reservation, where he hoped to obtain supplies and new recruits. Colonel Grierson and the Tenth Cavalry succeeded in driving him back into Mexico, where he and most of his band were cornered by Mexican forces and slain. (See Thrapp, *Victorio and the Mimbres Apaches*)

VOLKMAR, WILLIAM J., from Pennsylvania. West Point, class of 1864. Volkmar served in the Fifth Cavalry, where he rose to captain. From 1881 to 1885 he served as aide-de-camp to General Sheridan. By then he had been promoted to major and was assigned to the adjutant general's office. He retired as a colonel in 1898. (1:988)

WALSH, JAMES W., from Ireland. Walsh enlisted as a private in the army in 1850 and rose rapidly in rank during the Civil War. At the end of the war he was a brevet colonel in the Fifth Pennsylvania Cavalry. He was appointed a captain in the Tenth Cavalry in 1866 and died seven years later. (1:999)

WARD, CHARLES R., from Pennsylvania. West Point, class of 1867. Ward joined the Tenth Cavalry as a second lieutenant in 1867 and was promoted to first lieutenant in 1876. He was dismissed from the service in 1888. (1:1000)

WOODWARD, SAMUEL L., from New York. Woodward was a close friend of both Ben and Alice Grierson. He served under Grierson in the Sixth Illinois Cavalry during the Civil War and received brevets as captain and major for gallantry during the famous raids into Mississippi in 1863 and 1864. He was adjutant of the Tenth Cavalry for ten years. Although generally referred to as *Major* (his brevet rank), he was not promoted to captain until 1887. He retired in 1903 as lieutenant colonel of the Seventh Cavalry. (1:1059)

YARD, JOHN E., from Pennsylvania. Yard served in the Civil War in the Ninth Infantry as a second and later a first lieutenant. He was appointed a major in the Tenth Cavalry in 1867 and served in that capacity until 1870. He was reassigned to various infantry regiments until his death in 1889. (1:1065)

Abbreviations

Notes

Introduction

1. Benjamin H. Grierson, "The Kirkpatricks," 14, FDNHS; John Kirk to Alice Kirk, 17 October 1844, TTU; *Mahoning Free Democrat*, 29 September 1853, 24 May 1854; William H. Leckie and Shirley A. Leckie, *Unlikely Warriors: General Benjamin H. Grierson and His Family* (Norman: University of Oklahoma Press, 1984), 12–16.

2. Leckie and Leckie, *Unlikely Warriors*, 17–27; for information on the entry of young, middle-class women into school teaching between 1825 and 1860, see Nancy Cott, *The Bonds of Womanhood: "Woman's Sphere" in New England, 1780–1835* (New Haven: Yale University Press, 1977), 34–35.

3. Barbara Welter, "The Cult of True Womanhood, 1820–1860," *American Quarterly* 18 (1966): 151–74.

4. For an excellent discussion of nineteenth-century views of gender roles, see Carl Degler, *At Odds: Women Against the Family, From the Revolution to the Present Time* (Oxford: Oxford University Press, 1980), 30–32.

5. Alice to Ben, 1 September 1861, ISHL. In this attitude she was not really atypical. See Degler, *At Odds*, 259–69.

6. Alice to Ben, 13 April 1861, ISHL.

7. Leckie and Leckie, *Unlikely Warriors*, 28–46; Alice to John Kirk, 15 January 1856, ISHL.

8. Leckie and Leckie, *Unlikely Warriors*, 78–140; see also D. Alexander Brown, *Grierson's Raid* (Urbana: University of Illinois Press, 1962).

9. Leckie and Leckie, *Unlikely Warriors*, 140–46. See also William H. Leckie, *The Buffalo Soldiers: A Narrative of the Negro Cavalry in the West* (Norman: University of Oklahoma Press, 1967), 3–18.

10. Sandra Myres notes that most officers' wives were well educated and came from upper-middle-class families. See her Foreword in Teresa Griffin Viele, *"Following the Drum": A Glimpse of Frontier Life* (Lincoln: University of Nebraska Press, 1984), 1–3; *Westering Women and the Frontier Experience, 1800–1915* (Albuquerque: University of New Mexico Press, 1982), 6; "Romance and Reality on the American Frontier: Views of Army Wives," *Western Historical Quarterly* 13 (October 1982): 417–18.

11. Like Caesar's wife the commanding officer's wife had to be above reproach, as Patricia Stallard notes in *Glittering Misery: Dependents of the Indian Fighting Army* (San Rafael: Presidio Press, 1978), 103; Charles King, the army officer turned novelist, wrote: "There is only one social position harder to fill than that of a minister's wife," in his reference to the commanding officer's wife in *Under Fire* (Philadelphia: Lippincott, 1895), 143.

12. A number of army officers' wives left memoirs, journals, or compilations of letters describing their experiences at western frontier posts. All stressed the difficulty they encountered making a home in a masculine society ruled by army regulations unconcerned with their needs in a primitive setting.

Notable works by officers' wives include Ellen McGowan Biddle, *Reminiscences of a Soldier's Wife* (Philadelphia: Lippincott, 1907); Mrs. Oresmus Bronson Boyd, *Cavalry Life in Tent and Field* (New York: Tait, 1894); Frances C. Carrington, *My Army Life and the Fort Phil-Kearney Massacre with an Account of the Celebration of "Wyoming Opened"* (Philadelphia: Lippincott, 1910); Margaret Carrington, *Ab-sa-ra-ka: Home of the Crow* (Philadelphia: Lippincott, 1869); Elizabeth B. Custer, *"Boots and Saddles"; or, Life in Dakota with General Custer* (New York: Harper & Bros., 1885); *Following the Guidon* (New York: Harper & Bros., 1890); *Tenting on the Plains; or, General Custer in Kansas and Texas* (New York: Webster, 1887); Katherine Gibson Fougera, *With Custer's Cavalry: From the Memoirs of the Late Katherine Gibson* (Caldwell, Idaho: Caxton, 1940); Merrill Mattes, ed., *Indians, Infants, and Infantry: Andrew and Elizabeth Burt on the Frontier* (Denver: Old West, 1960); Lydia Spencer Lane, *I Married a Soldier: Or Old Days in the Old Army* (1893; reprint, Albuquerque: Horn & Wallace, 1964); Frances Roe, *Army Letters From an Officer's Wife, 1871–1888* (New York: Appleton, 1909); Martha Summerhayes, *Vanished Arizona: Recollections of the Army Life of a New England Woman* (1908; reprint, Philadelphia: Lippincott, 1963). Stallard's *Glittering Misery* ably summarizes the domestic difficulties encountered by these women.

13. Of the army wives who left memoirs, journals, diaries, or letters that have since been published, only Ellen Biddle confronted a problem similar to Alice Grierson's. Biddle bore six children; four survived to adulthood although one suffered a chronic heart condition.

14. Bruce Dinges, "Colonel Grierson Invests on the West Texas Frontier," *Fort Concho Report* 16 (Fall 1984): 9.

15. A number of army wives noted the changes in the West brought about by the arrival of the railroad and the passage of time. For example, when Martha Summerhayes and her family returned to Arizona in 1886, they traveled through the desert in a Pullman car in a matter of hours. In 1874 the journey had taken days. Along the way the number of former luxuries readily available at reasonable prices constantly surprised her. *Vanished Arizona*, 223–24.

16. Bruce J. Dinges, "Benjamin H. Grierson," *Soldiers West: Biographies From the Military Frontier*, ed. Paul Andrew Hutton (Lincoln: University of Nebraska Press, 1987), 160–65; Paul Andrew Hutton, *Phil Sheridan and His Army* (Lincoln: University of Nebraska Press, 1985), 230–39; Leckie and Leckie, *Unlikely Warriors*, 293, 303.

1. Early Years on the Frontier

1. Benjamin Grierson, 2 March 1866, "Testimony," House of Representatives, H.R. 30, 39 Cong., 1 sess, 1866, *Report of the Joint Committee on Reconstruction*, 121–24.

2. Leckie and Leckie, *Unlikely Warriors*, 139–42.

3. War Department, Surgeon General's Office, *Circular No. 4: A Report of Barracks and Hospitals with Descriptions of Military Posts* (Washington, D.C.: Government Printing Office, 1870), 284–85. Fort Leavenworth, established in 1827 by Colonel Henry Leavenworth, 3rd Infantry, to protect the Santa Fe Trail, is the oldest fort west of the Mississippi still operating today. Robert Frazer, *Forts of the West* (Norman: University of Oklahoma Press, 1965), 56.

4. Leckie and Leckie, *Unlikely Warriors*, 144–48.

5. Roe, *Army Letters*, 5.

6. Until 1878, laundresses were part of the military; they were carried on the company roster and received free transportation and rations. John B. Sibbald, "Camp Followers All," *American West* 3 (Spring 1866): 56–67; Miller J. Stewart, "Army Laundresses: Ladies of the 'Soap Suds Row,'" *Nebraska History* 61 (Winter 1980): 421–36.

7. Robert M. Utley, ed., *Life in Custer's Cavalry: Diaries and Letters of Albert and Jennie Barnitz, 1867–68* (New Haven: Yale University Press, 1977), 15; War Department, *Circular No. 4*, 287–89. Fort Riley was

founded in 1853 at a strategic point on the north bank of the Kansas River, close to the junction of the Republican and Smoky Hill rivers. Like Leavenworth, it is still in operation today. Frazer, *Forts of the West*, 57.

8. Marguerite Merington, ed., *The Custer Story: The Life and Intimate Letters of General George A. Custer and His Wife Elizabeth* (Lincoln: University of Nebraska Press, 1950), 210. The court-martial lasted from September 15 to October 11.

9. Sydney Ahlstrom provides excellent background on the Disciples of Christ, a thoroughly American offspring of Scotch Presbyterians and Baptists. See *A Religious History of the American People* (New Haven: Yale University Press, 1972), 447-49.

10. Summerhayes, *Vanished Arizona*, 109. She judged one army surgeon "much better versed in the sawing off of soldiers' legs than in the treatment of young mothers and babies." Marian Russell recorded that one army surgeon "was reduced to a hopeless wreck before my ordeal." See *Land of Enchantment: Memoirs of Marian Russell along the Santa Fe Trail*, ed. Garnet M. Brayer (Evanston: Branding Iron Press, 1954), 110. One scholar maintains that both regular and contract army physicians "lacked the competence of their brethren in civil life. Low pay and frontier discomforts discouraged able doctors from seeking a military career." Robert Utley, *Frontier Regulars: The United States Army and the Indians, 1866-1891* (New York: Macmillan, 1973), 87. There was a good chance that no physician would be in attendance, since doctors were often out in the field with the troops, according to Forrest R. Blackburn, "Army Families in Frontier Forts," *Military Review* 49 (October 1969): 23.

11. Lawrence A. Frost, *The Court-Martial of General George Armstrong Custer* (Norman: University of Oklahoma Press, 1968), 246.

12. Details of the Medicine Lodge Treaties are found in Charles J. Kappler, *Indian Affairs: Laws and Treaties*, 2 vols. (Washington, D.C.: Government Printing Office, 1903): 2:980-89. The Indian chiefs who signed the treaties misunderstood the terms. Promised the right to hunt buffalo south of the Arkansas River while also receiving annuities from the United States government, they did not comprehend the specification that they would become farmers and their children would be placed in schools. See Robert Utley, *The Indian Frontier of the American West, 1846-1890* (Albuquerque: University of New Mexico Press, 1982), 114-16.

13. J. W. Wilbarger, *Indian Depredations in Texas* (Austin: Hutchings, 1889), 633-36; Ben Grierson to John Grierson, 23 March 1868, Benjamin Grierson, Letters and Documents, Edward Ayer Collection, MS 343A, Newberry Library, Chicago, Illinois, two rolls, microcopy at TTU (hereafter referred to as MS 343A).

14. Fort Gibson, located on the Grand River in northeastern Indian Territory, was established in 1824 to expedite Indian removal. Following

the Civil War it declined in importance, becoming a quartermaster depot. See Brad Agnew, *Fort Gibson: Terminal on the Trail of Tears* (Norman: University of Oklahoma Press, 1980); W. Morrison, *Military Posts and Camps in Oklahoma* (Oklahoma City: Harlow, 1936), 28–47.

15. Elizabeth Custer, *Tenting on the Plains*, 320. Frances Roe, *Army Letters*, 77–78 and 103–4. For an examination of racial attitudes among army officers and their wives, see Erwin N. Thompson, "The Negro Soldier on the Frontier: A Fort Davis Case Study," *Journal of the West* 7 (April 1968): 231–32. I find no evidence in Alice Grierson's letters that she feared black soldiers.

Black soldiers of the Tenth received the name "buffalo soldiers" because their hair reminded the Cheyenne Indians of buffalo hair. Since the buffalo was sacred, the sobriquet was a mark of respect. They accepted the compliment proudly and even incorporated the buffalo into the regimental crest.

16. Army wives had two choices. They could leave their husbands at their posts for years and accompany their children back East. Or they could remain with their husbands and send their children away. Frances Boyd and Martha Summerhayes selected the first choice, and Ellen Biddle and Elizabeth Burt opted for the second. See Boyd, *Cavalry Life*, 292–93; Summerhayes, *Vanished Arizona*, 236; Biddle, *Reminiscences*, 139–41; Mattes, *Indians, Infants, and Infantry*, 256.

Army regulations of 1866 allowed schools on posts, but it was not until 1878 that regulations were revised to make schools mandatory beginning in 1881. Even then many posts remained without schools. See Stallard, *Glittering Misery*, 94, and Edward M. Coffman, *The Old Army: A Portrait of the American Army in Peacetime, 1784–1898* (New York: Oxford University Press, 1986), 323.

17. *Annual Report of the Commissioner of Indian Affairs for 1868*, 68–70.

18. Army regulations of 1861 specified one room for a lieutenant, two for a captain or chaplain, three for a lieutenant colonel, and four for a colonel, as well as a kitchen in each case. See War Department, *Revised United States Army Regulations of 1861* (Washington, D.C.: Government Printing Office, 1863), 159–60.

19. R. G. Carter, *On the Border with Mackenzie or Winning West Texas from the Comanches* (Washington, D.C.: Eynon, 1935), 257; Ben to Alice, 5 March 1869, ISHL.

20. Gillette Griswold, "Old Fort Sill: The First Seven Years," *Chronicles of Oklahoma* 36 (Spring 1958): 4; Wilbur S. Nye, *Carbine and Lance: The Story of Old Fort Sill* (Norman: University of Oklahoma Press, 1943), 89–93; War Department, *Circular No. 4*, 266. Grierson later received one thousand dollars from Congress to build a hospital.

21. Leckie and Leckie, *Unlikely Warriors*, 163.

The "humanitarian generals" were O. O. Howard, George Crook, John Pope, Ranald Mackenzie, Nelson Miles, and Benjamin Grierson. All demonstrated concern for the fate and well-being of the Indians they were forced to fight. See Richard Ellis, "The Humanitarian Generals," *Western Historical Quarterly* 3 (April 1972): 169–78.

22. Ben to Alice, 7 April 1869, MS 343A. See also Dinges, "Grierson," *Soldiers West*, 160–61, and Hutton, *Phil Sheridan*, 107–8.

23. The Griersons had hoped that Camp Wichita would be named for Major Joel Elliott, killed at the Battle of the Washita. Instead it was named for Brigadier General Joshua W. Sill, a close friend of Sheridan who had died at the Battle of Stone River, Tennessee, in December 1862; Ben to John Grierson, 23 July 1869, MS 343A.

24. Brian W. Dippie, *The Vanishing American: White Attitudes and U.S. Indian Policy* (Middletown, Connecticut: Wesleyan University Press, 1982), 144–46; Robert Utley, "The Celebrated Peace Policy of General Grant," *North Dakota History* 20 (July 1953): 121–42.

25. Leckie and Leckie, *Unlikely Warriors*, 172–73. R. G. Carter commented most favorably on the gracious hospitality the Griersons provided the Fourth Cavalry in 1871. Events included "breakfast, lunch, dinner, dancing and picnic parties—the latter to the Signal Station at Mt. Scott." *On the Border with Mackenzie*, 257.

26. Lawrie Tatum, *Our Red Brothers and the Peace Policy of President Ulysses S. Grant* (Lincoln: University of Nebraska Press, 1970), 24–31; Morrison, *Military Posts in Oklahoma*, 64.

27. Kiowa Files, Depredations, Indian Archives, Oklahoma State Historical Society, Oklahoma City, Oklahoma; Leckie and Leckie, *Unlikely Warriors*, 171–90.

28. Grierson, believing in accommodation and wishing to avoid a full-scale Indian war, had warned the Kiowas to move back onto the reservation in advance of Mackenzie's troops, an action that led Mackenzie to conclude that he had been "double cross[ed]" and that the Indians had escaped their just chastisement. Sheridan agreed with Mackenzie, and his animosity toward Grierson increased. Others, including the Commissioner of Indian Affairs and General John Pope, viewed Grierson's actions as wise and responsible. See Carter, *On the Border with Mackenzie*, 123–24, 129; Hutton, *Phil Sheridan and His Army*, 238–39; and Dinges, "Grierson," *Soldiers West*, 163.

29. War Department, *Circular No. 8, A Report of the Hygiene of the United States Army with Descriptions of Military Posts* (Washington, D.C.: Government Printing Office, 1875), 238.

30. William S. Soule became the official post photographer for Fort Sill in 1869 and retained that position for six years. His photographs are prominently displayed at the Fort Sill museum today.

31. Leckie and Leckie, *Unlikely Warriors*, 193–95; Stephen A. Forbes, *The Great Chicago Fire, October 8–10, 1871: Described by Eight Men and Women Who Experienced Its Horrors and Testified to the Courage of Its Inhabitants*, ed. Paul M. Angle (Chicago: Chicago Historical Society, 1971), 2–3. Stephen Forbes served under Grierson as a sergeant in the Seventh Illinois Cavalry during Grierson's 1863 raid through Mississippi. See Brown, *Grierson's Raid*, 20, 81.

32. [Susan] Ellen Kirk to Alice, 2 March 1870, TTU; Ben to Alice, 16 December 1871, ISHL.

33. By this time the *Revolution*, having passed into the hands of the *New York Christian Enquirer*, was being edited by Parker Pillsbury and Paulina Wright Davis. Its new masthead read: "What therefore God hath joined together let no man put asunder." Despite these changes, it still contained articles on "How to Get the Ballot" and "Men and Women Advocates." *The Revolution*, 12 October 1871. See also Elizabeth Griffith, *In Her Own Right: The Life of Elizabeth Cady Stanton* (New York: Oxford University Press, 1984), 131–33.

34. Theodore Tilton's "Victoria C. Woodhull: A Biographical Sketch" was the third publication in the *Golden Age Tract* series. For detailed information on Woodhull's appearance before the House Judiciary Committee on January 12, 1871, see *Woodhull & Claflin's*, 4 February 1871, 11 February 1871, and 18 February 1871. Her speech, which she stated was inspired by spirits, made a favorable impression upon the committee members. The majority, nonetheless, recommended tabling the Woodhull Memorial to Congress, and it died in committee. See also M. M. Marberry, *Vicky: A Biography of Victoria C. Woodhull* (New York: Funk & Wagnalls, 1967), 23.

35. Tilton, "Victoria C. Woodhull," 32.

36. Elizabeth Cady Stanton, "A Lecture to Ladies Only," *Woodhull & Claflin's*, 21 May 1870; Dr. R. T. Trail, "The Rights of Children," *Woodhull & Claflin's*, 6 May 1871. Trail argued that one of the most basic rights of children was the right to be wanted, adding: "The great majority of children are the offspring of chance. . . . Very frequently they are the most unwelcome guest that could be introduced into the family circle." For other articles on birth control, see *Woodhull & Claflin's*, 17 May 1871, 10 June 1871.

These arguments represented the beginning of the "voluntary motherhood" movement. In the mid-nineteenth century many women sought greater personal autonomy, and limiting the number of children they bore was an essential element in gaining more control over their lives. See Linda Gordon, "Voluntary Motherhood: The Beginnings of Feminist Birth Control Ideas in the United States," *Feminist Studies* 1 (1973): 5–22.

37. "Domestic feminism" sought greater power and autonomy for

women within marriage, especially in the all-important area of fertility. Influential writers such as Dr. William Acton and William Alcott aided this endeavor by arguing that the sexual needs of women were not as strong as those of men. By engaging in sexual relations, wives were, in effect, conferring favors on their husbands rather than fulfilling mutual desires. In this context men were exhorted to exercise more control over their own sexuality and to make fewer demands on their wives—resulting in fewer pregnancies. Thus what historians had earlier dismissed as Victorian prudery was oftentimes a growing assertion of female power. See Daniel Scott Smith, "Family Limitation, Sexual Control and Domestic Feminism in Victorian America," *Feminist Studies* 1 (1973): 40–57, and Degler, *At Odds*, 279–97.

38. Ben to Alice, 18 December 1871, ISHL.

39. With the exception of the anovulant pill, all the modern forms of contraception were available to Americans prior to the Civil War, but mechanical devices were expensive and to many "smacked of the brothel." Coitus interruptus was more readily accepted, largely because of Robert Dale Owen's *Moral Physiology; or, a Brief and Plain Treatise on the Population Question*, first published in 1831. This work, reprinted in numerous editions, sold well for decades. See Wilson Yates, "Birth Control Literature and the Medical Profession in Nineteenth-Century America," *Journal of the History of Medicine and Allied Sciences* 31 (January 1976): 42–54; Norman Himes, *Medical History of Contraception* (Baltimore: Williams & Wilkins, 1936), 440. One scholar notes that even on the frontier women were bearing fewer children. See Julie Roy Jeffrey, *Frontier Women: The Trans-Mississippi West, 1848–1890* (New York: Hill & Wang, 1979), 58.

40. Many nineteenth-century Americans, including feminists and radicals such as Woodhull and Claflin, were extremely fearful of the social consequences of contraception and counseled continence or periodic abstinence. See Gordon, "Voluntary Motherhood," 6–9; Tennie [Tennessee] C. Claflin, *The Ethics of Sexual Equality* (New York: Woodhull & Claflin, 1873), 27–31; James Reed, *From Private Vice to Public Virtue: The Birth Control Movement and American Society Since 1830* (New York: Basic Books, 1978), 22–23.

41. One historian estimates that by the middle of the nineteenth century there was one abortion for every five or six live births. James Mohr, *Abortion in America: The Origins and Evolution of National Policy* (New York: Oxford University Press, 1978), 5, 254.

42. Ben to Alice, [20] December 1871, ISHL.

43. Leckie and Leckie, *Unlikely Warriors*, 204–10.

2. Fort Concho: Life in "the Most God-Forsaken Part of Uncle Sam's Dominions"

1. This is the way Grierson interpreted his assignment. He believed that Sheridan had abused him as far back as the Civil War, largely to favor his "toadies" Wesley Merritt and George Armstrong Custer. Ben to Alice, 21 June 1875, TTU.

2. Bruce Dinges, "Scandals in the Tenth Cavalry: A Fort Sill Case History, 1874," *Arizona and the West* 28 (Summer 1986): 125–40.

3. John Grierson to Ben, 23 November 1874, TTU.

4. War Department, *Circular No. 4*, 200; Ben to Alice, 1 May 1875, 4 May 1875, 10 June 1875, ISHL; Medical History of Fort Concho, Records of the War Department, Adjutant General's Office, Record Group 94, National Archives and Records Service, Washington, D.C.

Fort Concho was established in 1867 as part of a line of posts extending from El Paso to the Red River to protect settlements and the mail route. It was located midway between the junction of the North and South Concho rivers and the present town of San Angelo. See Frazer, *Forts of the West*, 147.

Building the post was difficult since the only wood available was pecan, an extremely hard material. Other supplies had to be brought in by wagon from the military depot at San Antonio, 230 miles away, or from Fredericksburg, 160 miles away. J. Evetts Haley, *Fort Concho and the Texas Frontier* (San Angelo, Texas: *San Angelo Standard-Times*, 1952), 129–39.

5. Leckie and Leckie, *Unlikely Warriors*, 225–26; Ben to Charlie Grierson, 27 June 1875, TTU.

6. Leckie and Leckie, *Unlikely Warriors*, 230.

7. Olive McFarland to Robert Grierson, 24 September 1875, TGCHS.

8. By 1870 the preponderance of women to men in the 20–29-year-old age group in the Northeast and north-central region of the United States stood at 100 to 86. It would take a full generation of births after the Civil War, plus the replenishment brought about by the "new" immigration beginning in 1880, to redress these imbalances. Even then, many middle- and upper-class women would not find husbands, largely because their standards and expectations had risen along with their educational levels. U.S. Department of Commerce, Bureau of the Census, *Historical Statistics of the United States: Colonial Times to 1970*, 2 vols. (Washington, D.C.: Government Printing Office, 1975), 1:22; Degler, *At Odds*, 152.

9. Virginia Keyes, daughter of Lucien B. Maxwell, land baron of New Mexico, had eloped with Alexander Scammel Brooks Keyes, captain of the Tenth Cavalry, in 1870, much to her father's displeasure. The early years of her marriage were turbulent due to Keyes's fondness for alcohol and

his alleged affair with Lizzie Davidson, daughter of Lieutenant Colonel John Davidson. See Samuel Woodward to Colonel Grierson, 5 July 1874, 8 August 1874, ISHL.

10. Alice's comments that a college degree would not guarantee employment were accurate. By the mid-1870s business was still in the throes of a depression, opportunities were severely limited, and in this environment the college curriculum was viewed as irrelevant to the business world. Male enrollment was declining, and to counter this trend many institutions of higher learning began taking in larger numbers of female students. See Patricia A. Graham, "Expansion and Exclusion: A History of Women in Higher Education," *Signs* 3 (Summer 1978): 759–61, 766.

11. John E. Parsons, *The Peacemaker and Its Rivals: An Account of the Single Action Colt* (New York: William Morrow, 1950), 35.

12. Congress mistreated the army, reducing its pay after the Civil War to prewar levels despite the increase in the cost of living. In 1870 pay scales ranged from fourteen hundred dollars for a second lieutenant to thirty-five hundred dollars for a colonel, low amounts compared to civilian salaries for equivalent positions and responsibilities. Moreover, military life was more expensive than civilian because of the costs connected with continual moving and the higher prices on the frontier.

The matter of promotion was even more frustrating. An officer moved up in the ranks in his own regiment but only when a vacancy occurred through death or retirement. See Utley, *Frontier Regulars*, 20–22. Such a system proved especially irritating for wives. Martha Summerhayes noted that her husband served eleven years as a second lieutenant and another eleven as a first lieutenant (*Vanished Arizona*, 236–37). Even Elizabeth Custer, who generally enjoyed military life, expressed frustration in *Following the Guidon*, 282–86.

13. Several officers' wives commented on the important role the army played in protecting the railroad and the free or cut-rate tickets their families received so gratefully. See, for example, Biddle, *Reminiscences*, 91; Mary M. Carr, "Fort McPherson in 1870: A Note by an Army Wife," ed. James L. King, *Nebraska History* 45 (March 1964): 106.

14. Dinges, "Scandal in the Tenth Cavalry," 139–40.

15. Both Sherman and Sheridan recognized that destruction of the buffalo was the most effective means of defeating the Plains Indians, for it demolished the supply of food and materials on which they depended. Along with the incursion of the railroads into the Indian hunting grounds, the disappearance of the buffalo doomed the Indian way of life. By 1878 the buffalo had vanished from the southern plains, and five years later they were gone from the northern plains as well. See Philip H. Sheridan, *Personal Memoirs*, 2 vols. (New York: Webster, 1888), 2:297; Richard Bartlett,

The New Country: A Social History of the American Frontier, 1776–1890
(New York: Oxford University Press, 1974), 33–35.

16. The year 1877 represented the depth of the depression. After four years of hard times as many as five million people, or 15 percent of the labor force, were unemployed, according to Philip Foner, *The Great Labor Uprising of 1877* (New York: Monad Press, 1977), 24. The number of homeless increased markedly, and many of them were "white, literate and 'quite young.'" See Robert Bruce, *1877: Year of Violence* (Chicago: Quadrangle Books, 1970), 22–24.

17. Bringing young (and not so young) women servants to frontier posts was usually a futile exercise, as many of the army officers' wives noted. Within a matter of weeks even the homeliest received proposals. See Fougera, *With Custer's Cavalry*, 96. Lydia Lane's cook, "Old" Martha, "ugly as she was, was nonetheless soon proposed to by a stonemason" at Fort Union in New Mexico Territory. Lane, *I Married a Soldier*, 154–55.

18. The frontier army was a world unto itself. George A. Forsyth noted that "social intercourse, on account of the isolation and peculiar experiences, was without formality; companionship begat friendship and affection." *The Story of a Soldier* (New York: Appleton, 1900), 109. Frances Roe wrote of her pleasure in returning to a Montana post after a furlough. "The winter East was enjoyable and refreshing from first to last, but citizens and army people have so little in common, and this one feels after being with them a while, no matter how near and dear the relationship may be." See Roe, *Army Letters*, 333.

19. Congress had failed to pass an appropriation bill for the army when it adjourned on March 4, 1877, and no funds were allocated until Rutherford B. Hayes called Congress into special session in the fall. A bill was finally passed after heated debate on November 21. In the meantime most officers were forced to borrow money to tide themselves and their families over, and this recourse simply added the cost of interest to their other high living expenses. Sidney E. Whitman provides insights into this episode in *The Troopers: An Informal History of the Plains Cavalry, 1865–1890* (New York: Hastings House, 1962), 111–17. See also Utley, *Frontier Regulars*, 58–68.

20. Susan Bingham Kirk to Alice, 20 November 1853, TTU.

21. Physicians of the era often attributed mental illness in young people to overtaxing of the mind, which allegedly caused the entire nervous system to break down. Thus Colonel Grierson was voicing a common opinion when he attributed Charlie's illness to too much study. See Barbara Sicherman, *The Quest for Mental Health in America, 1880–1917* (New York: Arno Press, 1980), 155.

22. For the nicknames of officers of the Tenth Cavalry, see Fanny

Corbusier, *Verde to San Carlos: Recollections of a Famous Army Surgeon and His Observant Family on the Western Frontier, 1869–1886* (Tucson: Dale Stuart King, 1968), 218.

23. The railroad strikes were sparked by successive wage cuts during a time of depression. The major lines moving westward from West Virginia across Maryland, Pennsylvania, Ohio, Indiana, Illinois, and Missouri stopped shortly thereafter, not to reopen on a regular basis until mid-August, when the strikes were broken. As Ben predicted, federal troops were eventually placed at the disposal of governors in the states affected —namely, units from his own Division of the Missouri, as well as from the Division of the Atlantic. Paul Hutton provides an excellent overview of the role of the army in breaking the strikes. See *Phil Sheridan and His Army*, 169–77.

24. Susan Miles, "Fort Concho in 1877," *West Texas Historical Association Year Book* 35 (October 1959): 29–31; a full account of the Lost Expedition on the United Plains is given in Leckie, *Buffalo Soldiers*, 155–63. See also Curtis W. Nunn, "Eighty-six Hours Without Water on the Texas Plains," *Southwestern Historical Quarterly* 43 (January 1940): 356–64.

25. It was believed that nature had healing powers and, moreover, that directing energy into physical activities could alleviate mental strain. Thus hard physical labor in the out-of-doors was expected to restore health. See Joseph F. Kett, "Curing the Disease of Precocity," in *Turning Points: Historical and Sociological Essays on the Family*, ed. John Demos and Savanne Boocok, *Journal of Sociology* 84, Supplement, 1978 (Chicago: University of Chicago Press, 1978), s183–s211.

26. Leckie and Leckie, *Unlikely Warriors*, 250–51.

27. John Billings, assistant surgeon of the United States Army, wrote in 1870: "Fort Davis by reason of its delightful climate, its healthfulness and comfortable quarters, is one of the most desirable posts on the Texas frontier and its surrounding country may be called grand and picturesque." See War Department, *Circular No. 4*, 230.

Established in 1854 as an important communication link along the El Paso–San Antonio Road and as a critical point for overseeing the activities of Comanches and Apaches, the Fort was named for Jefferson Davis, then secretary of war. During the Civil War, Confederate troops occupied the post, but in 1867 the Ninth Cavalry moved in and rebuilt the fort, then in disrepair. See Frazer, *Forts of the West*, 148.

28. Typhoid fever is spread by contaminated water. John Billings noted in 1870 that the Main Concho "became so impregnated with putrefying animal matter as to be offensive both to taste and smell." Another source of water came from a spring at a bend above the Main Concho River close to the mail station. There troopers built a circular wall to contain the seepage, but since cattle and buffalo died in the river "the slightest rise

overflowed the spring and polluted the water." Nonetheless, this was the main source of drinking water for the post until cisterns were completed and tapped ground-level water by means of a steam-driven pump in 1879. See War Department, *Circular No. 4*, 201; Haley, *Fort Concho and the Texas Frontier*, 323–24.

29. Susan Miles, "Edith Clare Grierson, 1865–1878," *Fort Concho Report* 10 (Winter 1978): 6–7; Alice to Ben, 13 October 1878, TTU.

30. Transcript of the William H. Beck Trial, Records of the War Department, Office of the Judge Advocate General (Army), General Courts-Martial, 1812–1938, Record Group 153, National Archives and Records Service, Washington, D.C.

31. Transcript of the Thomas Little Trial, Records of the War Department, OJAG (Army), General Courts-Martial, 1812–1938, RG 153, National Archives and Records Service, Washington, D.C.; General Court-Martial Orders No. 81, Headquarters of the Army, 5 December 1877, Adjutant General's Office, RG 94, National Archives and Records Service, Washington, D.C.

32. Colonel Grierson found this court-martial duty particularly onerous. Stanley charged Hazen with cowardice during the Civil War, and Hazen accused Stanley of libel. The result was a double court-martial beginning in April 1879 in which Stanley was found guilty of "conduct unbecoming an officer and gentleman."

Such filings of charges and countercharges were only too common in this period and absorbed a great deal of the time and energy of commanding officers. Many of the accusations stemmed from the frustration brought on by the lack of promotion opportunities and the relatively low army pay. See Ben to Alice, 27 April 1879, 28 April 1879, TTU; Marvin E. Kroeker, "William B. Hazen," *Soldiers West*, 205; Utley, *Frontier Regulars*, 21.

33. Alice to Ben, 20 May 1879, TTU, 21 August 1879, ISHL.

34. General Court-Martial Orders No. 34, Headquarters of the Army, 30 May 1879, AGO, RG 94, National Archives and Records Service, Washington, D.C.

35. General Court-Martial Orders No. 61, Headquarters of the Army, 18 November 1879, AGO, RG 94, National Archives and Records Service, Washington, D.C.

36. Leckie and Leckie, *Unlikely Warriors*, 256. The army had given priority to educating black enlisted men since 1866, for most, having formerly been slaves, were illiterate. Regulations specified that chaplains were responsible for conducting literacy classes in black units. The needs of children at frontier posts remained secondary, although the regulations of 1866 did state that post schools could be established.

In 1878 Alexander McD. McCook was appointed army supervisor of education, and his unflagging efforts brought renewed interest and additional appropriations for post schools, which now became mandatory for the children of enlisted men and of the commanding officer. Attendance was optional for the children of junior officers, since compelling their attendance would break down the army caste system. It was assumed, however, that officers could afford to make other arrangements.

Mandating post schools was not the same as creating them, and by 1882 a survey under McCook's successor, George G. Mullins, revealed that 32 out of 137 posts were still without schools. And even where schools existed, the quality of education was questionable since teachers, drawn from the enlisted men, were paid the paltry sum of 35 cents per day. See War Department, *Regulations of the Army of the United States and the General Orders in Force on the 17th of February, 1881* (Washington, D.C.: Government Printing Office, 1881), 56–58; Coffman, *Old Army*, 323–27.

37. The United States government had removed these Mimbres Apaches from their Warm Springs home in New Mexico with the intent of forcing them onto the San Carlos Reservation in Arizona. In desperation the Indians turned themselves over to authorities at the Mescalero Reservation in New Mexico. However, they remained wary and insecure and finally, under the leadership of the chief Victorio, broke out in pursuit of freedom. Before long they were terrorizing the border area between northern Mexico and southwestern United States. See Dan L. Thrapp, *Victorio and the Mimbres Apaches* (Norman: University of Oklahoma Press, 1974), 181–200.

38. Leckie and Leckie, *Unlikely Warriors*, 258–61.

39. Ibid., 260–65.

40. Ibid., 266–67; Thrapp, *Victorio and the Mimbres Apaches*, 293–307.

41. The Whittaker case still appears bizarre today. It seems almost incomprehensible that anyone could injure himself that severely and still have the strength to tie himself to a bedpost.

Whittaker, who came from South Carolina, entered West Point in 1876, one year before Lieutenant Henry Flipper (the first black graduate of West Point) graduated. By 1879 he had been found deficient in his courses and a board recommended his dismissal. At General Schofield's suggestion, he was held back one year. In 1880, however, following his injuries, Whittaker failed his final examinations. General Schofield now concluded that blacks were incapable of competing with white students, and no more were admitted to West Point for many years. See Robert Ewell Greene, *Black Defenders of America, 1775–1973* (Chicago: Johnson, 1974), 120–21.

42. Leckie and Leckie, *Unlikely Warriors*, 269.

43. Ibid., 274; Robert to Alice, 8 October 1881, 19 November 1881, 21 December 1881, 27 December 1881, TTU. Twenty-six years earlier William Fitch had been married to Alice's sister, Mary, who died the following year.

44. The Kirk family showed a genetic predisposition to manic depressive psychosis. One of Alice's cousins, John Manning of Youngstown, required hospitalization in his youth. Both Alice's brother Henry and her sister Maria were committed to the asylum in Columbus, Ohio, at various times during their adolescence. Maria died of typhoid fever at seventeen, but Henry remained susceptible to debilitating depression all his life, as family correspondence indicated.

Grierson family members displayed emotional disturbances generally of a depressive nature without alternating periods of mania. Ben's deceased sister Mary, who died in 1861 at age thirty-six, was described as often "greatly depressed in spirit" for no apparent reason. Louisa Semple and John Grierson both periodically battled despondency. In their cases, however, there were usually ample financial and emotional reasons for feeling low. See Leckie and Leckie, *Unlikely Warriors*, 6, 9, 22, 168, 212, 302.

45. Alice's father encouraged her in this practice. In 1855, when Ben Grierson requested a loan from his father-in-law to purchase a partnership in John Walihan's country store in Meredosia, Illinois, John Kirk advanced him five hundred dollars, provided the 6 percent interest was paid Alice "to be used as she wishes." John Kirk to Ben and Alice, 31 December 1855, ISHL. See also Leckie and Leckie, *Unlikely Warriors*, 32–33.

46. Leckie and Leckie, *Unlikely Warriors*, 279–80.

3. The Final Years

1. Finding and keeping domestic help remained a problem for army wives. An 1870 law forbade the employment of off-duty soldiers, but the practice continued nonetheless. Increasingly, army wives turned to a new ethnic group, the Chinese, who won high praise for their energy and efficiency. The cultural gap between the army wife and her Chinese servant, however, often created misunderstanding and tension. See Roe, *Army Letters*, 184; Summerhayes, *Vanished Arizona*, 224, 231; and Boyd, *Cavalry Life*, 91–92.

2. Robert, like Charlie, owed his position to his father's influence. Such cases of nepotism were commonplace in the post–Civil War army and included Custer, who obtained commissions for his brother, Thomas, and his brother-in-law, James Calhoun, and Wesley Merritt, who managed to bring his younger brother into the Ninth Cavalry despite his inability to pass the qualifying examination. Sheridan himself saw that his younger brother, Michael, was kept permanently employed as a member of his staff until Michael's death.

3. Sally Johnson Ketcham, "Commanding Officer's Quarters, Fort Davis, Texas, Furnishing Plan." Typescript Manuscript, May 1974.

FDNHS. In all probability the new furniture was made in the Eastlake style, popular in the early 1880s.

4. Dinges, "Colonel Grierson Invests on the West Texas Frontier," 6–8.

5. Ibid., 9.

6. See James S. Brisbin, *The Beef Bonanza; or, How to Get Rich on the Plains, Being a Description of Cattle-Grazing, Sheep Farming, Horse-Raising and Dairying in the West* (Philadelphia: Lippincott, 1881), 24–25, 45–58; Edward Everett Dale, *The Range Cattle Industry: Ranching on the Great Plains from 1865 to 1925* (Norman: University of Oklahoma Press, 1960), 111.

7. John Grierson to Ben, 17 January 1883, TTU; Alice to Charlie, 29 July 1883, ISHL.

8. Dinges, "Colonel Grierson Invests on the West Texas Frontier," 9.

9. Leckie and Leckie, *Unlikely Warriors*, 285–86; Ellen Kirk Fuller to Alice, 26 September 1883, 31 December 1883, 31 January 1885, TTU.

10. Manuscript in possession of Dorothy Buell Dobbs. Typed copy on file at FDNHS.

11. Leckie and Leckie, *Unlikely Warriors*, 287. See also Martin F. Schmitt, ed., *General George Crook: His Autobiography* (Norman: University of Oklahoma Press, 1986), 253–60.

12. Dinges, "Colonel Grierson Invests on the West Texas Frontier," 9–10.

13. Bruce J. Dinges, "The Court-Martial of Lieutenant Henry O. Flipper: An Example of Black-White Relationships in the Army, 1881," *American West* 9 (January 1972): 12–17, 59–61; Leckie and Leckie, *Unlikely Warriors*, 274–75, 280.

14. Dinges, "Colonel Grierson Invests on the West Texas Frontier," 10–11.

15. Prescott was different from most mining towns. John Bourke, army officer turned ethnologist, recalled that in the 1880s "it was a village transplanted bodily from the center of the Delaware, the Mohawk, or the Connecticut Valley," and substantial and traditional homes dominated this territorial capital. *On the Border with Crook* (New York: Scribner's, 1891), 158. Ellen Biddle, army wife, was also favorably impressed with the "small but well built" Prescott when she arrived at Fort Whipple in 1876 and noted the many improvements inaugurated in the five years that she remained at the post. Biddle, *Reminiscences*, 162.

The post itself was established in 1863 twenty-four miles north of Prescott to protect the newly opened mines in the area. A year later it was moved to the left bank of Granite Creek, a mile northeast of Prescott, and named Camp Whipple in honor of Major General Amiel W. Whipple, killed at Chancellorsville. It became known as Whipple Barracks in 1879 and remained a key post in Arizona Territory until the turn of the century. Frazer, *Forts of the West*, 14–15; War Department, *Circular No. 4*, 457–58.

16. Whitman, *Troopers*, 50–51.

17. The three men appointed brigadiers in 1885 were N. H. Davis, John Gibbon, and Absalom Baird. Heitman, *Historical Register*, 1:27.

18. Utley, *Frontier Regulars*, 385–86.

19. Duty in Arizona was considered highly undesirable, but both Fanny Corbusier, a surgeon's wife, and Nannie [Hannah] Mills, wife of Major Anson Mills, wrote of the beauty of the Fort Grant area. They noted the tall pines, the heavy scent of balsam in the air, and the numerous meadows of wildflowers that awaited them as they climbed Mount Graham two miles away from the post. See Corbusier, *Verde to San Carlos*, 203–4, and Nannie Mills's letters in Anson Mills, *My Story* (Washington, D.C.: By the author, 1918), 194–95.

Fort Grant was established as Camp Grant in 1873 to replace an older, unhealthy camp sixty miles northwest. The new site in the Sierra Bonita (part of the Pinaleño range) served as a vantage point for controlling the Apache Indians and defending area settlers. It was abandoned as a military post in 1905. See Frazer, *Forts of the West*, 9.

20. Utley, *Frontier Regulars*, 387–96. Miles introduced the heliograph for transmitting messages, a device the British had used with success in India.

21. Alice to Ben, 16 November 1886, TTU.

22. Dale, *Range Cattle Industry*, 93–94.

23. War Department, Circular No. 4, 255–58; Paul Horgan, Introduction to *Santa Fe: The Autobiography of a Southwestern Town*, by Oliver La Farge with Arthur N. Morgan (Norman: University of Oklahoma Press, 1951), viii–ix.

24. Solomon Spiegelberg, the first Jewish settler to arrive in Santa Fe (in 1846), established a flourishing merchandising business. Other Jewish families followed and made a substantial contribution to the cultural activities in this old city. La Farge, *Santa Fe*, 334–35.

25. The penitentiary, described in the following letter, opened on August 7, 1885, and was hailed as "a magnificent structure" that demonstrated the territory's enlightened method of dealing with criminals. La Farge, *Santa Fe*, 124–25.

Edmund Ross, former senator from Kansas, became governor of New Mexico in 1885 and served until 1889. His tenure in office was marred by ongoing quarrels with the legislature, which he accused of corruption. See R. E. Twitchell, *The Leading Facts of New Mexican History*, 2 vols. (Cedar Rapids: Torch Press, 1911), 2:496–50.

Thomas B. Catron arrived in New Mexico in 1866 and began practicing law. By exploiting the confusion arising out of Spanish and Mexican land grants, he established himself as an expert on land disputes and became one of the largest landowners in the territory. A staunch Republican, he was "virtually a dictator of his party," according to Warren A. Beck. See *New Mexico: A History of Four Centuries* (Norman: University of Oklahoma Press, 1962), 300–301.

26. Leckie and Leckie, *Unlikely Warriors*, 293.

27. Gertrude Fuller to Alice, 22 November 1883; Ellen Fuller to Alice, 31 December 1883; Ben to Alice, 13 October 1884; Harvey B. Fuller, Jr., to Alice, 21 September 1885, TTU.

28. This was a common perception, but by the turn of the century, as Robert Utley notes, "the army's top leadership was heavy with generals who owed their regular army commission to Civil War volunteer service." Among them were Adna R. Chaffee, Henry W. Lawton, Nelson A. Miles, and William R. Shafter. *Frontier Regulars*, 18.

29. Neither gold nor silver mining proved very profitable in New Mexico. Because of the territory's geology, gold veins led not to a mother lode but instead to solid rock barriers. As for placer mining, the scarcity of water and the cost of machinery made it impractical. See Beck, *New Mexico*, 245–60.

30. General John Schofield stated in 1887: "Nothing else does so much to dampen military ardor as the sense of hopeless justice in respect to promotion." Utley, *Frontier Regulars*, 20. Utley notes that Schofield and others pushed for reform and that finally, in 1890, Congress passed legislation mandating promotion by seniority in arms rather than seniority in regiment.

31. Mills, *My Story*, 186; Douglas C. McChristian, *Garrison Tangles in the Friendless Tenth* (Bryan, Texas: Carroll, 1985), 26–27.

32. Many of the Kirks suffered from arthritis as they grew older, especially Alice's father, who constantly complained of a lame leg. Thus Alice dismissed her sore leg as an inherited condition. In the 1880s she suffered two minor injuries to her legs and concluded that these had aggravated her "arthritis," bringing on "sciatica." She consulted several physicians, but given the state of medical science, one diagnosed her as having a "broken bone in her leg" along with a developing tumor. A specialist was of the opinion that the condition would heal itself. It is impossible to state with certainty what her condition was, but it seems likely that she suffered from bone cancer. See Leckie and Leckie, *Unlikely Warriors*, 294–98.

33. Leckie and Leckie, *Unlikely Warriors*, 298–300; Benjamin H. Grierson, "The Lights and Shadows of Life, Including Experiences and Rememberances of the War of the Rebellion" (1892), ISHL.

34. Robert to Charlie, 17 August 1888, TTU.

35. Charles Grierson to Daisy Grierson, 10 April 1927, 14 April 1927, 6 May 1927, TTU.

36. Dinges, "Colonel Grierson Invests on the West Texas Frontier," 11.

37. Leckie and Leckie, *Unlikely Warriors*, 298–300.

Bibliography

I. Manuscript Materials

Fort Davis National Historic Site, Fort Davis, Texas
Grierson, Benjamin H. Miscellaneous Files.
Ketchum, Sally J. "Commanding Officer's Quarters Fort Davis, Texas, Furnishing Plan." Typescript, May 1974.
Illinois State Historical Library, Springfield, Illinois
Benjamin H. Grierson Papers.
Grierson, Benjamin H., Brigadier General. "The Lights and Shadows of Life, Including Experiences and Rememberances of the War of the Rebellion." 1892. Typescript.
National Archives and Records Service, Washington, D.C.
Courts-martial. Records of the Office of the Judge Advocate General (Army). Record Group 153.
Records of the War Department, Adjutant General's Office. Record Group 94.
Oklahoma Historical Society, Oklahoma City, Oklahoma
Indian Archives Division, Kiowa Files, Depredations.
Texas Technological University, Lubbock, Texas, Southwest Collection
Benjamin H. Grierson Papers, 1827–1941.
Grierson, Benjamin. Letters and Documents. Microcopy of MS 343A from Edward Ayer Collection, Newberry Library, Chicago, Illinois. Two rolls.

BIBLIOGRAPHY

Tom Green County Historical Society, San Angelo, Texas
Papers of Benjamin and Alice Grierson (on extended loan to Fort Concho Museum, San Angelo, Texas).

II. Government Publications

Annual Report of the Commissioner of Indian Affairs for 1868.
Heitman, Francis E. *Historical Register and Dictionary of the United States Army*, 2 vols. Washington, D.C.: Government Printing Office, 1899.
U.S. Department of Commerce. *Historical Statistics of the United States: Colonial Times to 1890.* 2 vols. Washington, D.C.: Government Printing Office, 1975.
U.S. War Department. Quartermaster General's Office. *Outline Description of U.S. Military Posts and Stations of the Year 1871.* Washington, D.C.: Government Printing Office, 1872.
————. *Regulations of the Army of the United States and General Orders in Force on the 17th of February, 1881.* Washington, D.C.: Government Printing Office, 1881.
————. *Revised United States Army Regulations of 1861.* With an Appendix Containing the Changes and Laws Affecting Army Regulations and Articles of War to June 25, 1863. Washington, D.C.: Government Printing Office, 1863.
————. Surgeon General's Office. *Circular No. 4: A Report on Barracks and Hospitals with Descriptions of Military Posts.* Washington, D.C.: Government Printing Office, 1870.
————. *Circular No. 8: A Report of the Hygiene of the United States Army with Descriptions of Military Posts.* Washington, D.C.: Government Printing Office, 1875.

III. Articles

Bigelow, John, Jr. "Tenth Regiment of Cavalry." In *The Army of the United States*, edited by Theodore F. Rodenbough and William L. Haskins, pp. 288–300. New York: Argonaut Press, 1966.
Blackburn, Forrest R. "Army Families in Frontier Forts." *Military Review* 49 (October 1969): 17–28.
Brackett, A. G. "Our Cavalry on the Frontier." *Army and Navy Journal* 20 (10 November 1883): 283–84.
Butler, Anne M. "Military Myopia: Prostitution on the Frontier." *Prologue* 13 (Winter 1981): 233–50.
Carr, Mary M. "Fort McPherson in 1870: A Note by an Army Wife." Edited by James L. King. *Nebraska History* 45 (March 1964): 99–107.
Degler, Carl N. "What Ought To Be and What Was: Women's Sexuality

in the Nineteenth Century." *American Historical Review* 79 (December 1974): 1467–90.

Dinges, Bruce J. "Colonel Grierson Invests on the West Texas Frontier." *Fort Concho Report* 16 (Fall 1984): 2–14.

———. "The Court-Martial of Lieutenant Henry O. Flipper: An Example of Black-White Relationships in the Army, 1881." *American West* 9 (January 1972): 12–17, 59–61.

———. "Scandal in the Tenth Cavalry: A Fort Sill Case History, 1874." *Arizona and the West* 28 (Summer 1986): 125–40.

Ellis, Richard. "The Humanitarian Generals." *Western Historical Quarterly* 3 (April 1972): 169–78.

Foner, Jack. "The Socializing Role of the Military." In *The American Military on the Frontier: Proceedings of the 7th Military History Symposium, United States Air Force Academy*, edited by James P. Tate, pp. 85–100. Washington, D.C.: Office of Air Force History, Headquarters, USAF and United States Air Force Academy, 1978.

Foreman, Carolyn Thomas. "General Benjamin Henry Grierson." *Chronicles of Oklahoma* 24 (Summer 1946): 195–217.

Gordon, Linda. "Voluntary Motherhood: The Beginnings of Feminist Birth Control Ideas in the United States." *Feminist Studies* 1 (1973): 5–22.

Graham, Patricia A. "Expansion and Exclusion: A History of Women in Higher Education." *Signs* 3 (Summer 1978): 759–73.

Griswold, Gillett. "Old Fort Sill: The First Seven Years." *Chronicles of Oklahoma* 36 (Spring 1958): 2–14.

Jensen, Joan M., and Miller, Darlis A. "The Gentle Tamers Revisited: New Approaches to the History of Women in the American West." *Pacific Historical Review* 49 (May 1980): 172–212.

Kett, Joseph F. "Curing the Disease of Precocity." In *Turning Points: Historical and Sociological Essays on the Family*, edited by John Demos and Savanne Boocok. *Journal of Sociology* 84, Supplement, 1978, s183–s211. Chicago: University of Chicago Press, 1978.

King, Charles. "Customs of the Service." *Army and Navy Journal*, 5 May 1883, 914.

Leonard, Thomas C. "Red, White and the Army Blue: Empathy and Anger on the American West." *American Quarterly* 26 (May 1973): 176–90.

Miles, Susan. "Edith Clare Grierson, 1865–1878." *Fort Concho Report* 10 (Winter 1978): 4–8.

———. "Fort Concho in 1877." *West Texas Historical Association Yearbook* 35 (October 1969): 47–57.

———. "Mrs. Buell's Journal, 1877." *Edwards Plateau Historian* 2 (1966): 33–43.

Millbrook, Minnie D., ed. "Mrs. General Custer at Fort Riley, 1866." *Kansas Historical Quarterly* 40 (Spring 1974): 63–71.

Miller, Darlis A. "Foragers, Army Women and Prostitutes." In *New Mexico Women: Intercultural Perspectives*, edited by M. Joan Jenson and Darlis A. Miller, pp. 141–68. Albuquerque: University of New Mexico Press, 1986.

Myres, Sandra L., ed. "Evy Alexander: The Colonel's Lady at McDowell." *Montana: The Magazine of Western History* (Summer 1974): 26–38.

———. "Romance and Reality on the American Frontiers: Views of Army Wives." *Western Historical Quarterly* 86 (July 1982): 49–80.

———. "A Woman's View of the Texas Frontier, 1874: The Diary of Emily K. Andrews." *Southwestern Historical Quarterly* 86 (July 1982): 49–80.

Nunn, Curtis W. "Eighty-Six Hours Without Water on the Texas Plains." *Southwestern Historical Quarterly* 43 (January 1940): 356–64.

Olmsted, Frederic Law. "Chicago in Distress." *Nation*, 9 November 1871, 302–5.

Rosenberg, Charles. "Sexuality, Class and Role in Nineteenth Century America." *American Quarterly* 25 (May 1973): 131–53.

Sheffy, L. F., ed. "Letters and Reminiscences of General Theodore A. Baldwin." *Panhandle-Plains Historical Review* (1938): 7–30.

Shields, Alice Mathews. "Army Life on the Wyoming Frontier." *Annals of Wyoming* 13 (October 1941): 331–43.

Sibbald, John R. "Camp Followers All." *American West* 3 (Spring 1966): 56–67.

Smith, Daniel Scott. "Family Limitation, Sexual Control and Domestic Feminism in Victorian America." *Feminist Studies* 1 (August 1973): 40–57.

Stage, Sarah H. "Out of the Attic: Studies of Victorian Sexuality." *American Quarterly* 27 (October 1975): 480–85.

Stewart, Miller J. "Army Laundresses: Ladies of the 'Soap Suds Row.'" *Nebraska History* 61 (Winter 1980): 421–36.

Temple, Frank M. "Discipline and Turmoil in the Tenth U.S. Cavalry." *West Texas Historical Association Yearbook* 43 (1982): 103–18.

Thompson, Erwin N. "The Negro Soldiers on the Frontier: A Fort Davis Case Study." *Journal of the West* 7 (April 1968): 217–35.

Tilton, Theodore. "Victoria C. Woodhull: A Biographical Sketch." *Golden Age Tract* No. 3, 1871.

Utley, Robert M. "Arizona Vanquished: Impressions and Reflections Concerning the Quality of Life on a Military Frontier." *American West* 6 (November 1969): 16–21.

———. "The Celebrated Peace Policy of General Grant." *North Dakota History* 20 (July 1953): 121–42.

Utley, Robert M., ed. "Campaigning with Custer: Letters and Diaries Sketch Life in Camps and Field During the Indian Wars." *American West* 14 (July/August 1977): 4–9, 58–60.

Welter, Barbara. "The Cult of True Womanhood: 1820–1860." *American Quarterly* 18 (Summer 1966): 151–74.

Yates, Wilson. "Birth Control Literature and the Medical Profession in Nineteenth-Century America." *Journal of the History of Medicine and Allied Sciences* 31 (January 1976): 42–54.

IV. Books

Agnew, Brad. *Fort Gibson: Terminal on the Trail of Tears*. Norman: University of Oklahoma Press, 1980.

Ahlstrom, Sydney. *A Religious History of the American People*. New Haven: Yale University Press, 1972.

Armes, George A. *Ups and Downs of an Army Officer*. Washington, D.C.: 1900.

Ashburn, Percy Morean. *A History of the Medical Department of the United States Army*. Boston: Houghton Mifflin, 1929.

Athearn, Robert G. *William Tecumseh Sherman and the Settlement of the West*. Norman: University of Oklahoma Press, 1956.

Bartlett, Richard A. *The New Country: A Social History of the American Frontier, 1776–1890*. New York: Oxford University Press, 1974.

Beck, Warren A. *New Mexico: A History of Four Centuries*. Norman: University of Oklahoma Press, 1962.

Biddle, Ellen McGowan. *Reminiscences of a Soldier's Wife*. Philadelphia: Lippincott, 1907.

Bourke, John. *On the Border with Crook*. New York: Scribner's, 1891.

Boyd, Mrs. Oresmus Bronson (Frances). *Cavalry Life in Tent and Field*. New York: Tait, 1894. Reprint, with introduction by Darlis A. Miller. Lincoln: University of Nebraska Press, 1982.

Brisbin, James S. *The Beef Bonanza: or, How to Get Rich on the Plains. Being a Description of Cattle-Growing, Sheep-Farming, Horse-Raising and Dairying in the West*. Philadelphia: Lippincott, 1881.

Brown, D. Alexander. *The Gentle Tamers: Women of the Old Wild West*. New York: Putnam, 1958.

———. *Grierson's Raid*. Urbana: University of Illinois Press, 1962.

Bruce, Robert V. *1877: Year of Violence*. Indianapolis: Bobbs-Merrill, 1959; Chicago: Quadrangle Books, 1970.

Carriker, Robert C., and Carriker, Eleanor R., eds. *An Army Wife on the Frontier: The Memoirs of Alice Blackwood Baldwin, 1867–1877*. Salt Lake City: Tanner Trust Fund, University of Utah Library, 1975.

Carrington, Frances C. *My Army Life and the Fort Phil-Kearney Massacre*, *with an Account of the Celebration of "Wyoming Opened."* Philadelphia: Lippincott, 1910.

Carrington, Margaret I. *Ab-sa-ra-ka, Home of the Crows: Being the Experiences of an Officer's Wife on the Plains.* Philadelphia: Lippincott, 1868.

Carter, R. G. *On the Border with Mackenzie or Winning West Texas from the Comanches.* Washington, D.C.: Eynon, 1935.

Claflin, Tennie [Tennessee] C. *The Ethics of Sexual Equality. A Lecture Delivered by Tennie C. Claflin, at the Academy of Music, New York, March 29, 1872.* New York: Woodhull & Claflin, 1873.

Coffman, Edward M. *The Old Army: A Portrait of the American Army in Peacetime, 1784–1898.* New York: Oxford University Press, 1986.

Corbusier, Fanny. *Verde to San Carlos: Recollections of a Famous Army Surgeon and His Observant Family on the Western Frontier, 1869–1886.* Tucson: Dale Stuart King, 1968.

Cott, Nancy F. *The Bonds of Womanhood: "Woman's Sphere" in New England, 1780–1835.* New Haven: Yale University Press, 1977.

Custer, Elizabeth Bacon. *"Boots and Saddles"; or, Life in Dakota with General Custer.* New York: Harper & Bros., 1885.

———. *Following the Guidon.* New York: Harper & Bros., 1890.

———. *Tenting on the Plains; or, General Custer in Kansas and Texas.* New York: Webster, 1887.

Dain, Norman. *Concepts of Insanity in the United States, 1789–1865.* New Brunswick: Rutgers University Press, 1964.

Dale, Edward Everett. *The Range Cattle Industry: Ranching on the Great Plains from 1865 to 1925.* Norman: University of Oklahoma Press, 1960.

Debo, Angie. *A History of the Indians of the United States.* Norman: University of Oklahoma Press, 1970.

Degler, Carl N. *At Odds: Women and the Family in America, From the Revolution to the Present.* Oxford: Oxford University Press, 1980.

Deutsch, Albert. *The Mentally Ill in America: A History of Their Care and Treatment from Colonial Times.* 2d ed. New York: Columbia University Press, 1949.

Dippie, Brian. *The Vanishing American: White Attitudes and U.S. Indian Policy.* Middletown, Connecticut: Wesleyan University Press, 1982.

Foner, Jack D. *The United States Soldier Between Two Wars: Army Life and Reforms, 1865–1898.* New York: Humanities Press, 1970.

Foner, Philip S. *The Great Labor Uprising of 1877.* New York: Monad Press, 1977.

Forbes, Stephen A. *The Great Chicago Fire, October 8–10, 1871: Described by Eight Men and Women Who Experienced Its Horrors and Testified to the Courage of Its Inhabitants.* Edited by Paul M. Angle. Chicago: Chicago Historical Society, 1971.

Forsyth, George A. *The Story of a Soldier.* New York: Appleton, 1900.

————. *Thrilling Days in Army Life.* New York: Harper & Bros., 1902.

Fougera, Katherine Gibson, ed. *With Custer's Cavalry, from the Memoirs of the Late Katherine Gibson, Widow of Captain Francis M. Gibson of the Seventh Cavalry, U.S.A. (Retired).* Caldwell, Idaho: Caxton, 1940. Reprint. Lincoln: University of Nebraska Press, 1986.

Frazer, Robert. *Fort of the West.* Norman: University of Oklahoma Press, 1965.

Frost, Lawrence A. *The Court-Martial of General George Armstrong Custer.* Norman: University of Oklahoma Press, 1968.

Glass, Major E. N., *History of the Tenth Cavalry.* Tucson: Acme, 1921.

Green, Bill. *The Dancing Was Lively: Fort Concho, Texas: A Social History, 1867–1882.* San Angelo, Texas: Green, 1974.

Greene, Duane Merritt. *Ladies and Officers of the United States Army: or, American Aristocracy. A Sketch of the Social Life and Character of the Army.* Chicago: Central, 1880.

Greene, Robert Ewell. *Black Defenders of America, 1775–1973.* Chicago: Johnson, 1974.

Griffith, Elisabeth. *In Her Own Right: The Life of Elizabeth Cady Stanton.* New York: Oxford University Press, 1984.

Haley, J. Evetts. *Fort Concho and the Texas Frontier.* San Angelo, Texas: *San Angelo Standard-Times,* 1952.

Himes, Norman. *Medical History of Contraception.* Baltimore: Williams & Wilkins, 1936.

Hooker, Forrestine C. *When Geronimo Rode.* New York: Doubleday, 1924.

Hutton, Paul Andrew. *Phil Sheridan and His Army.* Lincoln: University of Nebraska Press, 1985.

Hutton, Paul Andrew, ed. *Soldiers West: Biographies From the Military Frontier.* Lincoln: University of Nebraska Press, 1987.

Jeffrey, Julie Roy. *Frontier Women: The Trans-Mississippi West, 1848–1890.* New York: Hill & Wang, 1979.

Kappler, Charles V. *Indian Affairs: Laws and Treaties.* 2 vols. Washington, D.C.: Government Printing Office, 1903.

Knight, Oliver. *Life and Manners in the Frontier Army.* Norman: University of Oklahoma Press, 1978.

La Farge, Oliver (with Arthur N. Morgan). *Santa Fe: The Autobiography of a Southwestern Town.* Norman: University of Oklahoma Press, 1959.

Lane, Lydia Spencer. *I Married a Soldier: Or Old Days in the Old Army.* Philadelphia: Lippincott, 1893. Reprint, with foreword by Mrs. Dwight D. Eisenhower. Albuquerque: Horn & Wallace, 1964.

Leach, William. *True Love and Perfect Union: The Feminist Reform of Sex and Society.* New York: Basic Books, 1980.

Leckie, William H. *The Buffalo Soldiers: A Narrative of the Negro Cavalry in the West.* Norman: University of Oklahoma Press, 1967.

Leckie, William H., and Leckie, Shirley A. *Unlikely Warriors: General*

Benjamin H. Grierson and His Family. Norman: University of Oklahoma Press, 1984.

McChristian, Douglas C., ed. *Garrison Tangles in the Friendless Tenth: The Journal of First Lieutenant John Bigelow, Jr., Fort Davis, Texas*. Bryan, Texas: Carroll, 1985.

Marberry, M. M. *Vicky: A Biography of Victoria C. Woodhull*. New York: Funk & Wagnalls, 1967.

Mattes, Merrill, ed. *Indians, Infants, and Infantry: Andrew and Elizabeth Burt on the Frontier*. Denver: Old West, 1960.

Merington, Marguerite, ed. *The Custer Story: The Life and Intimate Letters of General George A. Custer and His Wife Elizabeth*. New York: Devon-Adair, 1950; Lincoln: University of Nebraska Press, Bison Books, 1987.

Mills, Anson. *My Story*. Washington, D.C.: By the author, 1918.

Mills, Charles K. *Harvest of Barren Regrets: The Army Career of Frederick William Benteen*. Glendale, California: Clark, 1985.

Mohr, James C. *Abortion in America: The Origins and Evolution of National Policy, 1800–1900*. New York: Oxford University Press, 1978.

Morrison, W. B. *Military Posts and Camps in Oklahoma*. Oklahoma City: Harlow, 1936.

Myres, Sandra. *Westering Women and the Frontier Experience, 1800–1915*. Albuquerque: University of New Mexico Press, 1982.

Myres, Sandra, ed. *Cavalry Wife: The Diary of Eveline M. Alexander*. College Station, Texas: Texas A & M University Press, 1977.

Nye, Wilbur S. *Carbine and Lance: The Story of Old Fort Sill*. Norman: University of Oklahoma Press, 1943.

Quaife, Milo M., ed. *Army Life in Dakota, Selections from the Journal of Philippe Régis Denis de Keredern de Trobriand*. Chicago: Lakeside Press, 1941.

Reed, James A. *From Private Vice to Public Virtue: The Birth Control Movement and American Society Since 1830*. New York: Basic Books, 1978.

Riley, Glenda. *Women and Indians on the Frontier, 1825–1914*. Albuquerque: University of New Mexico Press, 1984.

Roe, Frances M. A. *Army Letters from an Officer's Wife, 1871–1888*. New York: Appleton, 1909. Reprint, with introduction by Sandra L. Myres. Lincoln: University of Nebraska Press, Bison Books, 1981.

Russell, Marian. *Land of Enchantment: Memoirs of Marian Russell Along the Santa Fe Trail*. Edited by Garnet M. Brayer. Evanston, Illinois: Branding Iron Press, 1954.

Schmitt, Martin F., ed. *General George Crook: His Autobiography*. Norman: University of Oklahoma Press, 1946.

Scobee, Barry. *Fort Davis, Texas, 1583–1960*. El Paso: Hill, 1963.

Sheridan, Philip H. *Personal Memoirs*. 2 vols. New York: Webster, 1888.

Sicherman, Barbara. *The Quest for Mental Health in America. 1880–1917.* New York: Arno Press, 1980.

Spiller, Roger J.; Dawson, Joseph G.; and Williams, T. Harry, eds. *Dictionary of American Military Biography.* 3 vols. Westport, Connecticut: Greenwood Press, 1984.

Stallard, Patricia Y. *Glittering Misery: Dependents of the Indian Fighting Army.* San Rafael, California: Presidio Press, 1978.

Summerhayes, Martha. *Vanished Arizona: Recollections of My Army Life.* Philadelphia: Lippincott, 1908. Reprint, with introduction by W. Turrentine Jackson. Philadelphia: Lippincott, 1963.

Tatum, Lawrie. *Our Red Brothers and the Peace Policy of President Ulysses S. Grant.* Winston, 1899. Reprint. Lincoln: University of Nebraska Press, 1970.

Thrapp, Dan L. *Victorio and the Mimbres Apaches.* Norman: University of Oklahoma Press, 1974.

Toulouse, Joseph H., and James, R. *Pioneer Post of Texas.* San Antonio: Naylor, 1936.

Twitchell, Ralph E. *The Leading Facts of New Mexican History.* 2 vols. Cedar Rapids: Torch Press, 1911.

———. *Old Santa Fe: The Story of New Mexico's Ancient Capital.* Santa Fe: New Mexico Publishing, 1925.

Utley, Robert M. *Frontier Regulars: The United States Army and the Indian, 1866–1891.* The Macmillan Wars of the United States. New York: Macmillan, 1973.

———. *The Indian Frontier of the American West, 1846–1890.* History of the American Frontier. Albuquerque: University of New Mexico Press, 1984.

Utley, Robert M., ed. *Life in Custer's Cavalry: Diaries and Letters of Albert and Jennie Barnitz, 1867–1868.* New Haven: Yale University Press, 1977.

Vielé, Teresa Griffin. *"Following the Drum": A Glimpse of Frontier Life.* Lincoln: University of Nebraska Press, 1984.

Whitman, Sidney E. *The Trooper: An Informal History of the Plains Cavalry, 1865–1890.* New York: Hastings House, 1962.

Wilbarger, J. W. *Indian Depredations in Texas.* Austin: Hutchins, 1889.

Williams, Mary L., ed. and comp. *An Army Wife's Cookbook: With Household Hints and Home Remedies, Alice Kirk Grierson.* Globe, Arizona: Southwest Parks and Monuments Association, 1972.

Index

Acton, Dr. William: 226n.37
Alcott, William: 226n.37
Alvord, Mrs. Henry: 16, 22–24, 31
Alvord, Lieutenant Henry: 15, 17–18, 21, 24, 33, 45, 199
Andrews, Lieutenant Colonel George L.: 113, 199
Anthony, Susan B.: 59
Apaches: Lipan, 72, 112; Mescalero, 72, 232n.37; Mimbres, 232n.37; Warm Springs, 160
Atwood, Major Edwin B.: 104, 199–200
Arapaho Indians, Southern, 21

Badger, Chaplain Norman: 80, 200
Baldwin, Captain T. A.: 48, 54
Barber, Captain Merritt: 168, 200
Barnitz, Captain Albert: 18
Barnitz, Jennie (Mrs. Albert): 18
Bates, Lieutenant Alfred E.: 115, 200
Beck, Mamie: 116, 200
Beck, Rachel (Mrs. William): 43, 116, 120, 124–25
Beck, Captain William: 121–22, 125–26
Beck, Willie: 126
Bedal, Dr. Sylvester S.: 83, 200

Biddle, Ellen: 221n.13, 223n.16
Big Tree: 46, 200
Board of Indian Commissioners: 40, 41
Boggy Depot, Indian Territory: 54–55
Boyd, Frances: 223n.16
Brackett, Lieutenant Colonel Albert G.: 162, 201
Brevet rank: 15
Brisbin, Major James: 155
Bryant, Captain Montgomery: 23, 29, 34–35, 201
Buell, Colonel George P.: 132, 201
Buell, Dr. James: 96, 107, 201
Buell, Josie: 96, 98
Buffalo Soldiers, derivation of name: 223n.15
Burt, Elizabeth: 223n.16
Butler, Joseph: 45
Butler, Lizzie: 45
Byrne, Captain Edward: 17, 201

Cache Creek: 31, 56
Calhoun, Lieutenant James: 233n.2
Camp Supply: 132
Camp Wichita: 39–40, 224
Capps, Charles: 140, 176, 193

249

INDEX

Fort Huachuca, Arizona Territory: 195
Fort Leavenworth: 14–18, 221 n.3
Fort Lyon, Colorado Territory: 15
Fort McKavett, Texas: 154
Fort Riley, Kansas: 17–18, 221 n.7
Fort Sill, Indian Territory: 5, 40–41, 47,
  71, 81
Fort Stockton, Texas: 80, 154
Fort Thomas, Arizona Territory: 157
Fort Verde, Arizona Territory: 157
Fort Wallace, Kansas: 18
Fourth Cavalry: 47
Fuller, Ellen Kirk: 50, 55, 133, 139, 190–
  92; views on Robert and Charles's
  illness, 142–43; financial hardships,
  156–57, 183
Fuller, Gertrude: 191
Fuller, Harvey: 27, 140, 190, 193
Fuller, Harvey B., Jr.: 50, 56, 139–41,
  183
Fuller, Louisa: 124, 134, 186–87, 190
Fuller, Roger: 191
Fuller-Maxon Wedding: 150

Gardner, Major William F.: 102–3,
  205–6
Gardner, Dr. William H.: 154, 205–6
Garfield, President James A.: 136
Garrison, William Lloyd: 61
Gasman, Lieutenant Hans J.: 93, 98, 206
Gasman, Mrs. Hans J.: 98
Geronimo: 160, 206; surrender and
  escape from General Crook, 170;
  surrender to Nelson Miles, 174
Gillmore, Lieutenant Quincy O'Mahar:
  71, 206
Golden Age Tracts: 59, 61
Graham, Lieutenant George W.: 16, 206
Grand Canyon: 170
Grant, Ulysses S.: 13, 40, 132–33
Grierson, Alice Kirk: 1; character, 2–5,
  196–97; views on a military career,
  12; on marital roles, 13; frontier life
  at Fort Leavenworth, 14–18; gives
  birth at Fort Riley, 18–20; concern
  for Buffalo Soldiers, 22–24, 28, 30;
  separation from husband on frontier,
  24–40; gives birth at Fort Sill, 40;
  hardships following George's birth
  and birth and death of Mary Louisa,
  40–49; visit to Chicago, 50–69; life

at Fort Sill, 58–59, 66–67; interest
  in woman's rights movement, 60–
  61; views on child bearing, 61–64;
  relationship with her father, 64–65;
  return to Fort Sill, 69; the years in
  Saint Louis, 69; relocation to Fort
  Concho, 75–77; accounts of Fort
  Concho, 78–87, 93–109; visit to Centennial Celebration in Philadelphia,
  88; return to Jacksonville, 88–93;
  oldest son's breakdown, 101–12; description of Lost Expedition on the
  Staked Plains, 106, 110; loss of her
  daughter to typhoid fever, 115–19;
  response to Edie's death, 119–20;
  advice to Robert regarding proper
  behavior, 122; return to Jacksonville,
  124–27; improvements at Fort Concho, 127; husband's involvement in
  the Victorio campaign, 130–33; concerns over family back East, 133–36;
  Robert's mental breakdown, 139–43;
  assumption of Robert's care, 143;
  ideas regarding children's insanity,
  145–47; fear of loss of affection in
  her marriage, 147–49; move to Fort
  Davis, Texas, 151–54; anxiety over
  her husband's investments, 155, 176,
  184, 188–89; transferred to Whipple
  Barracks, Arizona, 157–72; onset
  of health problems, 6, 164; transferred to Fort Grant, 172–76; move
  to Santa Fe, 176–77; visits Santa Fe
  penitentiary, 180; views on husband's
  desire for promotion, 4–5, 185; visits
  mines near Sante Fe, 186–87; serious
  illness, 190–93; death, 194
Grierson, Benjamin Henry: 2, 11, 113,
  127, 137, 150, 152, 169, 172–73,
  180–81, 193–94; courtship and
  marriage, 1; as businessman, 3–6;
  joins Union Army, 3–4; commands
  Sixth Illinois Cavalry, 4; 1863 raid
  into Mississippi, 4; promotions
  during Civil War, 4; command of
  Tenth United States Cavalry, 4, 13–
  15; Colonel Custer's court martial,
  18; appointment to command District
  of Indian Territory, 21; site for new
  post, 30–31; as a "humanitarian
  general" supporting Indian Peace

251

INDEX

Stanton, Elizabeth Cady: 59

Summerhayes, Martha: 221n.15, 223n.16

Tatum, Lawrie: 46
Tatum, Mary Ann (Mrs. Lawrie): 44–46
Tear, Lieutenant Wallace: 106, 111–12, 117, 214
Tenth United States Cavalry: 4, 6, 13, 71, 108, 121; headquarters transferred to Fort Riley, 18; moved to Fort Concho, 71; in Victorio War, 130–31; transferred to Fort Davis, 150; headquarters moved to Whipple Barracks, 156–57; in Geronimo campaign, 160, 166, 172, 174
Terrazas, Colonel Joaquin: 131–32, 214
Third Cavalry: 161
Thompson, Lieutenant John M.: 45, 214
Tilden, Samuel J.: 92
Tilton, Theodore: 61, 225n.34
Tinaja de las Palmas (skirmish at): 130
Tishimingo, Indian Territory: 52, 54
Tres Castillos Mountains: 131
Turner, Lieutenant Edward P.: 94, 214
Twenty-Fourth Infantry: 132

Underground Railroad: 1

Valentine, Texas: 155
Vande Wiele, Captain John B.: 44, 214

Van Horn's Wells, Texas: 132
Van Vliet, Major Frederick: 178, 214
Victorio: 130–32, 214–15
Victorio War: 130–31
Volkmar, William J.: 169, 215

Walsh, Captain J. W.: 50, 215
Ward, Lieutenant Charles R.: 57, 108, 167, 215
Warm Springs Apache: 160
Washita, Battle of: 224n.23
West Point Military Academy: 69, 102, 105, 114, 120–21, 128–29
Whipple, General Amiel W.: 234–35n.15
Whipple Barracks, Arizona Territory: 6, 157, 165, 168–72, 235n.15
Whittaker, Cadet Johnson C.: 131–32, 232n.41
Wichita Mountains: 24, 31, 38
Willcox, Arizona Territory: 160
Woodhull, Victoria: 59
Woodhull & Claflin's Weekly: 59, 61, 225n.36
Woodward, Major Samuel: 15–16, 21–22, 28–29, 33–34, 37, 75, 80, 85, 151–52, 169–70, 176–77, 181–82, 189, 215

Yard, Major John E.: 45, 215
Yard, Mrs. John: 45
Youngstown, Ohio: 1

255

In the Women in the West series

Martha Maxwell, Rocky Mountain Naturalist
BY MAXINE BENSON

The Art of the Woman:
The Life and Work of Elisabet Ney
BY EMILY FOURMY CUTRER

Emily: The Diary of a Hard-Worked Woman
BY EMILY FRENCH
EDITED BY JANET LECOMPTE

The Adventures of the Woman Homesteader:
The Life and Letters of Elinore Pruitt Stewart
BY SUSANNE K. GEORGE

The Colonel's Lady on the Western Frontier:
The Correspondence of Alice Kirk Grierson
EDITED BY SHIRLEY A. LECKIE

A Stranger in Her Native Land:
Alice Fletcher and the American Indians
BY JOAN MARK

So Much to Be Done: Women Settlers
on the Mining and Ranching Frontier
EDITED BY RUTH B. MOYNIHAN,
SUSAN ARMITAGE, AND
CHRISTIANE FISCHER DICHAMP